I0438884

<u>Disclaimer</u>

Book Title: Performance of Structures During the Loma Prieta Earthquake of October 17, 1989 (NIST SP 778)

Book Author: Hai S. Lew;

Book Abstract: Immediately following the magnitude 7.1 Loma Prieta earthquake of October 17, 1989, a team representing the Interagency Committee on Seismic Safety in Construction surveyed the damage to buildings, utilities and transportation structures. This report is based primarily on the data gathered during the site survey and the results of preliminary analyses of structural failures. Most structures designed in accordance with modern codes and standards performed well without serious structural damage. However, there were many concrete and masonry buildings and highway structures in the San Francisco Bay area which were not designed according to modern seismic design codes and which did not perform well. The majority of damaged structures had not been strengthened to increase earthquake resistance. Except for two deaths from landslides and one from fire, the remainder of the 62 deaths from the earthquake was due to partial or total collapse of older structures. This investigation provided the basis for recommendations to improve design and construction practices for buildings and lifeline structures and to mitigate damage to existing structures in future earthquakes.

Citation: NIST SP - 778

Keyword: Bridges, buildings; codes; damage; earthquakes; fire safety; geology; highways;
housing; lifelines; seismic; specifications; structural engineering; viaducts.

NIST United States Department of Commerce
National Institute of Standards and Technology

NIST Special Publication 778   (ICCSSC TR11)

Performance of Structures During the Loma Prieta Earthquake of October 17, 1989

H. S. Lew, Editor

GENERAL DISCLAIMER

This document may have problems that one or more of the following disclaimer statements refer to:

- This document has been reproduced from the best copy furnished by the sponsoring agency. It is being released in the interest of making available as much information as possible.

- This document may contain data which exceeds the sheet parameters. It was furnished in this condition by the sponsoring agency and is the best copy available.

- This document may contain tone-on-tone or color graphs, charts and/or pictures which have been reproduced in black and white.

- The document is paginated as submitted by the original source.

- Portions of this document are not fully legible due to the historical nature of some of the material. However, it is the best reproduction available from the original submission.

PB 90 184599 IAS

NIST-114A (REV. 3-89)	U.S. DEPARTMENT OF COMMERCE NATIONAL INSTITUTE OF STANDARDS AND TECHNOLOGY BIBLIOGRAPHIC DATA SHEET	1. PUBLICATION OR REPORT NUMBER NIST/SP-778
		2. PERFORMING ORGANIZATION REPORT NUMBER
		3. PUBLICATION DATE January 1990

4. TITLE AND SUBTITLE

Performance of Structures During the Loma Prieta Earthquake of October 17, 1989

5. AUTHOR(S)

H. S. Lew, Editor

6. PERFORMING ORGANIZATION (IF JOINT OR OTHER THAN NIST, SEE INSTRUCTIONS) U.S. DEPARTMENT OF COMMERCE NATIONAL INSTITUTE OF STANDARDS AND TECHNOLOGY GAITHERSBURG, MD 20899	7. CONTRACT/GRANT NUMBER
	8. TYPE OF REPORT AND PERIOD COVERED Final

9. SPONSORING ORGANIZATION NAME AND COMPLETE ADDRESS (STREET, CITY, STATE, ZIP) Dept of the Interior U.S. Geological Survey 582 National Center Reston, VA 22092	NIST Category No. NIST- 140

10. SUPPLEMENTARY NOTES

Also Available from
GPO as SN003-003- 02988-2

☐ DOCUMENT DESCRIBES A COMPUTER PROGRAM; SF-185, FIPS SOFTWARE SUMMARY, IS ATTACHED.

11. ABSTRACT (A 200-WORD OR LESS FACTUAL SUMMARY OF MOST SIGNIFICANT INFORMATION. IF DOCUMENT INCLUDES A SIGNIFICANT BIBLIOGRAPHY OR LITERATURE SURVEY, MENTION IT HERE.)

Immediately following the magnitude 7.1 Loma Prieta earthquake of October 17, 1989, a team representing the Interagency Committee on Seismic Safety in Construction surveyed the damage to buildings, utilities and transportation structures. This report is based primarily on the data gathered during the site survey and the results of preliminary analyses of structural failures. Most structures designed in accordance with modern codes and standards performed well without serious structural damage. However, there were many concrete and masonry buildings and highway structures in the San Francisco Bay area which were not designed according to modern seismic design codes and which did not perform well. The majority of damaged structures had not been strengthened to increase earthquake resistance. Except for two deaths from landslides and one from fire, the remainder of the 62 deaths from the earthquake was due to partial or total collapse of older structures. This investigation provided the basis for recommendations to improve design and construction practices for buildings and lifeline structures and to mitigate damage to existing structures in future earthquakes.

12. KEY WORDS (6 TO 12 ENTRIES; ALPHABETICAL ORDER; CAPITALIZE ONLY PROPER NAMES; AND SEPARATE KEY WORDS BY SEMICOLONS)

Bridges, buildings; codes; damage; earthquakes; fire safety; geology; highways; housing; lifelines; seismic; specifications; structural engineering; viaducts.

13. AVAILABILITY	14. NUMBER OF PRINTED PAGES
X UNLIMITED	204
☐ FOR OFFICIAL DISTRIBUTION. DO NOT RELEASE TO NATIONAL TECHNICAL INFORMATION SERVICE (NTIS).	
X ORDER FROM SUPERINTENDENT OF DOCUMENTS, U.S. GOVERNMENT PRINTING OFFICE, WASHINGTON, DC 20402.	15. PRICE
X ORDER FROM NATIONAL TECHNICAL INFORMATION SERVICE (NTIS), SPRINGFIELD, VA 22161.	

ELECTRONIC FORM

NIST Special Publication 778

Performance of Structures During the Loma Prieta Earthquake of October 17, 1989

H. S. Lew, Editor

Center for Building Technology
National Engineering Laboratory
National Institute of Standards and Technology
Gaithersburg, MD 20899

Sponsored by:
U.S. Geological Survey
Department of the Interior
Reston, VA 22092

January 1990

U.S. Department of Commerce
Robert A. Mosbacher, Secretary

National Institute of Standards and Technology
Raymond G. Kammer, Acting Director

National Institute of Standards
and Technology
Special Publication 778
Natl. Inst. Stand. Technol.
Spec. Publ. 778
201 pages (Jan. 1990)
CODEN: NSPUE2

U.S. Government Printing Office
Washington: 1990

For sale by the Superintendent
of Documents
U.S. Government Printing Office
Washington, DC 20402

ABSTRACT

Immediately following the magnitude 7.1 Loma Prieta earthquake of October 17, 1989, a team representing the Interagency Committee on Seismic Safety in Construction surveyed the damage to buildings, utilities and transportation structures. This report is based primarily on the data gathered during the site survey and the results of preliminary analyses of structural failures. Most structures designed in accordance with modern codes and standards performed well without serious structural damage. However, there were many concrete and masonry buildings and highway structures in the San Francisco Bay area which were not designed according to modern seismic design codes and which did not perform well. The majority of damaged structures had not been strengthened to increase earthquake resistance. Except for two deaths from landslides and one from fire, the remainder of the 62 deaths from the earthquake was due to partial or total collapse of older structures. This investigation provided the basis for recommendations to improve design and construction practices for buildings and lifeline structures and to mitigate damage to existing structures in future earthquakes.

Key Words: Bridges; buildings; codes; damage; earthquakes; fire safety; geology; highways; housing; lifelines; seismic; specifications; structural engineering; viaducts.

The Loma Prieta earthquake struck the San Francisco Bay region at 5:04 p.m. (PDT) on October 17, 1989. Within a few hours, a decision was made to dispatch an interagency team representing the Interagency Committee on Seismic Safety in Construction (ICSSC). ICSSC is comprised of representatives of 25 Federal agencies with responsibilities for seismic safety of Federal or Federally assisted facilities. On October 18, 1989, the U.S. Senate Committee on Commerce, Science and Transportation and the U.S. House of Representatives Committee on Science, Space and Technology, Subcommittee on Science, Research and Technology requested the National Institute of Standards and Technology (NIST) to investigate earthquake damage including the elevated section of Interstate 880 (the Nimitz Freeway) and other bridge structures. Since NIST provides the secretariat for ICSSC, the team responded to the Congressional request. The team arrived in the San Francisco area on October 18, 1989, and carried out its investigation during the period of October 19 - 26, 1989. The team included civil, fire safety, geotechnical, and structural engineers. The team members were:

National Institute of Standards and Technology

Nicholas J. Carino
H. S. Lew, Team Leader
Harold E. Nelson
William C. Stone
Richard N. Wright
Felix Y. Yokel

Federal Highway Administration

James D. Cooper

Department of Housing and Urban Development

Lincoln M. H. Chang

U.S. Geological Survey

E. V. Leyendecker

The primary purposes of this report are to document perishable data and to identify opportunities to gain knowledge to improve practices for the seismic safety of new and existing buildings and lifelines.

The author or authors of each of the chapters are:

Chapter 1.	H. S. Lew
Chapter 2.	E. V. Leyendecker, Paul C. Thenhaus, Kenneth W. Campbell, Margaret G. Hopper, Stanley L. Hanson, S. T. Algermissen and David M. Perkins (USGS contributors)
Chapter 3.	Felix Y. Yokel
Chapter 4.	Nicholas J. Carino
Chapter 5.	William C. Stone, James D. Cooper and Nicholas J. Carino
Chapter 6.	Harold E. Nelson
Chapter 7.	Richard N. Wright and H. S. Lew

ACKNOWLEDGMENTS

The team acknowledges the logistical support provided by the Federal Emergency Management Agency's Region IX office. Ms. Laurie Friedman, who was assigned to the team by FEMA, made arrangements for the team to visit several sites in San Francisco and the epicentral region.

James H. Gates of the California Department of Transportation arranged the team's visit to the I-880 and other damage sites and made available the drawings of the bridge and highway structures. Frank Lew of the city of San Francisco guided the team through the Marina District in inclement weather and provided the building damage statistics. Ken Lewis, Senior Civil Engineer, city of Watsonville, provided subsurface information obtained from the Watsonville area.

Carl Stover and Glen Reagor, USGS, assisted in the interpretation of Modified Mercalli Intensity data collected from a mail survey for inclusion in Chapter 2. Phil Powers assisted with computer analysis of data and preparation of figures.

Many of the illustrations in this report were prepared by Keith F. Mackley of NIST.

The preparation of this report was partially supported by the U.S. Geological Survey, Department of the Interior.

CONTENTS

1. INTRODUCTION

by H. S. Lew

At 5:04 p.m., Pacific Daylight Time, on October 17, 1989, an earthquake with a surface-wave magnitude of 7.1 occurred with its epicenter located about 10 miles (15 km) northeast of Santa Cruz and 60 miles (95 km) south-southeast of San Francisco, California. According to the U.S. Geological Survey, the earthquake ruptured a segment of the San Andreas fault below the Santa Cruz Mountains. The hypocenter was about 11 miles (18 km) beneath the Earth's surface, and the rupture propagated about 25 miles (40 km) both northwest and southeast within a 10-second period. The earthquake was felt over an area of 400,000 square miles (1,000,000 sq km), from Los Angeles to the south, Oregon to the north, and western Nevada to the east. This earthquake, named the Loma Prieta earthquake, was the largest on the San Andreas fault since the great San Francisco earthquake of 1906 (M = 8.3) when a 275-mile (440-km) stretch of the fault ruptured.

Strong shaking lasted only about 10 to 15 seconds. Even so the destructive effects of the Loma Prieta earthquake were extensive. Wood-frame dwellings and unreinforced masonry buildings in communities near the epicenter and in isolated locations in San Francisco and Oakland sustained substantial damage. In Santa Cruz, Watsonville, and Los Gatos, there was extensive damage to old buildings in the downtown areas where small businesses are located. Elevated highway structures sustained severe damage in the Bay area, including the collapse of a section of Interstate 880 in Oakland which claimed 42 lives. The collapse of a 50-foot (15-m) link span of the San Francisco-Oakland Bay Bridge caused the bridge to remain closed for about a month. The Bay Area Rapid Transit System was in service immediately after the earthquake. However, damage to arterial highways and the bridge caused severe impacts on commuters and regional commerce.

As of December 28, 1989, the following statistics have been compiled by the California Governor's Office of Emergency Services:

- 62 confirmed deaths; 3,757 injuries.
- Over $6 billion property damage.
- Over 12,000 people displaced from their homes immediately following the earthquake.

This report presents an overview of the nature of the Loma Prieta earthquake and its effects and documents the damage. The geotechnical engineering aspects of the affected region are discussed in detail as they affect in large measure the distribution of the observed damage. Because of the significance of the damage to highway structures, the evolution of the design criteria for these structures is described. The collapse of the elevated portion of Interstate 880 is discussed in detail and preliminary analyses to determine the causes of the failure are presented. A detailed description of the nature of the damage sustained by buildings located in the Bay area and in the epicentral region is provided. The extent of fire damage and the performance of fire protection systems are presented. The lessons learned, or re-learned, from this earthquake are summarized. The report concludes with recommendations for actions to reduce risks from future earthquakes and for research to exploit opportunities provided by the Loma Prieta earthquake for learning and improving practices.

2. SEISMICITY AND STRONG MOTION DATA

by Edgar V. Leyendecker, Paul C. Thenhaus,
Kenneth W. Campbell, Margaret G. Hopper, Stanley L. Hanson,
S. T. Algermissen, and David M. Perkins

2.1 Introduction

The October 17, 1989 Loma Prieta earthquake (M_s 7.1) was the largest earthquake to strike the San Francisco Bay area since the great San Francisco earthquake of 1906. Numerous investigations were initiated as a consequence of this earthquake. One of these investigations involved collection of Modified Mercalli (MM) intensity data and collection of damage statistics for loss estimation research (see Leyendecker and others, 1988, for a description of field procedures). These data and data collected by an investigation team from the Interagency Committee in Seismic Safety in Construction formed part of a data base that led to the preliminary interpretation of the distribution of Modified Mercalli intensities presented here. Strong motion records collected by the U.S. Geological Survey (USGS) and the State of California's Division of Mines and Geology, provided basic ground-motion data that are discussed in conjunction with the intensity data.

2.2 Earthquake Mechanism

The epicenter was located 10 miles (15 km) northeast of Santa Cruz and was 60 miles (95 km) south-southeast of San Francisco at 37.036° N. latitude, 121.883° W. longitude (Ward and Page, 1989). Earthquake rupture initiated at 5:04:15 p.m., Pacific Daylight Time, at a depth of 11.4 miles (18.4 km) on the Southern Santa Cruz Mountains segment of the San Andreas fault (fig. 2.2.1(a)). Coseismic rupture propagated up-dip to a depth of 3.7 miles (5.9 km) and bilaterally along the fault northwest to just south of Los Gatos, and southeast to a point just south of Watsonville for a rupture length of 25 miles (40 km). From the south, the San Andreas fault bends to a more northwesterly course through this segment and results in a high degree of compression across the right-slip fault system. The fault plane dipped approximately 70° to the southwest and had a strong west-over-east thrust component (fig. 2.2.1(b)). Geodetic surveys following the earthquake indicate that slip at the hypocenter had a right-lateral horizontal component of 6.2 feet (1.9 m) and a vertical component of 4.3 feet (1.3 m) that resolve to a total oblique-slip displacement of 7.5 feet (2.3 m) (Plafker and Galloway, 1989). Deformation at the surface consisted of 14 inches (0.35 m) of uplift southwest of the fault's surface trace and echelon tensional cracks in the uplifted southwest block (fig. 2.2.1(c)). Surface fault displacement has not yet been identified unequivocally, but the lack of surface fault displacement would be consistent with the top of the rupture zone being at a depth of about 4 miles (6 km).

The southern Santa Cruz Mountains segment of the San Andreas fault was identified in 1988 as having a 30 percent probability of rupturing in a magnitude 6.5 earthquake within the next 30 years (U.S. Geological Survey, 1988). Figure 2.2.2 is a cross section of seismicity along the San Andreas fault as recorded during the past 20 years for an area extending from just south of Parkfield to north of San Francisco. Much of the fault zone between Parkfield and San Juan Batista is characterized by a high rate of low-magnitude seismicity associated with the well documented creep mechanism of fault slip in this segment. North and south of this area, however, seismicity is distributed both horizontally and vertically in fairly discrete patches along the fault plane. Areas deficient in earthquakes are areas of assumed strain accumulation and, therefore, are considered the most likely areas of major earthquakes in the near future. Three such seismic gaps are labeled in figure 2.2.2(a). Figure 2.2.2(b) illustrates how the Loma Prieta earthquake and its aftershocks filled a previously recognized seismic gap.

2.3 Strong Ground Motion

The earthquake triggered over 130 strong-motion instruments operated by the USGS (Maley et al., 1989) and the California Division of Mines and Geology (Shakal et al., 1989). Station locations are shown in figure 2.3.1. The amplitude of the larger of the two peak horizontal components of acceleration is shown adjacent to each station (units are fraction of gravity). The stations in the vicinity of San Francisco and Oakland are shown more clearly in figure 2.3.2. The larger of the two peak horizontal acceleration components at each station are shown graphically in figure 2.3.3 with the acceleration amplitude in proportion to the diameter of the circle.

The accelerograms recorded at 10 strong-motion stations, along with their peak accelerations, epicentral distances, and geologic site conditions, are shown in figure 2.3.4. The location of these 10 stations are identified by an alphabetic designation (A-J) in figures 2.3.1, 2.3.2, and 2.3.3.

The duration of strong shaking for two rock sites located over the inferred rupture zone of the earthquake (e.g., Lexington Dam, station D, and Corralitos, station A) is approximately 5 to 7 seconds. This duration is consistent with bilateral rupture over a total distance of about 25 miles (40 km), and with interpretations of the geodetic data. The estimated 25 mile (40 km) rupture length almost exactly coincides with the geographical limits of the MM intensity VIII contour inferred for the epicentral region (fig. 2.3.5).

Within the epicentral source region, peak accelerations were observed to be relatively independent of surface geology. However, outside of this region (especially beyond distances of 50 km or so), surface geology appears to strongly influence the amplitude of ground motion: sites located on crystalline rock and rocks of the Franciscan Complex have the lowest accelerations, sites located on soft rock and alluvium have intermediate accelerations, and sites located on artificial fill and Bay Mud have the highest accelerations. The differences in horizontal acceleration at hard-rock and Bay-Mud sites were best demonstrated in the San Francisco and Oakland areas, where differences of 100% to 260% were observed.

Within the epicentral source region of the earthquake, many sites recorded nearly equal amplitudes for the vertical and horizontal components of peak acceleration. This is consistent with limited observations from past earthquakes, having a strike-slip mechanism.

Peak acceleration was observed to be strongly dependent on geographical area and azimuth (see fig. 2.3.3), especially outside of the near-source region (about 30 miles (48 km) as defined by Campbell, 1981, 1989). For example, sites underlain by a given surface geology located to the northwest of the epicenter in the direction of San Francisco and Oakland had consistently higher accelerations than sites located to the north of the epicenter in the direction of San Jose, Hayward, and Livermore Valley. This observation is consistent with the overall distribution of MM intensities shown in figure 2.3.5. The combined effects of source directivity and radiation pattern may be partly responsible for this pattern, although some bias may be introduced to the overall damage pattern by the northwest trending corridor of cultural development along major highways. Also, the instrumentation array is relatively sparse in the Diablo Range to the northeast and in the western Santa Cruz Mountains southwest of the epicenter.

2.4 The Modified Mercalli Scale and MM Assessments

The Modified Mercalli intensity (MM) scale of 1931 (Wood and Neuman, 1931) groups observations on earthquake effects into similar levels of shaking and then ranks the shaking levels into ascending order I through XII (see table 2.1). Ground failure phenomena, such as landslides, sand blows, rock falls and liquefaction are generally relegated to MM level IX and higher. However, research and observations since the scale was developed in 1931 show that such effects can occur at much lower intensity levels depending on a number of physical properties of the surficial materials, such as moisture content, permeability, and texture, and the slope angles of hillsides and bluffs. Accordingly, where possible, the MM intensities have been assigned on the basis of shaking damage to buildings and structures and not on the basis of ground failure effects. This exercise becomes difficult, however, where structural damage from ground failure and shaking are inextricably mixed, as was the case for certain structures located in the communities of

Redwood Estates, Santa Cruz and the Marina District of San Francisco. In these cases, assessments of nearby structures and other items such as water towers and telephone poles, apparently not influenced by local ground failure effects, were used to corroborate overall assessments. However, damage resulting from the possible amplification of ground motion by surficial geologic materials and local topography is legitimately classed as shaking damage in these assessments, since amplification is believed to be unrelated to ground failure.

Areas assigned MM VI are characterized by broken windows and minor cracking to unreinforced masonry chimneys and plaster walls. For convenience, MM VII can be characterized as the threshold of architectural damage to buildings; negligible damage to well-designed and built ordinary buildings but considerable damage to poorly designed and built buildings. Falling of weak chimneys at the roof-line is characteristic of MM VII damage. MM VIII is characterized generally as the threshold of structural damage to buildings. Damage is considerable to ordinary substantial buildings. Some wood-framed houses are racked and move or fall off of foundations. Such damage at this level is usually because 1) the houses are unattached to the foundation, 2) the pile-foundation or wooden sills resting on a masonry or concrete foundation are badly decayed, or 3) there is insufficient lateral bracing of cripple studs which support the floor joists of the first story. Unreinforced masonry walls fall. MM IX is marked by considerable damage to structures designed to withstand earthquakes.

Figure 2.3.5 shows a preliminary map of the regional distribution of Modified Mercalli intensity resulting from the Loma Prieta earthquake. More detailed assessments in the San Francisco and Oakland areas are shown in the map in figure 2.4.1. Considerable work remains, however, to finalize the details of this initial assessment. Except for the MM VI assessments in Brentwood, Banta, Manteca, Vernalis, and some areas along state Highway 1, the evaluations are based on primary observations and data collected by the field parties. A secondary source of information for the above locations was early responses to a mail survey of postmasters, police and fire departments conducted by the U.S. Geological Survey's National Earthquake Information Center.

While the epicentral intensity of the Loma Prieta earthquake was assigned an MM VIII based on substantial damage to wood-framed dwellings and unreinforced masonry buildings in communities near the epicenter, the highest intensity levels (MM IX) were assigned to isolated sites in San Francisco and Oakland. The collapse of the elevated portion of I-880 in Oakland and the considerable damage to the Embarcadero Freeway in San Francisco warrant MM IX. Both of the reinforced concrete freeway structures were built under seismic design requirements of the then-existing codes. The Marina District in northern San Francisco also was assigned MM IX. Ground failure and shaking both played a role in some apartment collapses in the district. However, other collapses occurred in areas of no apparent ground failure. The collapse and widespread structural damage to these substantial buildings is reason for a tentative assignment of MM IX to the Marina District.

In all of the above areas, amplification of ground motions by surficial geologic materials may have played a significant role in causing the observed damage. Notably, intensity levels in eastern and northern San Francisco (known areas of thick sediments and Bay Mud; Joyner, 1982) exhibit intensity levels one to three units higher than the central-city areas. An exception is the extreme western margin of San Francisco where thick sediments have been documented but intensity levels are no higher than in the central area (fig. 2.4.1). These large differences in MM intensity are also consistent with the observed 100% to 200% difference in peak horizontal accelerations recorded on Bay Mud and Franciscan rock sites in the San Francisco and Oakland areas.

In the MM VIII epicentral area, wood-framed houses on laterally unbraced cripple studs performed poorly, as was the case in the May 2, 1983 Coalinga, California earthquake (Hopper et al., 1983). In Los Gatos, stately refurbished Victorian houses were thrown off their foundations. Decayed and rotted sills at the foundation connection of these older homes indicate a need for structural rehabilitation as well as cosmetic remodelling. Retrofitting decayed sills at the foundation level and laterally bracing cripple studs below the first-floor level would help to mitigate similarly extreme residential damage expected in future earthquakes. It is noted that many residences of post-1950 construction, when improved anchoring to the foundations began to be required, sustained far less damage than residences of earlier periods of construction.

The MM intensities along state Highway 1 on the Pacific Coast were assigned values of 6 and 7. Thus, the closure of the isoseismal between MM VI and MM VII between Monterey and Half Moon Bay seems likely to be located at or near the coastline (fig. 2.3.5).

The maps in figures 2.3.5 and 2.4.1 were originally developed by the authors and published by the USGS in a Circular on the Loma Prieta earthquake (Plafker and Galloway, 1989). Additional data obtained since the original publication indicate the need for some modifications. However, rather than modify the maps at this time on the basis of incomplete data, some of the additional data are shown highlighted on the maps to indicate trends.

As an example of the wealth of data available, figure 2.4.2 shows some of the safety inspection results available for San Francisco (Lew, 1989). These represent 378 inspected buildings using post-earthquake safety evaluation procedures developed by the Applied Technology Council (ATC, 1989). These are only for buildings posted as unsafe to enter (posted "Red" by the ATC procedures). The preliminary contour is shown for comparison. Additional data are available for San Francisco and other cities, such as Oakland, and will be used to modify the isoseismals in the future.

2.5 Summary

In the epicentral region of the earthquake, many sites recorded nearly equal amplitudes for the vertical and horizontal components of peak acceleration. This is consistent with observations of past strike-slip earthquakes. The peak horizontal acceleration of 0.64g was measured in the epicentral region at Corralitos. The peak vertical acceleration at this location was 0.47g. Duration of strong ground motion in the epicentral area was on the order of 5 to 7 seconds and 10 to 15 seconds in San Francisco and Oakland. The inferred rupture length of 25 miles (40 km) almost coincides with the geographical limits of the MM intensity VIII contour for the epicentral region.

Peak accelerations were observed to be strongly dependent on geographical area and azimuth, especially outside of the near-source region. For example, sites of a given surface geology located to the northwest of the epicenter in the direction of San Francisco and Oakland had consistently higher accelerations than sites located to the north of the epicenter in the direction of San Jose, Hayward, and Livermore Valley. This observation is also consistent with the overall distribution of MM intensities.

The epicentral intensity of the Loma Prieta earthquake was assigned an MM VIII based on substantial damage to wood-framed dwellings and unreinforced masonry buildings in communities near the epicenter. The highest intensity levels (MM IX) were assigned to isolated sites in San Francisco and Oakland some 55 to 60 miles (90 to 100 km) from the epicenter. Amplification of ground motions by surficial geologic materials may have played a significant role in causing these high intensities at such large distances. Notably, intensity levels in eastern and northern San Francisco, known areas of thick sediments and Bay Mud, exhibited intensity levels one to three units higher than the central San Francisco area. The large differences in MM intensity are consistent with the observed differences in peak accelerations. In the San Francisco-Oakland area, differences of 100% to 260% were observed in peak horizontal accelerations recorded on Bay Mud and Franciscan rock sites.

In the MM VIII epicentral area, wood-framed houses on laterally unbraced cripple studs performed poorly, as was the case in past earthquakes. Many residences of post-1950 construction, when improved anchoring to the foundations began to be required, sustained less damage than residences of earlier periods of construction.

2.6 References

Applied Technology Council. 1989a. Procedures for postearthquake safety evaluation of buildings. Applied Technology Council, ATC-20. 152 p.

Applied Technology Council. 1989b. Field Manual: Postearthquake safety evaluation of buildings. Applied Technology Council, ATC-20-1. 114 p.

Campbell, K. W. 1981. Near-source attenuation of peak horizontal acceleration. Bull. of the Seis. Soc. of Am. 68:828-843.

Campbell, K. W. 1989. Empirical prediction of near-source ground motion for the Diablo Canyon power plant site, San Luis Obispo County, California. U.S. Geological Survey Open-File Report 89-484, 115 p.

Hopper, M. G., Thenhaus, P. C., Barnhard, L. M., and Algermissen, S. T. 1983. Damage survey in Coalinga, California for the earthquake of May 2, 1983. The 1983 Coalinga, California earthquake. California Department of Conservation, Division of Mines and Geology. Special Publication 66, p. 5-8.

Joyner, W. B. 1982. Map showing the 200-foot thickness contour of surficial deposits and the landward limit of bay mud deposits of San Francisco, California: U.S. Geological Survey Miscellaneous Field Studies Map MF-1376, 1 plate, scale 1:24,000.

Lew, Frank. 1989. Department of Public Works, City and County of San Francisco, Personal communication with reports on earthquake-related building inspections.

Leyendecker, E. V., Highland, L. M., Hopper, M. G., and Arnold, E. P., Thenhaus, P. C., and Powers, P. 1988. The Whittier Narrows, California earthquake of October 1, 1987--Early results of isoseismal studies and damage surveys. Earthquake Spectra, v. 4, p. 1-10.

Maley, R., Acosta, A., Ellis, F., Etheredge, E., Foote, L., Johnson, D., Porcella, R., Salsman, M., and Switzer, J. October 1989. Strong-motion records from the Northern California (Loma Prieta) earthquake of October 17, 1989. U.S. Geological Survey Open-File Report 89-568. 85 p.

Plafker, G. and Galloway, J. 1989. Lessons learned from the Loma Prieta, California earthquake of October 17, 1989. U.S. Geological Survey Circular 1045. 48 p.

Shakal, A., Huang, M., Reichle, M., Ventura, C., Cao, T., Sherburne, R., Savage, M., Darragh, R., and Peterson, C. November 1989. CSMIP strong-motion records from the Santa Cruz Mountains (Loma Prieta), California earthquake of 17 October 1989. California Division of Mines and Geology, California Strong Motion Instrumentation Program Report No. OSMS 89-06. 196 p.

Stover, Carl. 1989. U.S. Geological Survey. Personal communication on evaluation of responses to an incomplete mail survey of MMI.

U.S. Geological Survey. 1988. Probabilities of large earthquakes occurring in California on the San Andreas fault. U.S. Geological Survey Open-File report 88-398. 62 p.

Ward, P. and Page, R. 1989. The Loma Prieta earthquake of October 17, 1989. U.S. Geological Survey pamphlet. 16 p.

Wood, H. O., and Neuman, F. 1931. Modified Mercalli intensity scale of 1931. Seismological Society of America Bulletin, v. 21. p. 277-283.

Table 2.1 Modified Mercalli intensity scale of 1931 (Wood and Neuman, 1931).

I Not felt, or, except rarely under especially favorable circumstances. Under certain conditions, at and outside the boundary of the area in which a great shock is felt: sometimes birds, animals, reported uneasy or disturbed; sometimes dizziness or nausea experienced; sometimes trees, structures, liquids, bodies of water, may sway--doors may swing, very slowly.

II Felt indoors by few, especially on upper floors, or by sensitive or nervous persons. Also, as in grade I but often more noticeably: sometimes hanging objects may swing, especially when delicately suspended; sometimes trees, structures, liquids, bodies of water, may sway, doors may swing very slowly; sometimes birds, animals, reported uneasy or disturbed; sometimes dizziness or nausea experienced.

III Felt indoors by several, motion usually rapid vibration. Sometimes not recognized to be an earthquake at first. Duration estimated in some cases. Vibration like that due to passing of light, or lightly loaded trucks, or heavy trucks some distance away. Hanging objects may swing slightly. Movements may be appreciable on upper levels of tall structures. Rocked standing motor cars slightly.

IV Felt indoors by many, outdoors by few. Awakened few, especially light sleepers. Frightened no one, unless apprehensive from previous experience. Vibration like that due to passing of heavy, or heavily loaded trucks. Sensation like heavy body striking building, or falling of heavy objects inside. Rattling of dishes, windows, doors; glassware and crockery clink and clash. Creaking of walls, frame, especially in the upper range of this grade. Hanging objects swung, in numerous instances. Disturbed liquids in open vessels slightly. Rocked standing motor cars noticeably.

V Felt indoors by practically all, outdoors by many or most; outdoors direction estimated. Awakened many, or most. Frightened few slight excitement, a few ran outdoors. Building trembled throughout. Broke dishes, glassware, to some extent. Cracked windows in some cases, but not generally. Overturned vases, small or unstable objects in many instance, with occasional fall. Hanging objects, doors, swing generally or considerably. Knocked pictures against walls, or swung them out of place. Opened, or closed, doors, shutters, abruptly. Pendulum clocks stopped, started, or ran fast, or slow. Moved small objects, furnishings, the latter to slight extent. Spilled liquids in small amounts from well-filled open containers. Trees, bushes, shaken slightly.

VI Felt by all, indoors and outdoors. Frightened many, excitement general, some alarm, many ran outdoors. Awakened all. Persons made to move unsteadily. Trees, bushes, shaken slightly to moderately. Liquid set in strong motion. Small bells rang--church, chapel, school, etc. Damage slight in poorly built buildings. Fall of plaster in small amount. Cracked plaster somewhat, especially fine cracks, chimneys in some instances. Broke dishes, glassware, in considerable quantity, also some windows. Fall of knickknacks, books, pictures. Overturned furniture in many instances. Moved furnishings of moderately heavy kind.

VII Frightened all, general alarm, all ran outdoors. Some, or many, found it difficult to stand. Noticed by persons driving motor cars. Trees and bushes shaken moderately to strongly. Waves on ponds, lakes, and running water. Water turbid from mud stirred up. Incaving to some extent of sand or gravel stream banks. Rang large church bells, etc. Suspended objects made to quiver. Damage negligible in buildings of good design and construction, slight to moderate in well-built ordinary buildings, considerable in poorly built or badly designed buildings, adobe houses, old walls (especially where laid up without mortar), spires, etc. Cracked chimneys to considerable extent, walls to some extent. Shook down loosened brickwork and tiles. Broke weak chimneys at the roof-line (sometimes damaging roofs). Fall of cornices from towers and high buildings. Dislodged bricks and stones. Overturned heavy furniture, with damage from braking. Damage considerable to concrete irrigation ditches.

VIII Fright general, alarm approaches panic. Disturbed persons driving motor cars. Trees shaken strongly--branches, trunks, broken off, especially palm trees. Ejected san and mud in small amounts. Changes: temporary, permanent; in flow of springs and wells; dry wells renewed flow; in temperature of spring and well waters. Damage slight in structures (brick) built especially to withstand earthquakes. Considerable in ordinary substantial buildings, partial collapse: racked, tumbled down, wooden houses in some cases; threw out panel walls in frame structures, broke off decayed piling. Fall of walls. Cracked, broke, solid stone walls seriously. Wet round to some extent, also ground on steep slopes. Twisting, fall, of chimneys, columns, monuments, also factory stacks, towers. Moved conspicuously, overturned, very heavy furniture.

IX Panic general. Cracked ground conspicuously. Damage considerable in (masonry) structures built especially to withstand earthquakes: threw out of plumb some wood-frame houses built especially to withstand earthquakes; great in substantial (masonry) buildings off foundations, racked frames; serious to reservoirs; underground pipes sometimes broken.

X Cracked ground, especially when loose and wet, up to widths of several inches; fissures up to a yard in width ran parallel to canal and stream banks. Landslides considerable from river banks and steep coasts. Shifted sand and mud horizontally on beaches and flat land. Changed level of water in wells. Threw water on banks of canals, lakes, rivers, etc. Damage serious to dams, dikes, embankments. Severe to well-built wooden structures and bridges, some destroyed. Developed dangerous cracks in excellent brick walls. Destroyed most masonry and frame structures, also their foundations. Bent railroad rails slightly. Tore apart, or crushed endwise, pipelines buried in earth. Open cracks and broad wavy folds in cement pavements and asphalt road surfaces.

XI Disturbances in ground many and widespread, varying with ground material. Broad fissures, earth slumps, and land slips in soft, wet ground. Ejected water in large amount charged with sand and mud. Caused sea-waves ("tidal" waves) of significant magnitude. Damage severe to wood-frame structures, especially near shock centers. Great to dams, dikes, embankments, often for long distances. Few, if any, (masonry), structures remained standing. Destroyed large well-built bridges by the wrecking of supporting piers, or pillars. Affected yielding wooden bridges less. Bent railroad rails greatly, and thrust them endwise. Put pipe lines buried in earth completely out of service.

XII Damage total--practically all works of construction damaged greatly or destroyed. Disturbances in ground great and varied, numerous shearing cracks. Landslides, falls of rock of significant character, slumping of river banks, etc., numerous and extensive. Wrenched loose, tore off, large rock masses. Fault slips in firm rock, with notable horizontal and vertical offset displacements. Water channels, surface and underground, disturbed and modified greatly. Dammed lakes, produced waterfall, deflected rivers, etc. Waves seen on ground surfaces (actually seen, probably, in some cases). Distorted lines of sight and level. Threw objects upward in the air.

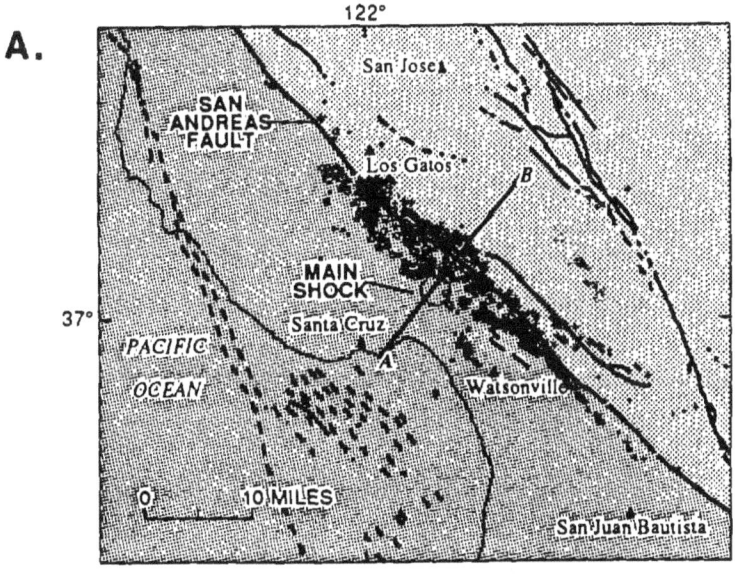

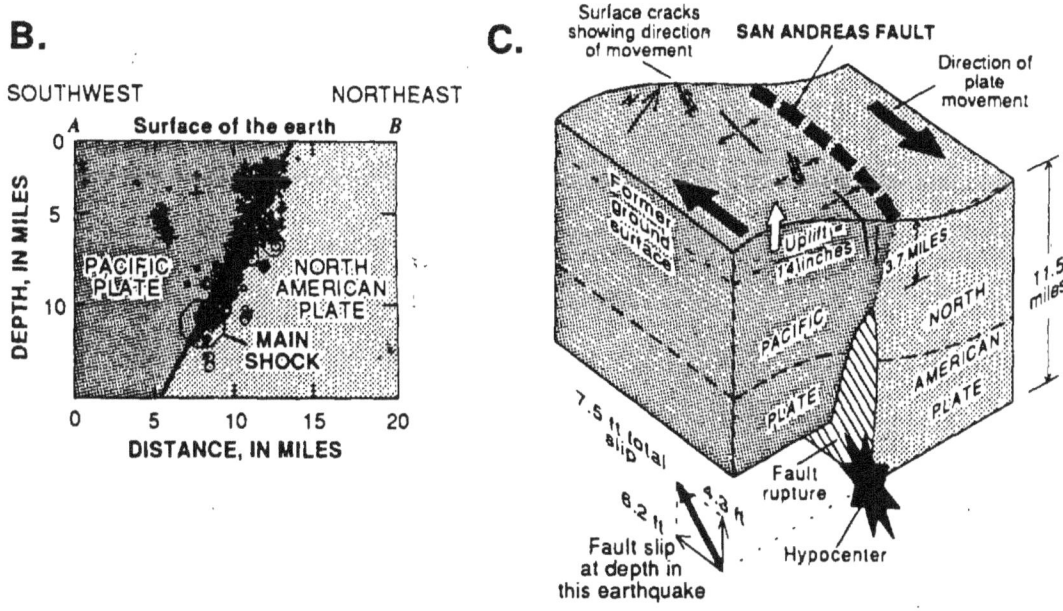

Figure 2.2.1   (A) Location map of the Loma Prieta mainshock and aftershock distribution. The size of the earthquake symbols is relative to magnitude. Black lines are faults, dashed where inferred. (B) Cross section along the line A-B in (A) showing the mainshock hypocenter and the vertical distribution of aftershocks. Note that the dip of the San Andreas fault is about 70° to the southwest. (C) Schematic block diagram showing the major geologic features in the earthquake area and coseismic deformation (from Ward and Page, 1989).

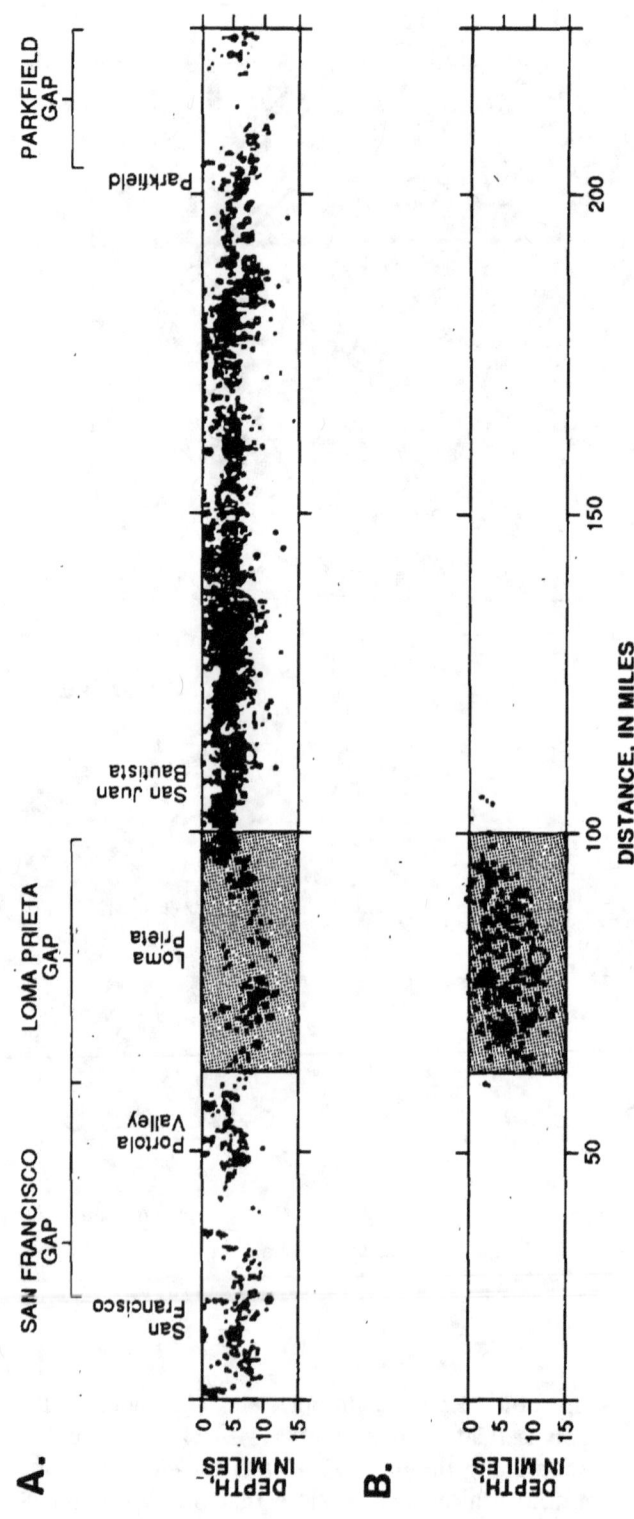

Figure 2.2.2 (A) Longitudinal section of the San Andreas fault plane showing the spatial distribution of seismicity since 1969. Inferred seismic gaps are labeled. (B) Section as in (a), the southern Santa Cruz Mountains segment following the Loma Prieta earthquake and its associated aftershocks that filled the Loma Prieta gap (from Ward and Page).

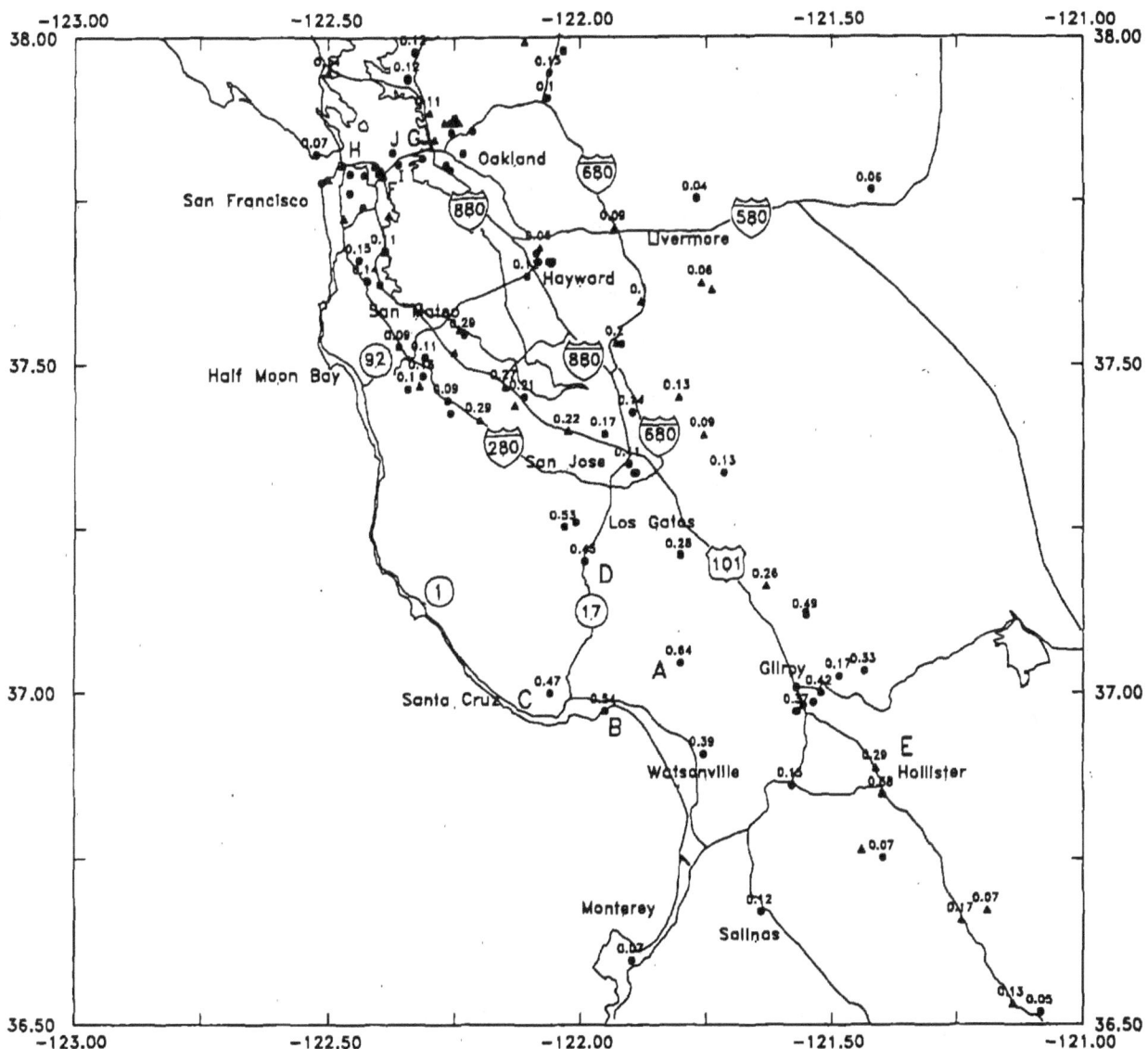

Figure 2.3.1   Location of strong motion instrumentation. USGS stations are designated by triangles
while CDMG stations are designated by circles. The peak horizontal acceleration as a
fraction of gravity is shown adjacent to the station. The area near San Francisco and
Oakland is shown enlarged in figure 2.3.2. The records for the 10 sites indicated by the
letters A-J are shown in figure 2.3.4.

2-11

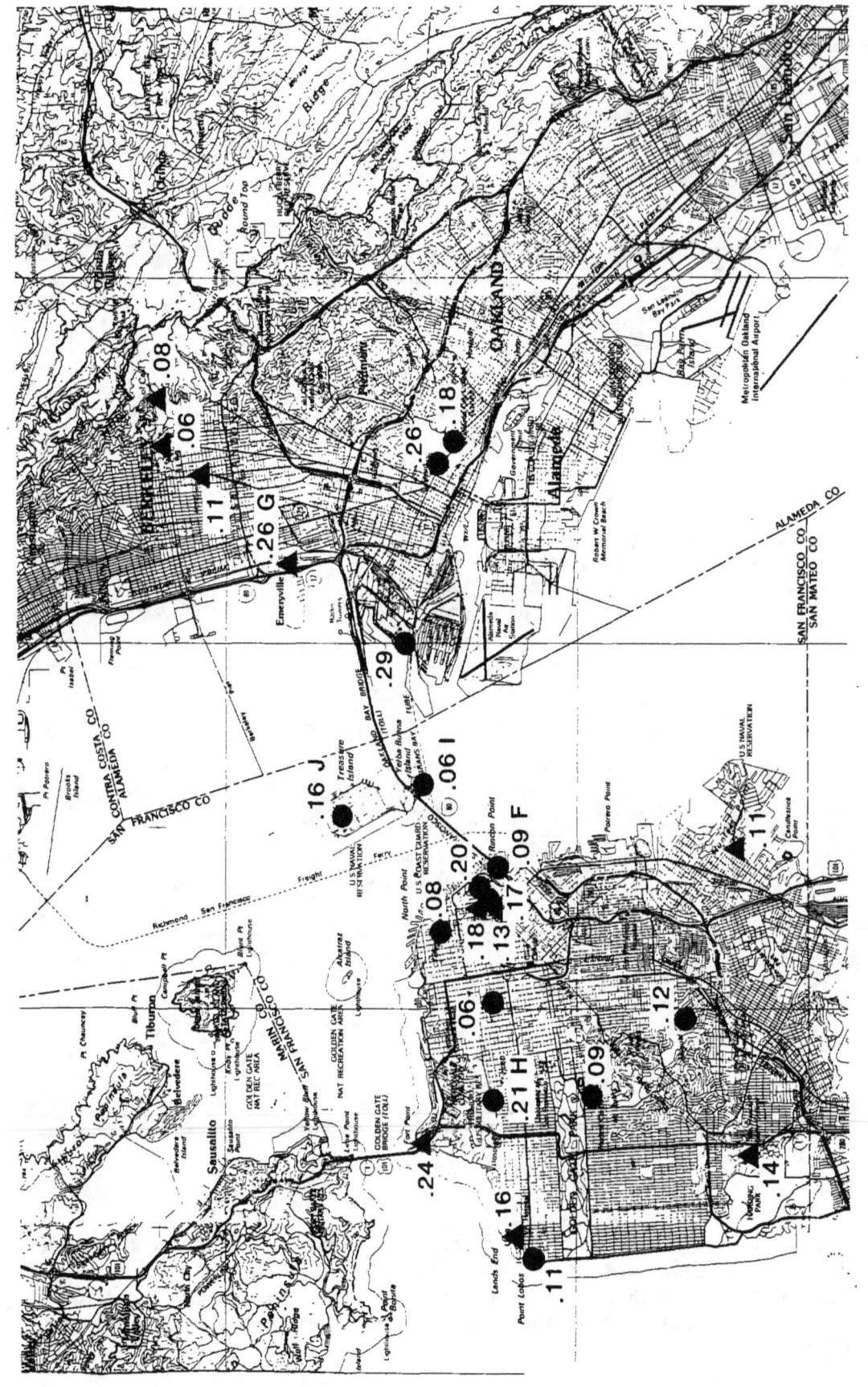

Figure 2.3.2　Strong motion instrumentation in the area of San Francisco and Oakland. USGS stations are designated by triangles while CDMG stations are designated by circles. The peak horizontal acceleration as a fraction of gravity is shown adjacent to the station. The records for the sites indicated by the letters are shown in figure 2.3.4.

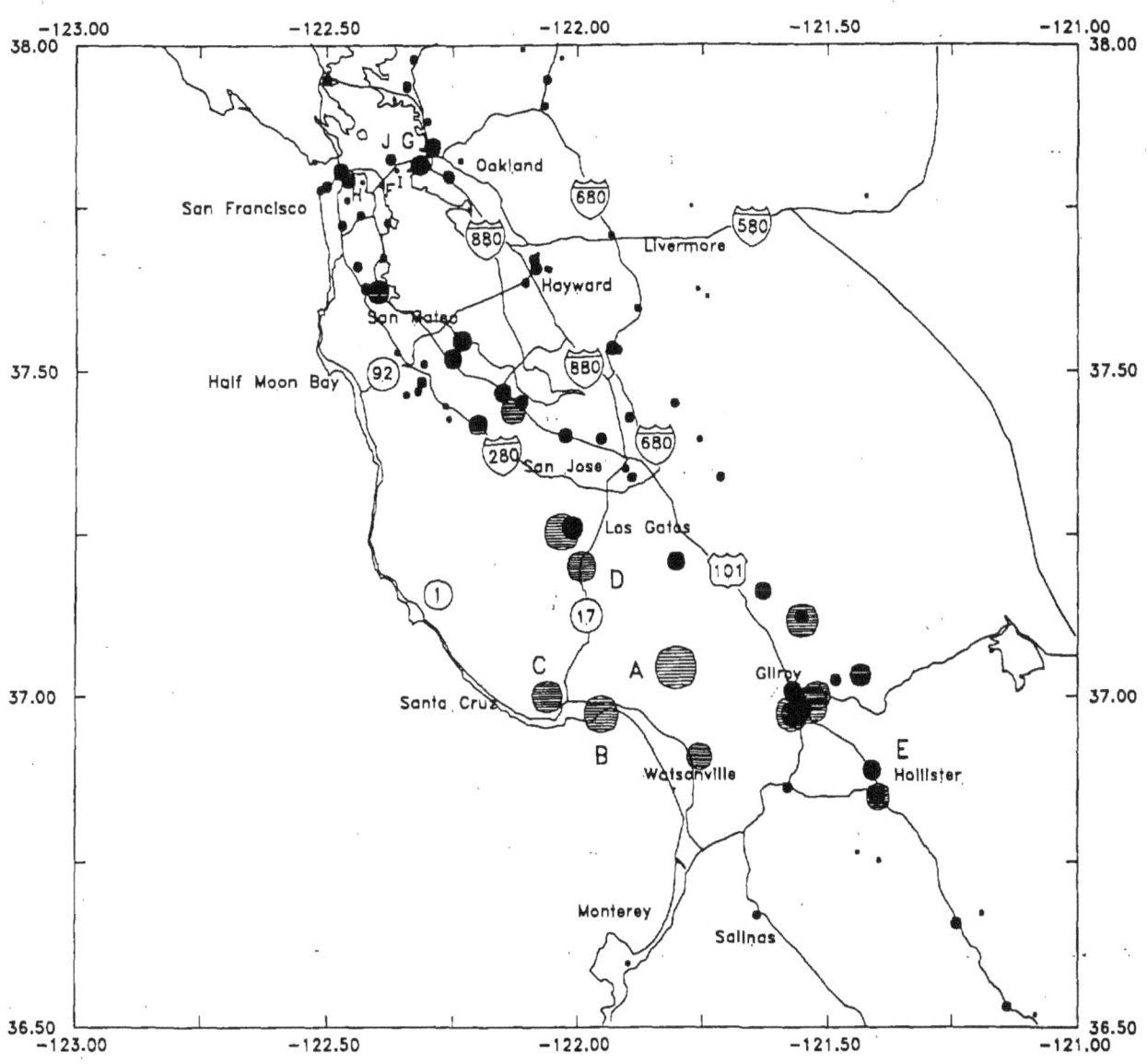

Figure 2.3.3   The relative peak horizontal acceleration is shown at each of the stations identified in figure 2.3.1 by the diameter of the circles. The largest circle at site A represents an acceleration of 0.64 g.

2-13

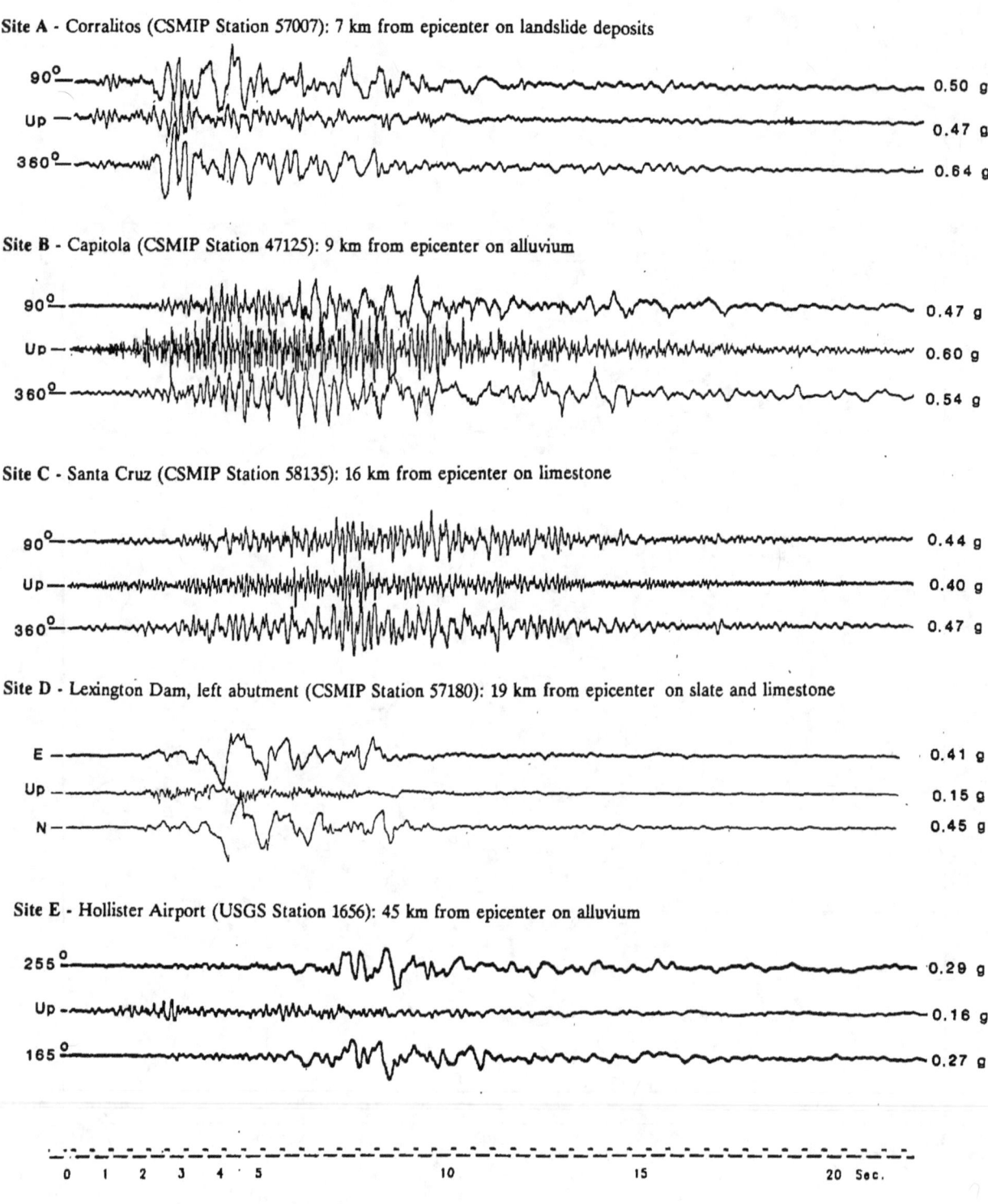

Site A - Corralitos (CSMIP Station 57007): 7 km from epicenter on landslide deposits

90° .... 0.50 g
Up .... 0.47 g
360° .... 0.64 g

Site B - Capitola (CSMIP Station 47125): 9 km from epicenter on alluvium

90° .... 0.47 g
Up .... 0.60 g
360° .... 0.54 g

Site C - Santa Cruz (CSMIP Station 58135): 16 km from epicenter on limestone

90° .... 0.44 g
Up .... 0.40 g
360° .... 0.47 g

Site D - Lexington Dam, left abutment (CSMIP Station 57180): 19 km from epicenter on slate and limestone

E .... 0.41 g
Up .... 0.15 g
N .... 0.45 g

Site E - Hollister Airport (USGS Station 1656): 45 km from epicenter on alluvium

255° .... 0.29 g
Up .... 0.16 g
165° .... 0.27 g

0 1 2 3 4 5   10   15   20 Sec.

Figure 2.3.4   Ground accelerations for the stations designated A-J in figure 2.3.1. The distance from the epicenter and the site geology are indicated.

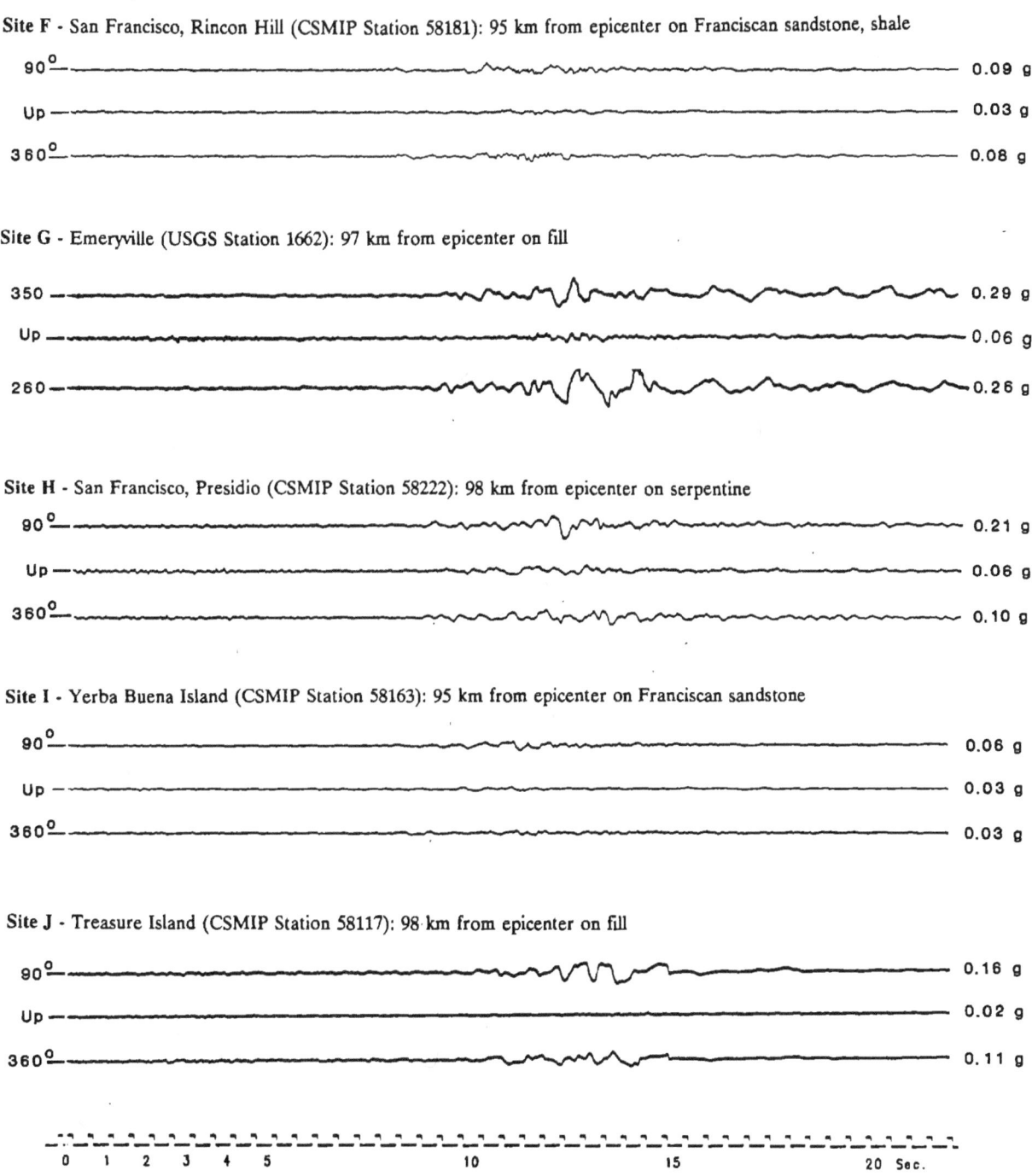

Site F - San Francisco, Rincon Hill (CSMIP Station 58181): 95 km from epicenter on Franciscan sandstone, shale

90° ———————————————————————————— 0.09 g

Up ———————————————————————————— 0.03 g

360° ———————————————————————————— 0.08 g

Site G - Emeryville (USGS Station 1662): 97 km from epicenter on fill

350 ———————————————————————————— 0.29 g

Up ———————————————————————————— 0.06 g

260 ———————————————————————————— 0.26 g

Site H - San Francisco, Presidio (CSMIP Station 58222): 98 km from epicenter on serpentine

90° ———————————————————————————— 0.21 g

Up ———————————————————————————— 0.06 g

360° ———————————————————————————— 0.10 g

Site I - Yerba Buena Island (CSMIP Station 58163): 95 km from epicenter on Franciscan sandstone

90° ———————————————————————————— 0.06 g

Up ———————————————————————————— 0.03 g

360° ———————————————————————————— 0.03 g

Site J - Treasure Island (CSMIP Station 58117): 98 km from epicenter on fill

90° ———————————————————————————— 0.16 g

Up ———————————————————————————— 0.02 g

360° ———————————————————————————— 0.11 g

0 1 2 3 4 5   10   15   20 Sec.

Figure 2.3.4 *(Cont'd)*   Ground accelerations for the stations designated A-J in figure 2.3.1. The distance from the epicenter and the site geology are indicated.

2-15

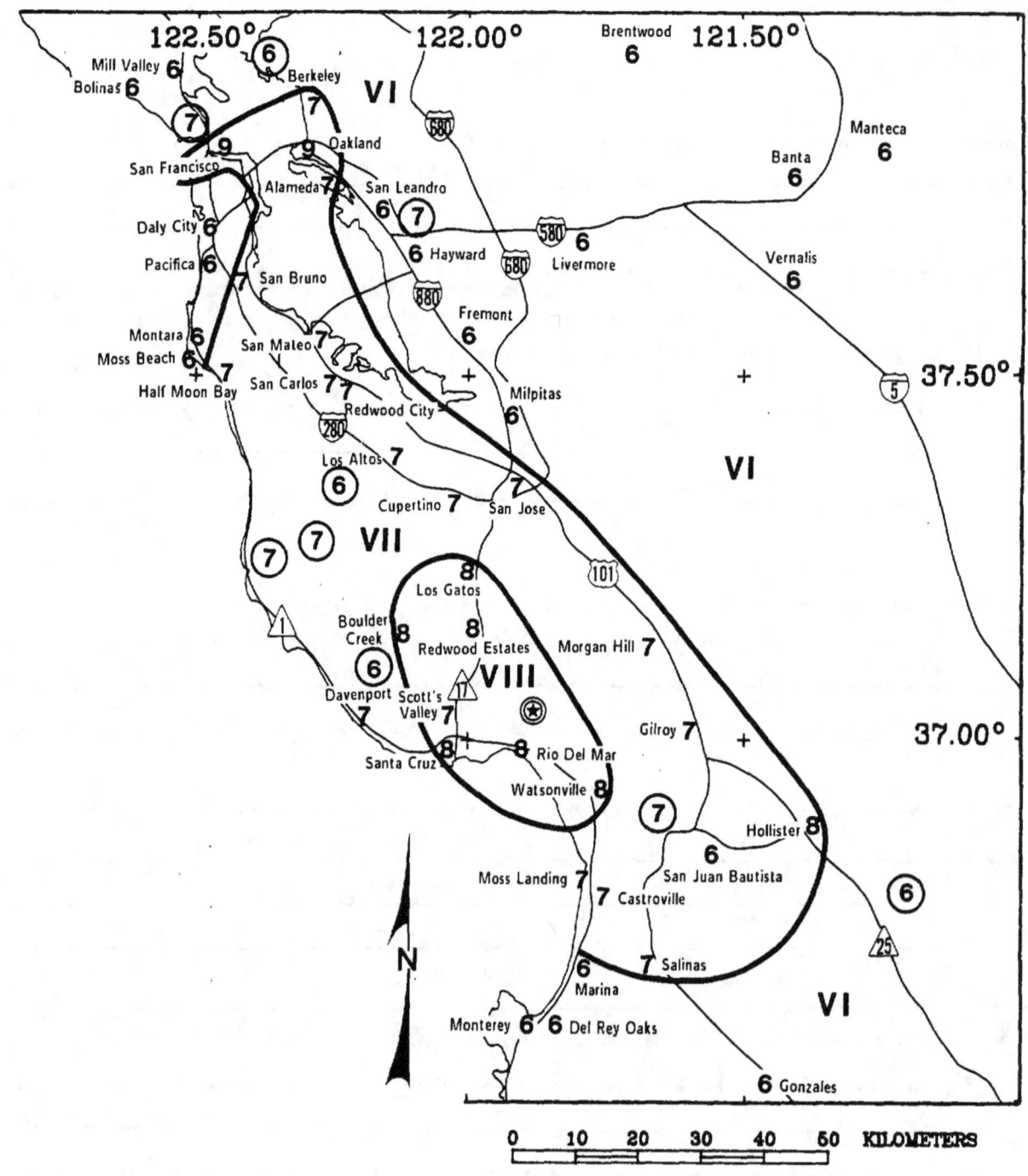

Figure 2.3.5   Preliminary map showing the distribution of Modified Mercalli intensity for the October 17, 1989 Loma Prieta, California earthquake. Intensity values for localities are given in Arabic numbers. Roman numerals represent the intensity level between isoseismal lines. Location of the earthquake epicenter is shown by the circled star. Numbers enclosed in circles have been added since original publication (Plafker and Galloway, 1989). Figure 2.4.1 shows more detailed assessments in the cities of San Francisco and Oakland, California.

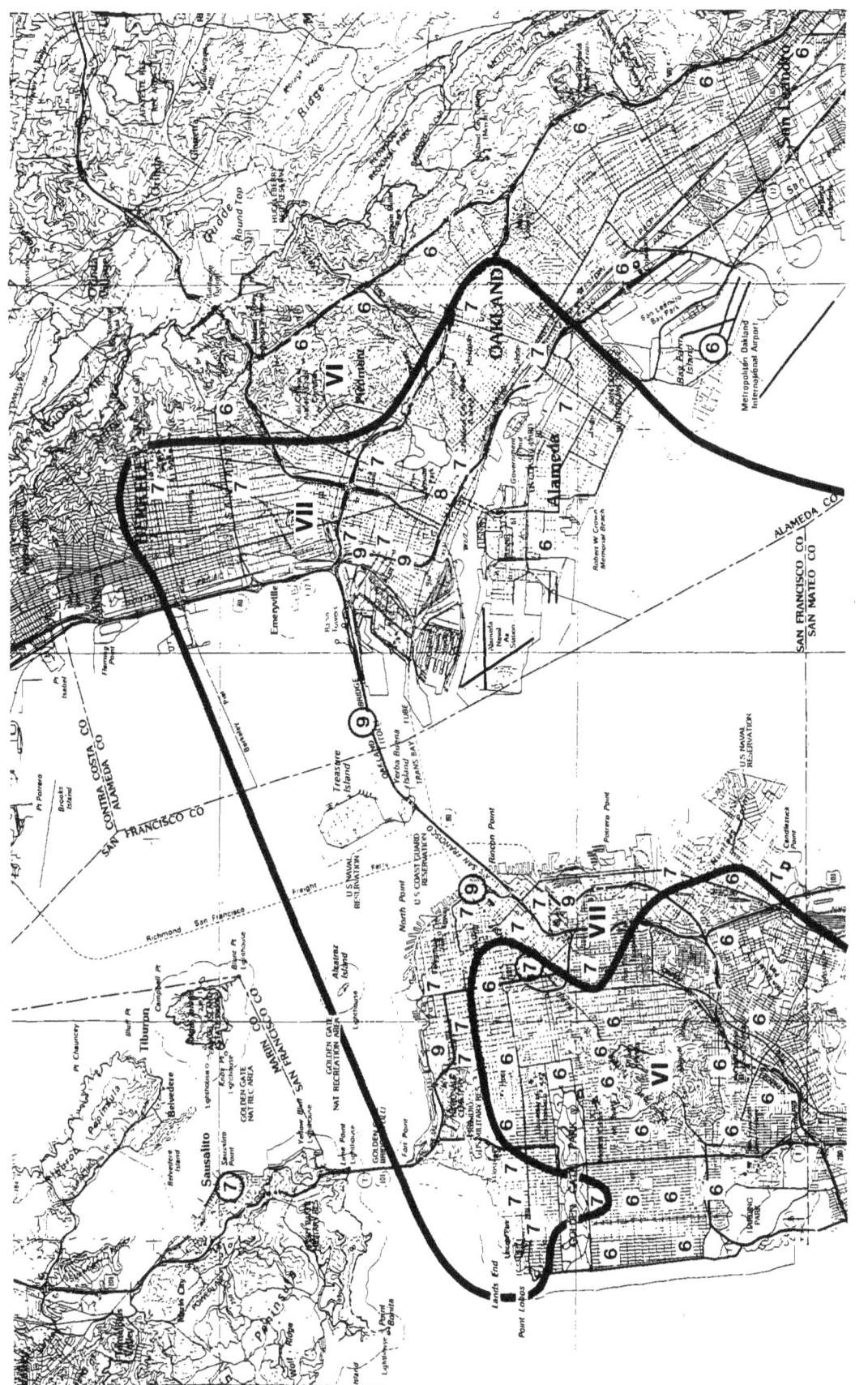

Figure 2.4.1   Detailed Modified Mercalli intensity for the San Francisco and Oakland areas. Numbers enclosed in circles have been added
since original publication (Plafker and Galloway, 1989).

2-17

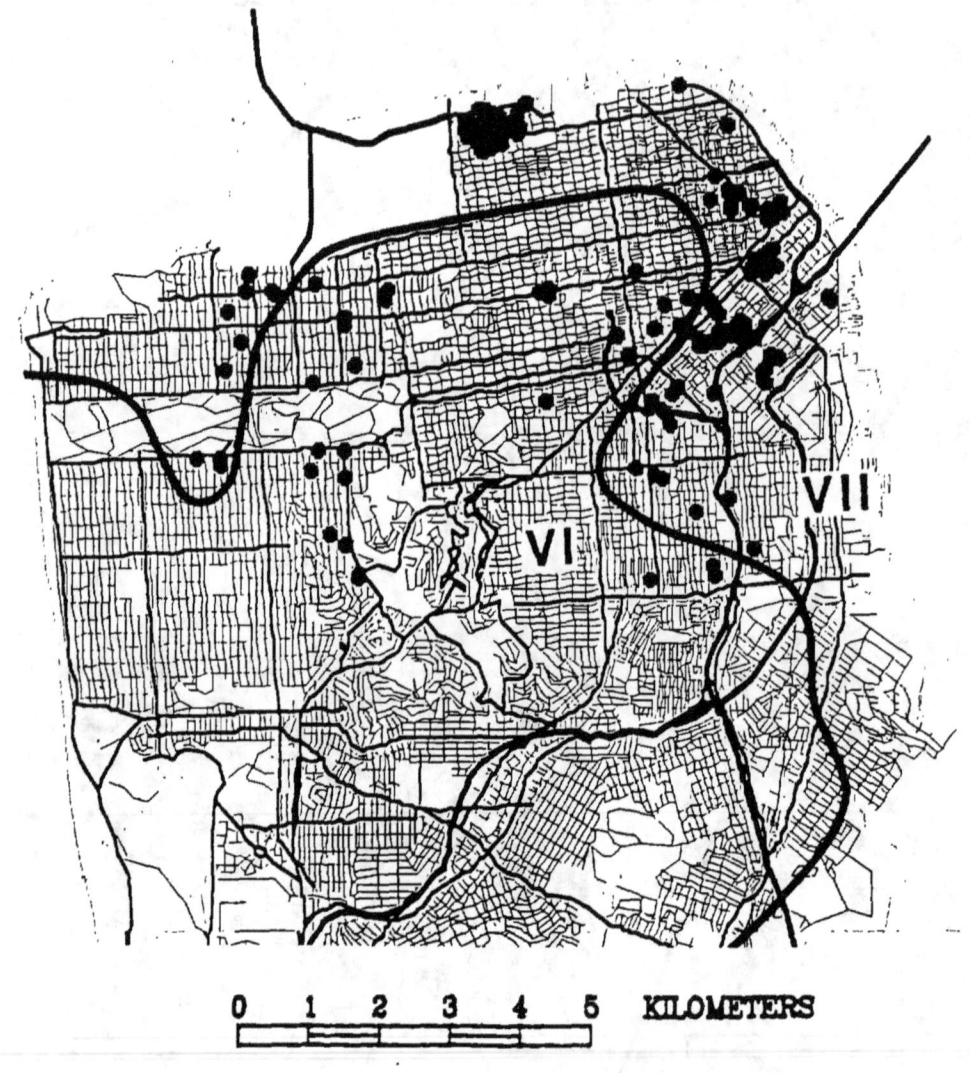

Figure 2.4.2   Damage inspections for San Francisco. The figure shows 378 inspections judged as "red" using the ATC postearthquake safety evaluation procedures (ATC, 1989a,1989b). Damage judged sufficiently for a "Red" designation may be caused by either ground shaking, ground failure, or be in a dangerous area. The preliminary intensity contour based on ground shaking effects from figure 2.4.1 is shown for comparison.

3. SURFICIAL GEOLOGY AND FOUNDATION FAILURES

by Felix Y. Yokel

3.1 Introduction

This chapter describes observed soil displacements and failures, foundation failures, and the effect of subsurface conditions on the severity of the observed earthquake damage.

The Loma Prieta earthquake is characterized by a selective damage pattern. While many structures in areas of relatively shallow, competent soil deposits in the hilly sections of the Los Gatos and Santa Cruz areas, approximately 10 miles (15 km) from the epicenter, remained undamaged or suffered only relatively minor damage, other structures located in areas of deep Bay Mud or alluvium in San Francisco and Oakland, over 60 miles (95 km) from the epicenter, suffered serious damage. Even though a variety of conditions, such as the age, stiffness and lateral load resistance of the affected structures, contributed to this selective damage pattern, it is evident from an examination of the surficial geology in areas where major earthquake damage occurred that the subsurface conditions in these areas were a major contributing factor.

3.2 Ground Failures

Figure 3.2.1 shows the approximate locations of observed ground failures. Four failure categories are identified: (1) fault zone ground cracking; (2) ground failures; (3) liquefaction; and (4) tension cracks. The observations compiled in the map were recorded by the U.S. Geological Survey in Menlo Park, CA, (prior to October 23, 1989), the University of California at Berkeley (Abolhassan et al., 1989), the U.S. Army Corps of Engineers, and the ICSSC team.

The fault zone ground cracking locations were identified by the USGS teams. Most of the fissures are located in the vicinity of the San Andreas and Sargent faults, within a zone extending approximately 12 miles (20 km) to the north and 18 miles (30 km) to the south from the epicenter. Some isolated cracks were observed in the vicinity of the Calaveras fault near the Anderson and Coyote Reservoirs, and in the vicinity of the Hayward fault near Fremont.

Ground failures, most of which were documented by the USGS teams, include landslides, tension cracks, and observable settlements. Liquefaction was identified by telltale signs such as sand boils, ground cracking, buckled sidewalks and lateral spreading. Some tension cracks, mostly in embankments, were

3-1

documented by the U.S. Corps of Engineers, and the ICSSC team. The failure categories identified in figure 3.2.1 are not mutually exclusive. For instance tension cracks in embankments may be attributable to a stability failure, in which case they would fall under "ground failures," or to liquefaction.

Most identifiable ground failures occurred within a distance of about 12 miles (20 km) from the epicenter. However, liquefaction was observed as far as 70 miles (110 km) from the epicenter (Abolhassan et al., 1989). This is because most liquefaction phenomena occurred in areas of deep soil deposits. In these deposits the low-frequency components of the earthquake motion were amplified (Maley et al., 1989, Shakal et al., 1989, Plafker and Galloway, 1989). These low-frequency components decay much more slowly with distance from the epicenter than the high-frequency components, and thus can cause damage and trigger liquefaction at great distances from the epicenter.

3.3 Relation of Subsurface Conditions to Earthquake Damage

3.3.1 San Francisco

Figure 3.3.1 shows the surficial geology of the San Francisco area. The information was derived from Borcherdt and Gibbs, 1975, and supplemented with information from Joyner, 1982. The boundaries between the various soil types are only approximately drawn. Four types of subsurface conditions are identified: Bay Mud; alluvium deeper than 90 ft (30 m); alluvium from 0 - 90 ft (0 - 30 m) deep; and shallow bedrock.

The Bay Mud, also referred to as the "new" Bay Mud is a deposit of recent geological origin and consists of normally consolidated (except for the surcharge effects of man-made fill and structures) organic-rich silty marine clays with some sands with water contents of 50% or more and unconfined compression strengths on the order of 600 psf (30 kPa) near the surface and increasing with depth at the rate of approximately 50 psf (2.4 kPa) per meter. The new Bay Mud layer is up to 130 ft (40 m) thick and has typically shear-wave propagation velocities on the order of 300 - 425 ft/s (90 - 130 m/s) (Borcherdt and Gibbs, 1975). In most on-shore locations the Bay Mud is overlain by about 20 ft (7 m) of man-made fill, which consists of a mixture of rubble and hydraulically placed silty and clayey sands.

The alluvium comprises older Bay sediments, including "old" Bay Mud which consist mostly of stiff silty sandy clays, and granular deposits of medium to dense silty and clayey sands, sands, and gravels. The old Bay Mud is the oldest unconsolidated deposit (Pleistocene) and is also identified as the "Alameda Formation" (Radbruch, 1957). The old Bay Mud was overconsolidated by desiccation during the glacial periods and typically has water contents of less than 40%. It is therefore much denser than the new Bay Mud. The old Bay Mud, wherever it occurs, comprises the lowest layer of alluvium and rests on bedrock. Granular deposits, also identified as "Merritt Sands" (Radbruch, 1957) sometimes form an intervening layer between the new and the old Bay Mud. Typical shear wave propagation velocities in the alluvial deposits are 600 ft/s (200 m/s) at the surface and increase with depth. Thicknesses of the alluvium range up to 1800 ft (600 m) (Borcherdt and Gibbs, 1975).

Figure 3.3.2 shows the approximate location of observed earthquake damage in the San Francisco region together with information on subsurface conditions which was derived from the Joyner map referred to previously. The Joyner map was prepared for the purpose of microzonation on the basis of borehole information. The map shows two details: the boundaries of the area underlain by "Bay Mud"; and the boundaries of the 200 ft (60 m) depth contour of surficial deposits. Within the 200 ft depth contour in the Bay Mud area, the new Bay Mud rests on a layer of alluvium.

Two locations where major highway damage occurred, I-280 and Evans Avenue (1), and I-480 and Market Street (4), are within the Bay Mud area, as well as in the 200-ft contour. An examination of available boring logs indicates, that the I-280 site where damage occurred, is underlain by about 10 ft (3 m) of loose gravel fill, resting on a 40 ft (13 m) thick layer of new Bay Mud, which in turn rests on an layer of alluvium consisting mainly of dense fine to medium sands in its upper part and stiff clays in its lower part. Bedrock is at a depth of 190 ft (58 m). From this site the Bay Mud layer increases to a thickness of approximately 90 ft (30 m) toward the northbound direction of I-280.

Borings from I-480, the Embarcadero section (4), indicate that the Bay Mud layer is between 100-120 ft (30-37 m) thick and bedrock is at a depth of approximately 240 ft (75 m). The alluvial layer between the new Bay Mud and the bedrock consists of old Bay Mud, overlain by a layer of granular deposits.

Highway damage location (2) on I-280 and Channel Street where joints of bents sustained damage is also in the Bay Mud area, but not within the 200 ft depth contour. The damage in location (2) is more localized than that in locations (1) and (4). One of the highway damage areas shown, U.S. Rt. 101 and Fell Street (6), is near the edge of the 200 ft contour and within the area of alluvial deposits, but not in the Bay Mud area.

Extensive liquefaction damage was evident in the Marina District within the boundaries of the cross-hatched area at location (8) in figure 3.3.2. The most intensive damage was concentrated in an area which was filled between 1913 and 1915 in preparation for a 1915 exposition. The fill consists of approximately

30 ft (10 m) of hydraulically placed loose sand (Standard Penetration Test blow counts of 1 to 6), and is underlain by approximately 60 ft (20 m) of new Bay Mud and another 60 ft of dense sand (alluvium). Microseismic measurements in the Marina District reported by Watabe (1989), indicate a maximum site period of 1.2 s.

The most prominent telltale sign of liquefaction are sand boils. These occur as a result of piping, caused by hydrostatic excess pressures. A typical sand boil is shown in figure 3.3.3. Note that the sand was washed out through the joint between the sidewalk tile and the brick wall retaining the stair case. Similar sand boils were observed in many other locations throughout the Marina District. While some of the sand probably was washed out by ruptured water mains, there are many locations, some within buildings, where the sand boils could have been caused only by the presence of excess pore water pressures resulting from the ground shaking.

Typical liquefaction damages observed were buckled sidewalks (fig. 3.3.4) ruptured pipelines, and tension cracks (fig. 3.3.5). The pipeline ruptures, which occurred in more than 100 locations in the Marina District, obviously were caused by excessive ground displacements, associated with liquefaction or cyclic mobility. In some locations there was heave in the pavement on top of pipelines, which either did not settle with the surrounding soil or were uplifted by buoyancy (fig. 3.3.6).

Extensive structural damage to buildings coincided with the liquefaction area in the Marina District. The structural damage in the Marina District is discussed in detail in Chapter 4 of this report. Further studies are needed to determine the mechanism by which liquefaction caused this damage or contributed to it. While some settlement and tilting of foundations was observed by others (Abolhassan et al., 1989) the structural failure mode observed by the ICSSC team was shear failure in the lowest story. The residential structures that failed in the Marina District are for the most part three or four stories high. These structures, under normal conditions, have resonant frequencies on the order of 3 Hz, while the characteristic frequency of the ground motion is less than 1 Hz. Thus resonance between the ground motion and the dynamic response of these building normally would not contribute to the initiation of structural failures. However, in this instance, loss of foundation stiffness could have modified the dynamic response characteristics of the structures.

Other areas underlain by Bay Mud deposits where liquefaction was observed and where a great number of buildings had to be condemned because of structural failures are on Market Street near 1st Street (11), on Folsom Street between 4th and 10th street (5), on S. Van Ness Ave. near U.S. Rt. 101 (10), and on Bluxome Street (3).

Damage location (9) and other building damage locations, which are shown in the figure but not identified by numbers, and which are remote from Bay Mud deposits, are generally located in the deep alluvial deposit area shown in figure 3.3.1. In the case of damage location (9), the damaged buildings were reported to be located in a man-made fill area.

In summary, most of the damages to structures and lifeline systems in San Francisco occurred in areas of Bay Mud deposits. The most likely reason for the damages are the amplification of the ground motion by the Bay Mud and the underlying alluvial deposits and soil liquefaction. The amplification of the ground motion also contributed to the widespread liquefaction of fill areas. In many areas, liquefaction of the man-made fill covering the Bay Mud deposits coincided with major structural damage to buildings and utilities (damage locations (3), (4), (5), (8), and (10) in fig. 3.3.2).

3.3.2 Oakland

Figure 3.3.7 shows the surficial geology of the areas in Oakland where damage occurred. Three types of subsurface conditions are identified in the figure: (1) Bay Mud, which is similar to the new Bay Mud area identified in figure 3.3.1; (2) alluvium; and (3) shallow bedrock. The information in figure 3.3.7 is taken from Gibbs and Borcherdt (1974), and from a map prepared by Radbruch (1957). In the figure, the alluvial deposits are not differentiated by their characteristics. However Radbruch's map shows two types of surficial alluvial deposits: fine silty and clayey sands with lenses of sandy clay and clay, identified as "Merritt Sands"; and clayey gravels, sandy and silty clays, and sand-clay-silt mixtures with pebbles, identified as the "Temescal Formation." These surficial alluvial deposits, as well as the Bay Mud deposits, rest on a deep layer of old Bay Muds, identified by Radbruch as the "Alameda Formation." The upper portion of this layer has been overconsolidated by desiccation during the glacial periods. Most available boring logs, including those taken in conjunction with the construction of I-880, do not penetrate to bedrock. However, a boring on the Naval Reserve to the south of the inner Harbor (Boring 88 in Radbruch's map) indicates a depth to bedrock of 440 ft (135 m), and another boring at Adeline Street in Oakland, not far from the collapsed I-880 viaduct, indicates a depth of 550 ft (167 m) to bedrock (Radbruch, 1957).

The most prominent failure in the Oakland area is collapse of the I-880 viaduct which is discussed in Chapter 5. As indicated in figure 3.3.7, the collapsed part of the viaduct is located near the outer boundary of the Bay Mud area. An examination of available boring logs indicates that near the north end of the collapsed area there is 5 ft (1.5 m) fill, 6 ft (2 m) of Bay Mud and 60 ft (17 m) of alluvium, which consists of stiff silty clays (Temescal Formation). The borings stopped in a compact layer of coarse sand and gravel and were not carried to bedrock. Toward the south end of the collapsed area the thickness of the Bay Mud layer increases to 25 ft (8 m) and there is a layer of dense sands and gravels (Merritt Sand) to a depth of 100 ft (32 m). All borings taken stopped in a layer of compact sands and gravels and did not penetrate into the underlying layer of old Bay Mud. However the information previously discussed indicates that the depth to bedrock is very great.

The area of extensive building damage in Oakland, identified in figure 3.3.7 is in the surficial alluvial deposit identified by Radbruch as Merritt Sand and is in the vicinity of the Bay Mud deposits surrounding Lake Merritt. Radbruch's information indicates that this area is also underlain by a deep layer of the Alameda Formation.

It is of interest that three strong motion stations in the Oakland area, shown in figure 2.3.2 recorded peak accelerations of 0.26g, 0.26g and 0.29g. These stations provide a measure of the amplification of the earthquake motion attributable to the deep alluvial deposits in the area, and also indicate that over this area of deep alluvial deposits the strong motion did not vary substantially. The strong motion records indicate dominant site periods from 1 to 1.5 s (Maley et al., 1989).

3.3.3 Watsonville

The damaged area in Watsonville is located in the deep alluvial soil deposits of the Pajaro River valley. The subsurface conditions in the Watsonville area have been extensively studied (Dupré and Tinsley, 1979, and Dupré, 1975). The building damage in Watsonville is in a formation of fluvial, estuarine and alluvial fan deposits designated by Dupré and Tinsley as "older floodplain deposits." These deposits are characterized as "unconsolidated, relatively finegrained deposits of sand and silt, commonly including relatively thin layers of clay." In accordance with the information utilized by Dupré these deposits are coarser grained at the bottom and become more finegrained toward the surface, and their depth is on the order of 220 ft (67 m) or more. The surface deposits near the Pajaro River where fissures were observed are designated as "younger floodplain deposits." These deposits are similar to the older floodplain deposits, but they are more susceptible to liquefaction.

Extensive tension cracking was observed along the embankments of the Pajaro River (fig. 3.2.1). Figure 3.3.8 shows a 2 ft (600 mm) wide tension crack near the bridge of Main Street over the Pajaro River. The crack was parallel to the river between the dike and the river. There was a second parallel crack nearer the river which was approximately 6 in (150 mm) wide. There were also some tension cracks outside the embankment and parallel to it (fig. 3.3.9). The tension cracks in the soil parallel to the embankment are attributable to spreading of the embankment, probably caused by liquefaction. The bridge itself had to be closed to traffic because of structural damage. The bridge which was built in 1947 is supported by 40 ft (12 m) long untreated wood piles. Preliminary survey information from the City of Watsonville indicates that the bridge and a manhole in its vicinity settled approximately 6 in (150 mm). The Pajaro River bridge is located in the area designated by Dupré and Tinsley as younger floodplain deposits.

Extensive structural and pipeline damage was observed in downtown Watsonville in the areas of the older floodplain deposits. Shallow pits excavated for utility pipe repair contained deposits of fine sands, interbedded with clays (fig. 3.3.10). The observation made in these pits corroborates the observations recorded by Dupré and Tinsley. No telltale signs of liquefaction were observed in the damage area in downtown Watsonville and no groundwater was observed in the excavated pits (about 7 ft (2 m) deep). Borings taken in March 1966 at the fire station in the downtown area show 2-3 ft (0.6 m) of silt, underlain by a 5 ft (1.5 m) layer of clay, which in turn rests on sand. The deepest boring terminated in sandy soils at a depth of 28 ft (8.5 m). The groundwater level at the time of boring was 17.5 - 21.5 ft (5.3 - 6.5 m) below surface. A local building official mentioned that 1989 was a dry year prior to the earthquake. Thus, it is unlikely that the ground water level was much closer to the surface during the earthquake to cause liquefaction near the base of the footings in the downtown area of Watsonville. Typically, the buildings in downtown Watsonville are supported by shallow spread footings.

3.3.4 Santa Cruz

Extensive building damage occurred at the Pacific Garden shopping mall which parallels the San Lorenzo river. No specific subsurface information has been obtained to date, however the damaged area is located on the alluvial deposits of the San Lorenzo River valley, which are similar to the "older and younger floodplain deposits" previously described (Dupré, 1975). Not much damage was observed in the hilly sections of Santa Cruz. Microseismic measurements in the Pacific Garden mall area (Watabe, 1989) indicate a maximum site period of 3.26 s, which would be associated with deep soil deposits.

Many of the damaged buildings were stiff masonry shear wall structures which are judged to have natural frequencies much higher than the characteristic frequency of the site. While widespread liquefaction was observed by others in the Santa Cruz area (i.e. Abolhassan et al., 1989), no telltale signs of liquefaction were observed by the ICSSC team in the Pacific Garden mall area.

3.3.5 Los Gatos

Most of the earthquake damage in Los Gatos occurred in the flat terrain adjacent to the Los Gatos Creek. This is also the area where most of the unreinforced brick structures are located. The subsurface information obtained on the site is from shallow pits dug to repair the extensive damage to utilities. The soils in these pits were granular (sands and gravels) and stratified, indicating that these are alluvial deposits (fig. 3.3.11). No groundwater accumulated in the 7 ft (2 m) deep pits.

The Los Gatos area was mapped by Dibblee and Brabb (1978). In accordance with their map, most of the damage occurred in an area of surficial deposits of recent (Holocene) alluvium, resting on older, Pleistocene alluvial deposits. No information was obtained on the depth of these deposits.

3.4 Summary

The pattern of earthquake damage was closely correlated with subsurface conditions. Most structural and lifeline damage occurred in areas of deep soil deposits. Heavy concentrations of damage to structures and utilities were associated with soil liquefaction.

In San Francisco most of the damage occurred in areas underlain by new Bay Mud, but there also were damages in areas of deep alluvial deposits. The damage in Oakland covered in this report occurred in an area of deep alluvial deposits, which exhibited approximately uniform amplification of the ground motion over a large region. At the collapsed I-880 viaduct these alluvial deposits were covered with a 6-24 ft (2-8 m) thick layer of Bay Mud. It is not yet known whether this soft layer contributed to the collapse. In Watsonville and Santa Cruz most of the earthquake damage occurred in areas of deep alluvium. In Los Gatos most of the damage also is in an alluvial area, however there is no information on the depth of the deposit.

The effect of the subsurface conditions on the damage pattern observed in this earthquake is mostly attributed to amplification of the earthquake motion by the underlying soil deposits (Plafker and Galloway, 1989). When maximum accelerations from rock sites of roughly comparable epicentral distance are compared with those from sites of new Bay Mud deposits and sites of alluvial deposits the average amplification ratios observed in this earthquake are 1.8 and 2.6 for vertical and horizontal accelerations, respectively, for Bay Mud sites, and 1.9 and 1.8 for vertical and horizontal accelerations, respectively, for alluvial sites (EERI, 1989). These amplifications of maximum accelerations are associated with much greater amplifications of velocities and displacements in the horizontal direction, because of the long characteristic period of the horizontal components of the earthquake motion in the deep soil deposits.

The long characteristic period of the deep soil deposits also is a reason why severe damage occurred in areas with epicentral distances of approximately 60 miles (95 km). Low-frequency components of the earthquake motion decay more slowly with epicentral distance than high-frequency components and can be strongly amplified by deep soil deposits. The probability of experiencing severe shaking is increased in areas of deep soil deposits because strong shaking can occur from distant as well as nearby earthquakes.

Strong correlations between subsurface conditions and damage patterns have been observed in many other earthquakes. For instance, in the September 19, 1985 Mexico City earthquake most of the structural damage occurred in areas of the lakebed area where the depth of the soft clay deposits ranged from 100 - 125 ft (30 - 38 m) (Stone et al., 1987). However, in the Mexico City earthquake, most of the damage was caused by resonance between the ground motion and the dynamic response of the damaged buildings. In the Loma Prieta earthquake, relatively stiff buildings also were damaged in areas of deep soil deposits, while similar buildings in areas of shallow, competent soil deposits remained undamaged. The vulnerability of these latter structures cannot be attributed to amplification resulting from resonance between the ground motion and the initial dynamic response of the structures.

At present, design criteria recognize the effect of site characteristics on structures having long natural periods. However, for structures with natural periods less than approximately 0.6 s no site amplification is recognized, and for soil profiles containing soft clay, recommended design spectra actually stipulate a reduced seismic design coefficient (FEMA, 1988, NEHRP Section 4.2.1). These provisions and those for retrofit of existing structures should be re-examined.

3.5 References

Abolhassan et al. 1989, Preliminary Report on Seismological and Engineering Aspects of the October 17, 1989 Santa Cruz (Loma Prieta) Earthquake, University of California at Berkeley, Report No. UBC/EERI-89/14.

Borcherdt, R. D. and Gibbs, J. F., 1975, "Prediction of Maximum Earthquake Intensities for the San Francisco Bay Region," U.S. Geological Survey Open File Report 75-180.

Federal Emergency Management Agency, 1988, "NEHRP Recommended Provisions for the Development of Seismic Regulations for New Buildings," FEMA 95.

California Division of Mines and Geology, 1989, "Strong Ground Shaking from the Loma Prieta Earthquake of October 17, 1989 and its Relation to Near-Surface Geology in the Oakland Area," November, 1989.

Dibblee, Jr., T. W. and Brabb, E. E., 1978, "Preliminary Geologic Maps of the Chittenden, Los Gatos, and Watsonville East Quadrangles," U.S. Geological Survey Open File Report 78-453.

Dupré, W. R., 1975, "Quaternary History of the Watsonville Lowlands, North-Central Monterey Bay Region," Doctoral Dissertation, Stanford University.

Dupré, W. R. and Tinsley III, J. C., 1975, "Maps Showing Geology and Liquefaction Potential of the Northern Monterey and Southern Santa Cruz Counties, CA," U.S. Geological Survey Misc. Field Studies, Map MS-648.

Earthquake Engineering Research Institute and National Research Council, 1989, "Loma Prieta Earthquake, October 17, 1989, Preliminary Reconnaissance Report," EERI 89-03.

Gibbs, J. F. and Borcherdt, R. D., 1974, "Effects of Local Geology on Ground Motion in the San Francisco Bay Region, A Continued Study," U.S. Geological Survey Open File Report 74-22.

Joyner, W. B., 1982, "Map Showing the 200-foot Thickness Contour of Surficial Deposits and the Landward Limit of Bay Mud Deposits of San Francisco, CA", U.S. Geological Survey Misc. Field Studies Map MF-1376, 1 Plate, Scale 1:24,000.

Maley, R., et al., 1989, "U.S. Geological Survey Strong-Motion Records from the Northern California (Loma Prieta) Earthquake of October 17, 1989," Open-File Report 89-568, U.S. Geological Survey.

Plafker, G. P. and Galloway, J. P., Eds., 1989, "Lessons Learned from the Loma Prieta, CA, Earthquake of October 17, 1989.," U.S. Geological Survey Circular 1045, U.S. Government Printing Office.

Radbruch, D. H., 1975, "Areal and Engineering Geology of the Oakland West Quadrangle, CA," U.S. Geological Survey Misc. Geologic Investigations, Map I-239.

Shakal, A., et al., 1989, "November 1989 CSMIP Strong Motion Records from the Santa Cruz (Loma Prieta) CA Earthquake of 17 October 1989," California Division of Mines and Geology, Report OSMS 89-06.

Stone, W. C., Yokel, F. Y., Celebi, M., Hanks, T., and Leyendecker, E. V., 1987, "Engineering Aspect of the September 19, 1985 Mexico Earthquake," NBS Building Science Series 165, National Bureau of Standards.

Watabe, M., 1989, "San Francisco Earthquake," Tokyo Metropolitan University.

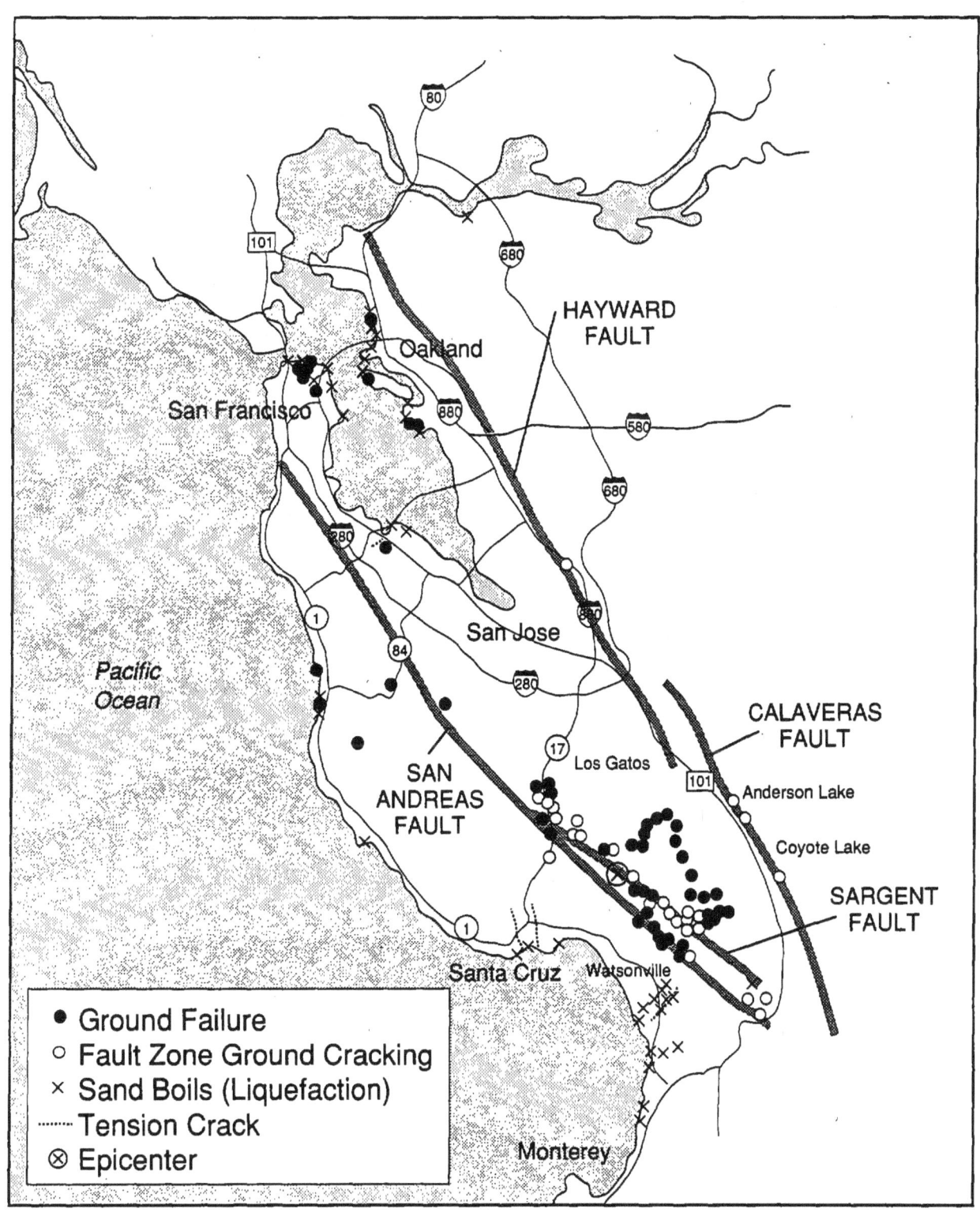

Figure 3.2.1   Ground failures caused by the Loma Prieta earthquake.

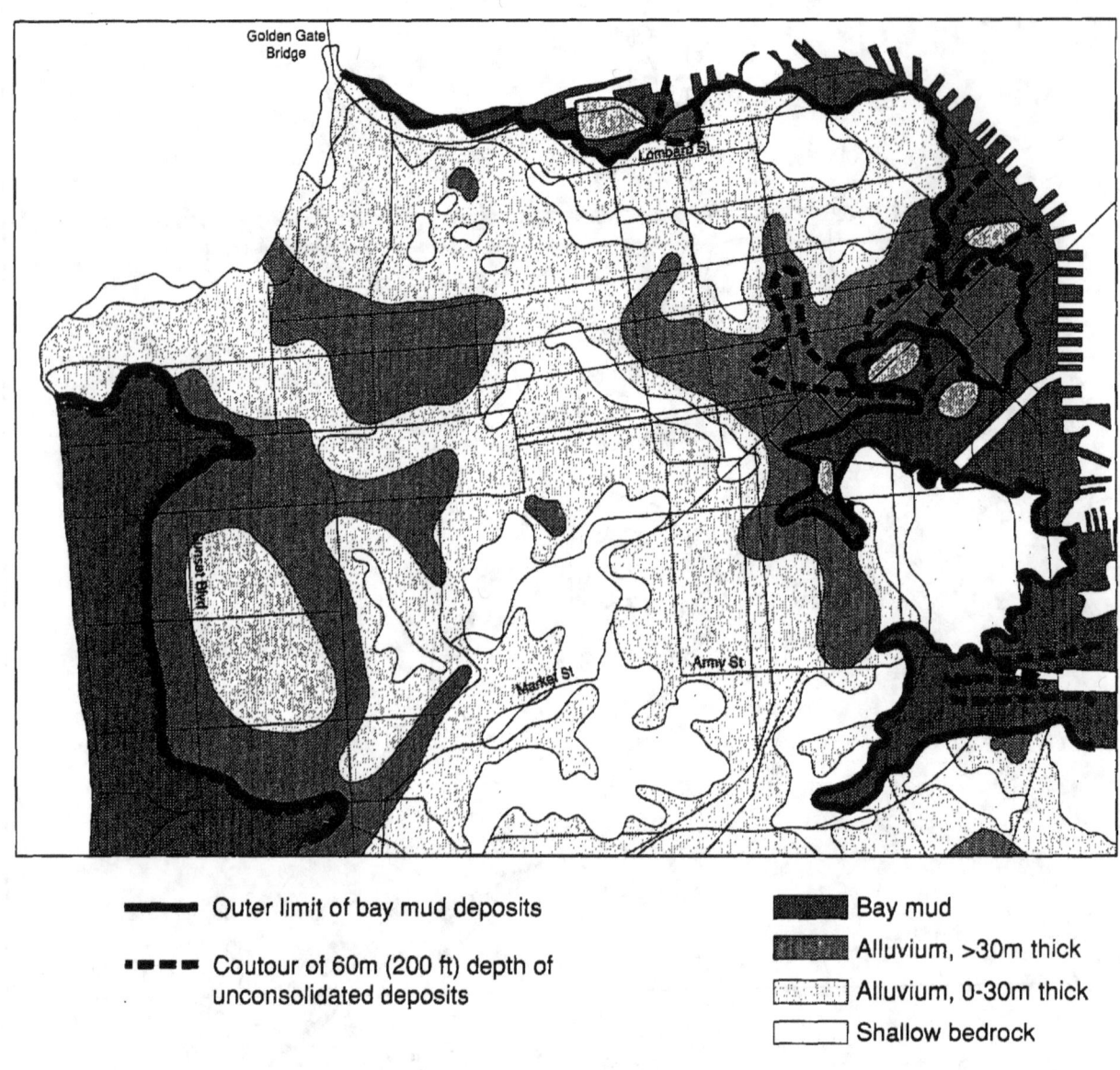

———	Outer limit of bay mud deposits
▪▪▪▪	Coutour of 60m (200 ft) depth of unconsolidated deposits

■	Bay mud
▓	Alluvium, >30m thick
░	Alluvium, 0-30m thick
□	Shallow bedrock

Figure 3.3.1   Surficial geology of the San Francisco area.

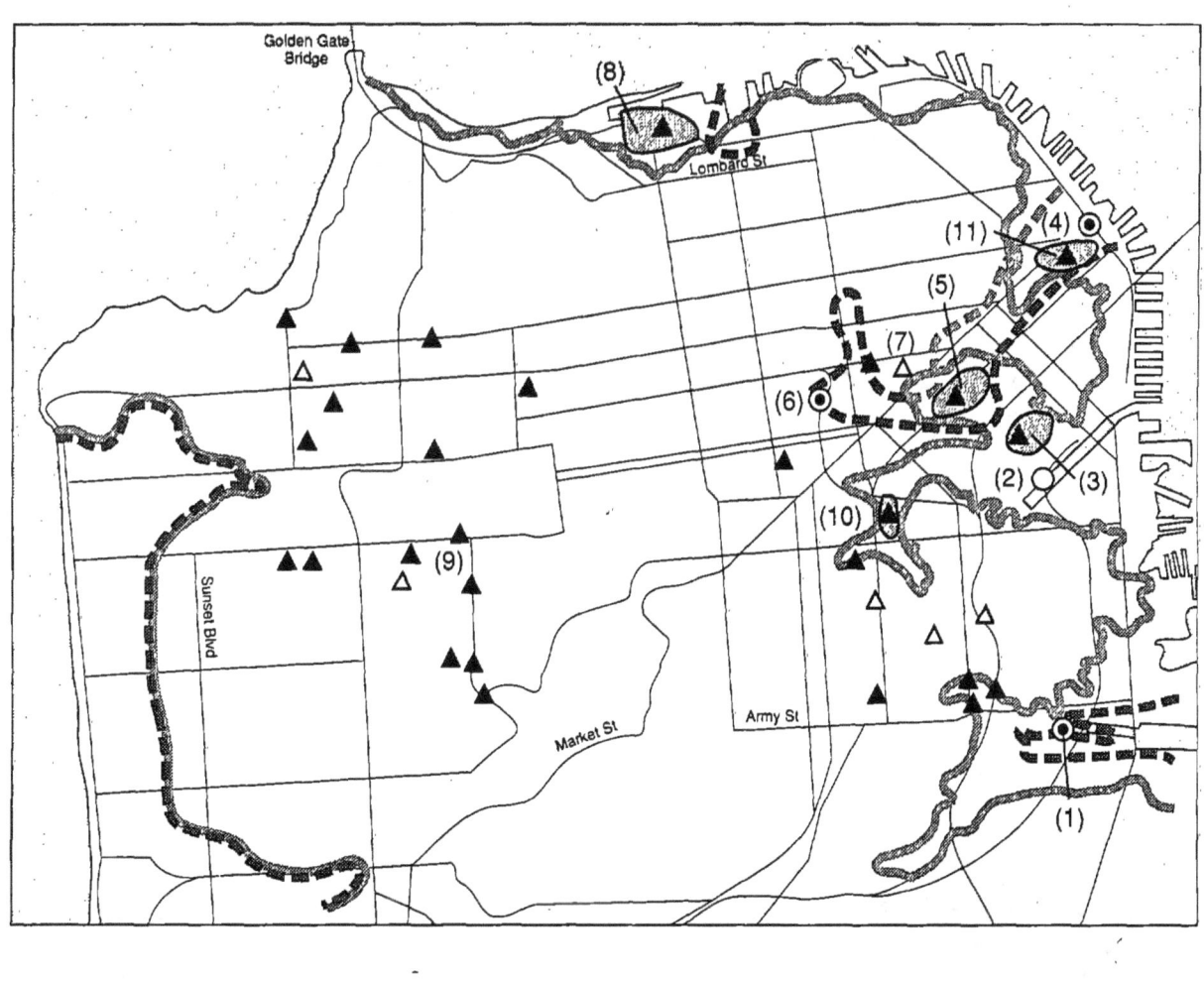

▬▬▬ Outer limit of bay mud deposits	⊙ Major damage to highway structures
■ ■ ■ Coutour of 60m (200 ft) depth of unconsolidated deposits	○ Minor damage to highway structures
⬭ Area of damage concentration	▲ Major damage to buildings
	△ Minor damage to buildings

Figure 3.3.2   Correlation of damage patterns and surficial geology in the San Francisco area.

Figure 3.3.3   Sand boil in the Marina District of San Francisco.

Figure 3.3.4   Typical liquefaction damage in the Marina District of San Francisco.

3-14

Figure 3.3.5   Tension crack at Mission Street and Embarcadero Freeway.

Figure 3.3.6   Pavement heave over utility pipe.

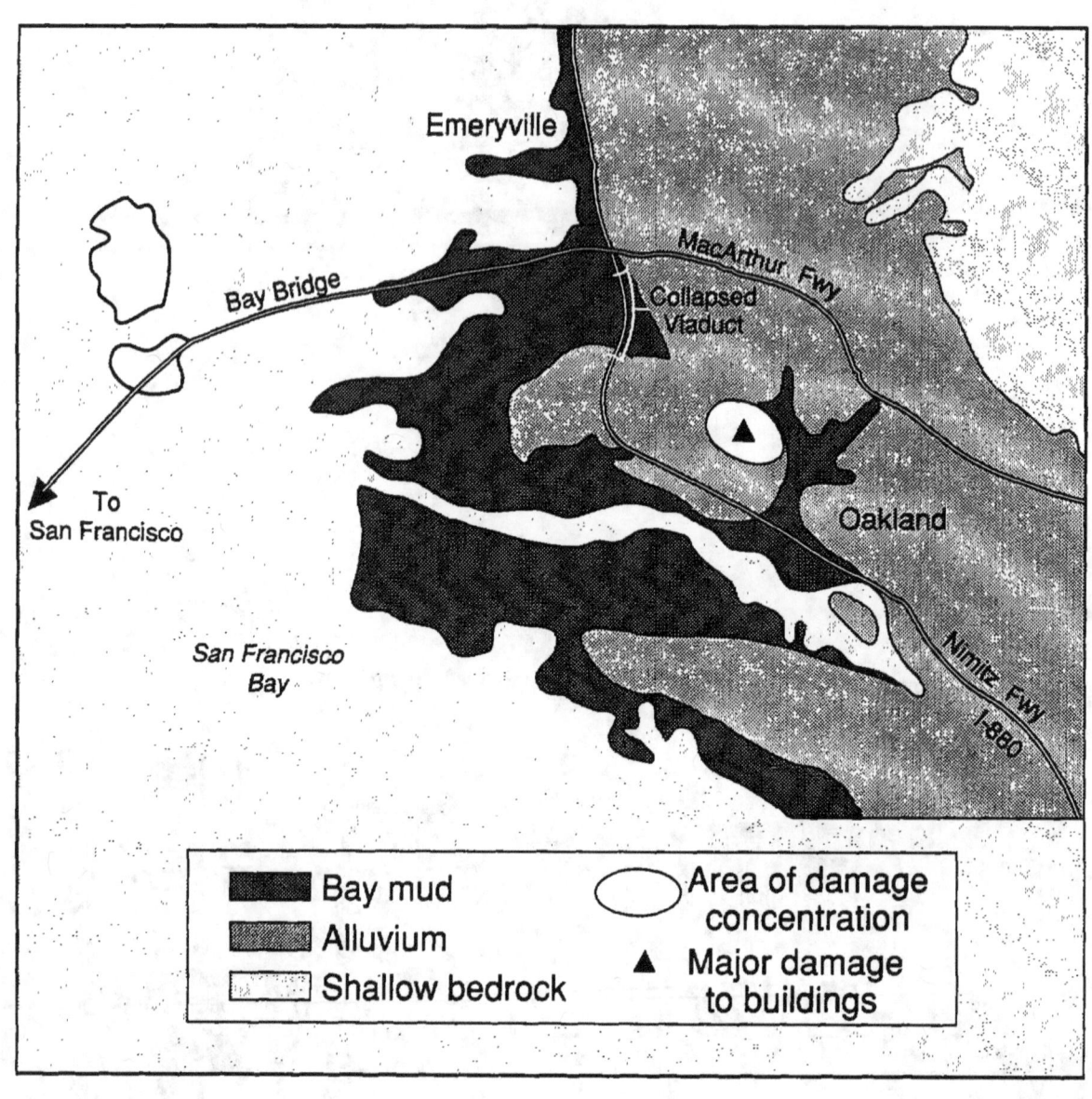

Figure 3.3.7   Surficial geology of the Oakland Area.

Figure 3.3.8   Tension cracks on Pajaro River bank in Watsonville.

Figure 3.3.9   Tension cracks behind Pajaro River levee.

Figure 3.3.10   Excavated pit in Watsonville.

Figure 3.3.11   Excavated pit in Los Gatos.

3-18

4. PERFORMANCE OF BUILDINGS

by Nicholas J. Carino

4.1 Introduction

This chapter describes the performance of buildings within the Bay area and within the epicentral region. Because of the large area in which buildings were damaged, the inspections concentrated on those regions which experienced a large amount of severe damage. As discussed in Chapter 3 the most serious damage was concentrated in areas of deep soil deposits.

Most structures designed according to modern codes and standards performed well without structural damage. The majority of the damaged structures were either wood-framed dwellings or unreinforced masonry buildings which had not been strengthened to increase their seismic resistance. It should be noted that the Loma Prieta earthquake was not a severe test of buildings designed according to modern seismic criteria. Except for the epicentral region, peak ground accelerations were less than implied by modern building codes. Also, the duration of strong ground shaking was only 10 to 15 seconds. Thus, the favorable performance of the majority of modern buildings can not be used as evidence that current seismic design criteria are adequate.

There were isolated failures in modern structures to which the team did not gain access. Detailed investigations of the circumstances associated with these failures can provide opportunities to improve design standards if it is found that the failures occurred where standards were met. The Loma Prieta earthquake also provided opportunities to evaluate the performance of the various seismic strengthening methods used within the affected region. The team observed many instances of successful strengthening measures, but there were also examples of unsuccessful measures.

This chapter provides examples of the type of damage observed in the more severely affected regions. Probable failure mechanisms are discussed where possible, but no attempt is made to provide in-depth explanations of the underlying factors leading to the observed damage.

4.2 San Francisco

The following areas in San Francisco sustained the most severe damage and were investigated: the Marina District, the Financial District, the Civic Center District, and South of Market District. Following the earthquake, building officials and volunteer engineers inspected over 8500 buildings. It has been reported by the Department of Public Works[1] of the city of San Francisco that about 260 buildings were given the status "unsafe" and about 1400 were classified as "limited entry."

4.2.1 Marina District

Figure 4.2.1 is a map of the Marina District showing the approximate areas covered by aerial photographs (numbered 1 through 4) to be shown. Figure 4.2.2 is an aerial view (#1 in fig. 4.2.1) of the northwestern quadrant of the Marina District. This photograph gives a general impression of the type of construction in this area. Most buildings are of wood frame construction with stucco or brick masonry veneer exteriors. The majority of the buildings are three or four stories tall. In general, the buildings at the corners of the blocks are four-story, apartment buildings with garages at the first story level. The mid-block buildings tend to be three stories and are built with little, if any, clearance between them.

Figure 4.2.3 is a map showing the area (bounded by Baker Street, Marina Boulevard, Fillmore Street, and Chestnut Street) which was secured by the police to control access to the zone of severe damage. The table in figure 4.2.3, lists the numbers of buildings that were subsequently declared unsafe by the Department of Public Works. While the damage was concentrated within the area shown on the map, buildings with severe damage were scattered throughout the District.

The degree of damage ranged from total collapse to cosmetic damage to the building exteriors. Figure 4.2.4 is an aerial view (#2 in fig. 4.2.1), looking northwest, of the intersection of Fillmore Street and Cervantes Boulevard. The heap of rubble is the remains of a collapsed four-story building, which was subsequently demolished for safety reasons. Three residents, including a 3-month-old child, were killed in the collapse. Figure 4.2.5 is an aerial view (#3 in fig. 4.2.1), looking toward the southeast, of the intersection of Divisadero and Beach Streets. A building collapsed at the northeast corner of Beach and Divisadero and was subsequently demolished for safety reasons. The dark area on the northwest corner of Beach and Divisadero is the site of the large fire in which one person died. Other severely damaged buildings can also be seen in the photograph.

Figure 4.2.6 shows the portion of the Marina District that was examined, and the numbers indicate the locations of buildings highlighted in the report. Figures 4.2.7 and 4.2.8 show two examples of building which collapsed. The two four-story buildings (location #14) shown in figure 4.2.7 were severely damaged

---

[1]Database provided by Franklin Lew, Seismic Safety Program Manager, Department of Public Works, San Francisco.

by the earthquake, and 5 days later, the first stories of both buildings collapsed as shown in the photograph. These buildings were subsequently demolished. The collapsed building shown in figure 4.2.8 (location #3) is also believed have been four-stories tall, but in this case the lower three stories collapsed. During the collapse, the building moved a large distance toward the south.

Figures 4.2.9 through 4.2.14 are examples of buildings which suffered severe damage but did not collapse. Examination of the building geometries and locations (figure 4.2.6) reveals that the buildings had the following common characteristics: (1) they were four stories tall; (2) the first story contained many openings for garages; and (3) they were located at the corners of intersecting streets.

Figure 4.2.15(a) is an elevation view of a schematic representation of one of these typical corner buildings. The garage door openings in the first story results in buildings with low lateral stiffness and strength. Because of their corner locations, these buildings are free to move in two perpendicular directions. Because of these factors, horizontal movement of the foundation during an earthquake would be expected to cause large distortions in the garage story, as illustrated in figure 4.2.15(b). Figure 4.2.16 is a close-up view of the lower story at the corner of the building shown in figure 4.2.11. The brick veneer and the wood sheeting have been stripped form the studs, revealing the ineffective lateral bracing in the only solid wall portion of the first story.

Failure of brick masonry veneers were common throughout the Marina District. While such failures may not be structurally significant, falling bricks posed a life hazard during the earthquake. Figure 4.2.17 shows a four-story building (location #2) with multiple garages on the first story. Shaking of the building did not result in large distortions as seen in the previous examples, but it was strong enough to dislodge a large portion of the masonry facade. The building shown in figure 4.2.18 (location #10) is also a four-story building with garages, in which more than two stories of brick facade fell. The final example (location #12) shown in figure 4.2.19(a) is the same type of structure, and the brick masonry veneer peeled off at a corner (similar to failure shown in fig. 4.2.16, but less severe). Figure 4.2.19(b) is a close-up of the failed corner showing the condition of the wooden boards behind the brick. The wood is decayed and there is no evidence of effective ties between the wood sheeting and brick veneer. At other buildings with masonry facade failures, it was observed that ordinary nails had been used to tie the masonry to the building. The nails were badly corroded and provided no anchorage to the masonry.

The above examples have illustrated the severity of damage to some of the buildings in the Marina District. According to the Department of Public Works database, about 100 buildings were "red-tagged," which means that they were judged to be unsafe to enter. Thus the majority of the buildings in this district were undamaged or suffered only minor damage. For example, figure 4.2.20 shows an undamaged four-story building on Broderick Street (location #7) opposite from the severely damaged building shown in figure 4.2.12. As can be seen in the aerial photograph (view #4) shown in figure 4.2.21, these two buildings have about the same overall shapes. Apparently, the undamaged building had been retrofitted and some of the garage doors were removed and replaced with solid wall, thereby increasing the lateral strength of the first story. Another example of building (location #8) with excellent performance is shown in figure 4.2.22 (a). This three-story building had been retrofitted by using a moment resisting steel frame as shown in figure 4.2.22(b). The only damage to the building was a broken pane of glass, although the four-story building on the right (see fig. 4.2.22 (a)) was leaning on it.

In summary, dwellings in the Marina District suffered varying degrees of damage. The severe damage tended to be concentrated within two blocks from the intersection of Beach and Divisadero Streets. There was evidence of liquefaction and large soil displacements within the damage zone, but damages were generally consistent with strong ground shaking rather than foundation failures. The most severe damage occurred to four-story apartment buildings with garages in the first story and located at street corners. Brick veneers collapsed due to inadequate anchorage to the wood framing.

4.2.2 Financial, South of Market, and Civic Center Districts

Figure 4.2.23 shows the locations of the other districts in San Francisco that were investigated. Also shown in the figure are those areas which have a high concentration of unreinforced masonry (URM) buildings. As can be seen the three districts have a large number of URM structures. As was previously discussed, another important feature of these districts is that they include areas underlain by deep soft soil deposits, which amplified the ground motion. The combination of seismically vulnerable URM buildings and large ground movements resulted in extensive damage within these districts. As of October 28, the South of Market District was reported to have had 30 structures posted as "unsafe," the second highest number in a San Francisco district[2].

Figure 4.2.24 shows the locations of structures discussed in this section. As shown in figure 4.2.23, Chinatown contains many URM buildings. Because these buildings are founded on firm ground, they were subjected to small ground movements and none of them were damaged as severely as the collapsed wooden structures in the Marina District. However, significant cracking was observed in some buildings. Figure

---

[2]San Francisco Examiner, October 28, 1989

4.2.25 shows a two-story building (location #1) with severe diagonal cracking in the masonry piers between the first-story windows.

The most severe damage observed in the Financial District was concentrated in the circled region shown in figure 4.2.24. There were indications of large ground displacements within this zone. Figure 4.2.26(a) is a view along Davis Street, between Sacramento and California Streets (location #2), which shows distortions in the sidewalk. The close-up view in figure 4.2.26(b) shows that there is about 1 in. (25 mm) of permanent settlement of the sidewalk relative to the retaining wall. The horizontal scrape mark on the wall suggests that the sidewalk moved upwards about 3 in. (75 mm) during the earthquake. The sidewalk was adjacent to a building of modern construction which had no signs of damage, even though it had many windows in the ground story.

Two historic URM structures on Front Street experienced severe structural damage. Figure 4.2.27(a) shows the six-story Marine Building (location #3) on the northeast corner of Front and California Streets. While there does not appear to be much damage, the close-up view of the northwestern corner in figure 4.2.27(b) shows severe cracking, which starts at a level coincident with the roof line of the adjacent two-story structure. Thus pounding between the two buildings may have contributed to the damage of the Marine Building. The damage was so extensive that the building was subsequently demolished.

Figure 4.2.28(a) shows the structural damage suffered by the Golden State Bank building (location #4). The southeast corner of the third story was destroyed along with the lintel. The northeast corner was also severely damaged as seen in figure 4.2.28(b). There also appears to have been pounding between this building and the adjacent building (location of Harrington's Restaurant).

Figure 4.2.29(a) shows the historic, four-story DeBernardi warehouse building on the corner of Front and Sacramento Streets (location #5). This building is adjacent to Harrington's Restaurant shown in the previous photograph. In 1972, the structure was seismically upgraded by the addition of the X-bracing which can be seen through the windows. Figure 4.2.29(b) is a close-up view of one of the braces showing some damage, which indicates that they were subjected to large loads during the earthquake. Thus the retrofit measure performed its intended function of protecting the structure.

A final example of the type of damage within the Financial District is shown in figure 4.2.30. The Bank of California building, at the corner of California and Sansome Streets (location #6), suffered major cracking of its stone facade.

Figure 4.2.31 is an aerial view of a portion of the South of Market District. The view is toward the southwest and the elevated highway is the ramp structure connecting the Embarcadero Freeway and the San Francisco-Oakland Bay Bridge. As was shown in figure 4.2.23, there are many URM buildings in this district, and a large number are used commercially. As a result, besides suffering loss of property, this district sustained a great loss in business activity.

During the drive through the South of Market District, damaged URM buildings were observed. In addition, there was damage to engineered structures with masonry facades. An example is the eight-story Wells Fargo Bank Building shown in figure 4.2.32 (location #7), which suffered extensive cracking to the masonry cladding. In 1969, San Francisco enacted the Parapet Ordinance requiring the strengthening of parapets to resist seismic loads. As a result, a majority of the parapets have been braced and survived the shaking.

Damage was observed in the reinforced concrete building at the corner of Fremont and Howard Streets (location #6) shown in figure 4.2.33(a). This building can be seen at the bottom right-hand corner of the aerial photograph (fig. 4.2.31). The building is of flat-slab construction (with column capitals) and shear walls around the stairwell. It originally served as a warehouse, but was converted to an office building. Extensive damage occurred to most of the spandrels on the side of the building facing Howard Street. The cracking tended to be horizontal, except near the corners were X-cracks were formed as seen in figure 4.2.33(b).

The greatest loss of life due to a building failure occurred at a large URM structure on Bluxome Street (location #8). The structure consisted of two similar wings. Figure 4.2.34(a) shows the appearance of the middle of the structure where the two wings joined. The fourth-story wall of the wing to the right collapsed into the courtyard area. The building had undergone previous strengthening as indicated by the large bolts on the facade. These bolts went through the building, tying together the front and rear walls. However, similar bolts were not used in the other direction, and as a result wall failures occurred. Figure 4.2.34(b) shows the exterior wall facing Sixth Street. The entire fourth-story exterior wall collapsed. Unfortunately, people were driving their cars along the street, and five persons were crushed to death by the falling masonry. Reports in the local newspapers indicated that this building had undergone engineering evaluations as early as 1982, and it had been identified as being seismically deficient. In March of 1986, bricks were reported to have fallen from the building causing damage to a car.

The Civic Center area was the other location surveyed by the team. Damage was observed to the masonry exterior of the Public Library, a steel-framed building. However, according to subsequent reports, the structural frame was not damaged. Some cosmetic damage was also observed in the interior of City Hall. The team inspected the interior of the Old Federal Building (location #9) and noted damage to interior partitions. The most serious damage in the Old Federal Building occurred to the elevators. As shown in figure 4.2.35, the counterweight jumped out its track during the shaking and collided with the upward moving cab.

In summary, unreinforced masonry buildings, masonry infilled walls, and masonry cladding sustained damage in the Financial, South of Market, and City Center Districts. A contributing factor appears to be the amplification of ground motion by the deep soil deposits in these districts. Buildings on firmer ground sustained little or no damage. Parapets braced and anchored to the roof framing performed well.

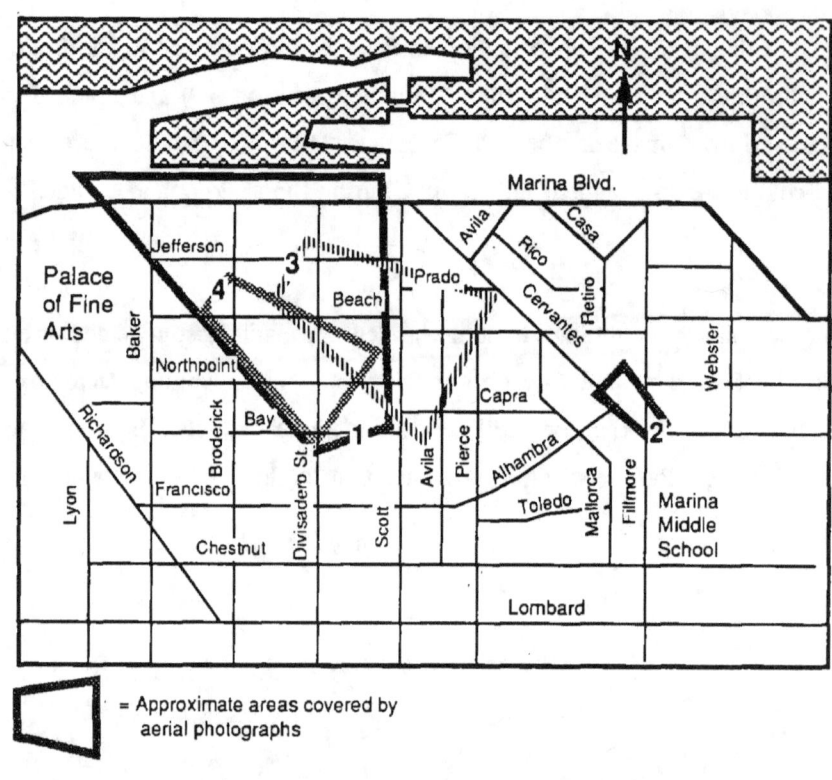

Figure 4.2.1   Map of Marina District showing approximate areas covered by aerial photographs.

Figure 4.2.2   Aerial view (#1) of the western portion of the Marina District, view is toward the north.

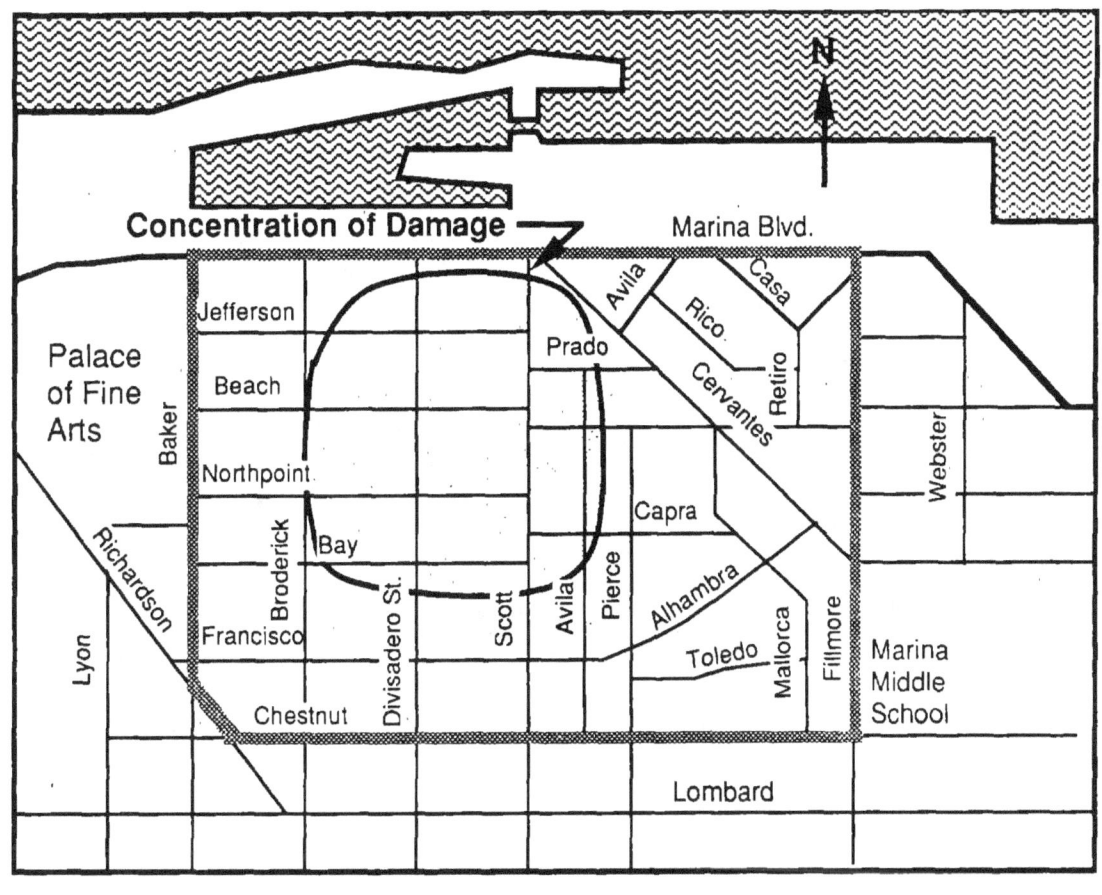

Limited access zone

Approximate Number of Buildings Declared Unsafe

Alhambra	2	Fillmore	4
Avila	10	Francisco	7
Bay St.	13	Jefferson	10
Beach	8	Marina	3
Broderick	2	Northpoint	7
Capra	1	Prado	2
Cervantes	11	Scott	18
Divisadero	12		

Source: San Francisco Department of Public Works

Figure 4.2.3   Map of Marina District showing region of concentrated damage.

Figure 4.2.4   Aerial view (#2) of demolished building at the intersection of Fillmore St. and Cervantes Blvd.

Figure 4.2.5   Aerial view (#3) of portion of the Marina District which suffered extensive damage; dark zone is location of the fire.

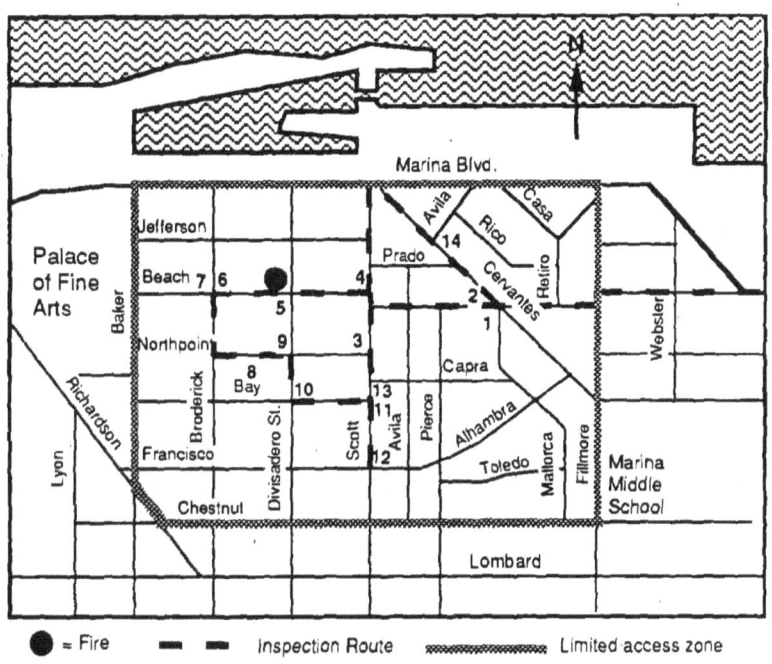

Figure 4.2.6   Map of the Marina District showing locations of buildings mentioned in this report.

Figure 4.2.7   Two four-story buildings which suffered total collapse of their first stories (location #14).

Figure 4.2.8   Four-story building which suffered total collapse of its lower stories (location #3).

Figure 4.2.9   Example of four-story building with multiple garages in the first story (location #1).

Figure 4.2.10   Example of four-story building with multiple garages in the first story (location #4).

Figure 4.2.11   Example of four-story building with multiple garages in the first story (location #5).

Figure 4.2.12   Example of four-story building with multiple garages in the first story (location #6).

Figure 4.2.13   Example of four-story building with multiple garages in the first story (location #9).

Figure 4.2.14   Example of four-story building with multiple garages in the first story (location #13).

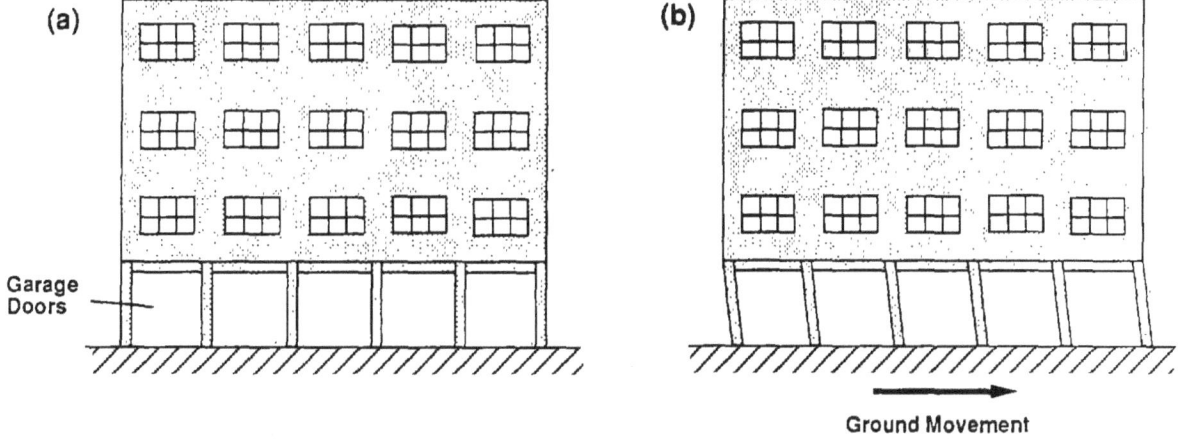

Ground Movement

Figure 4.2.15   (a) Schematic elevation view of a four-story building with multiple garages and (b) expected building distortion due to ground motion.

Figure 4.2.16   Detail of ineffective framing system in corner of building at the intersection of Beach and Divisadero Streets (location #5).

Figure 4.2.17   Example of building with failure of brick masonry facade (location #2).

Figure 4.2.18   Example of building with failure of brick masonry facade (location #10).

Figure 4.2.19   (a) Example of building with failure of brick masonry facade (location #12) and (b) close-up view of corner showing damaged wood and lack of anchorage to the masonry.

4-18

Figure 4.2.20   An undamaged four-story building on the corner of Broderick and Beach Streets (location #7).

Figure 4.2.21   Aerial view (#4) of the buildings shown in figures 4.2.12 and 4.2.20.

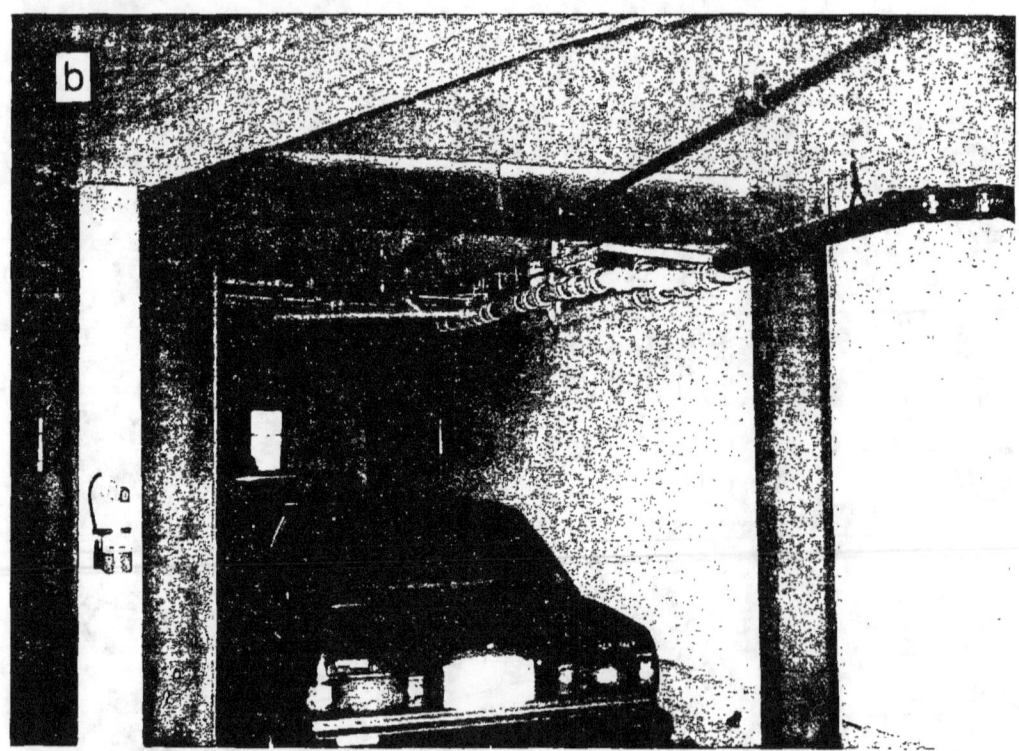

Figure 4.2.22   (a) An undamaged, three-story building (location #8) and (b) view of the moment-resting frame used for retrofitting.

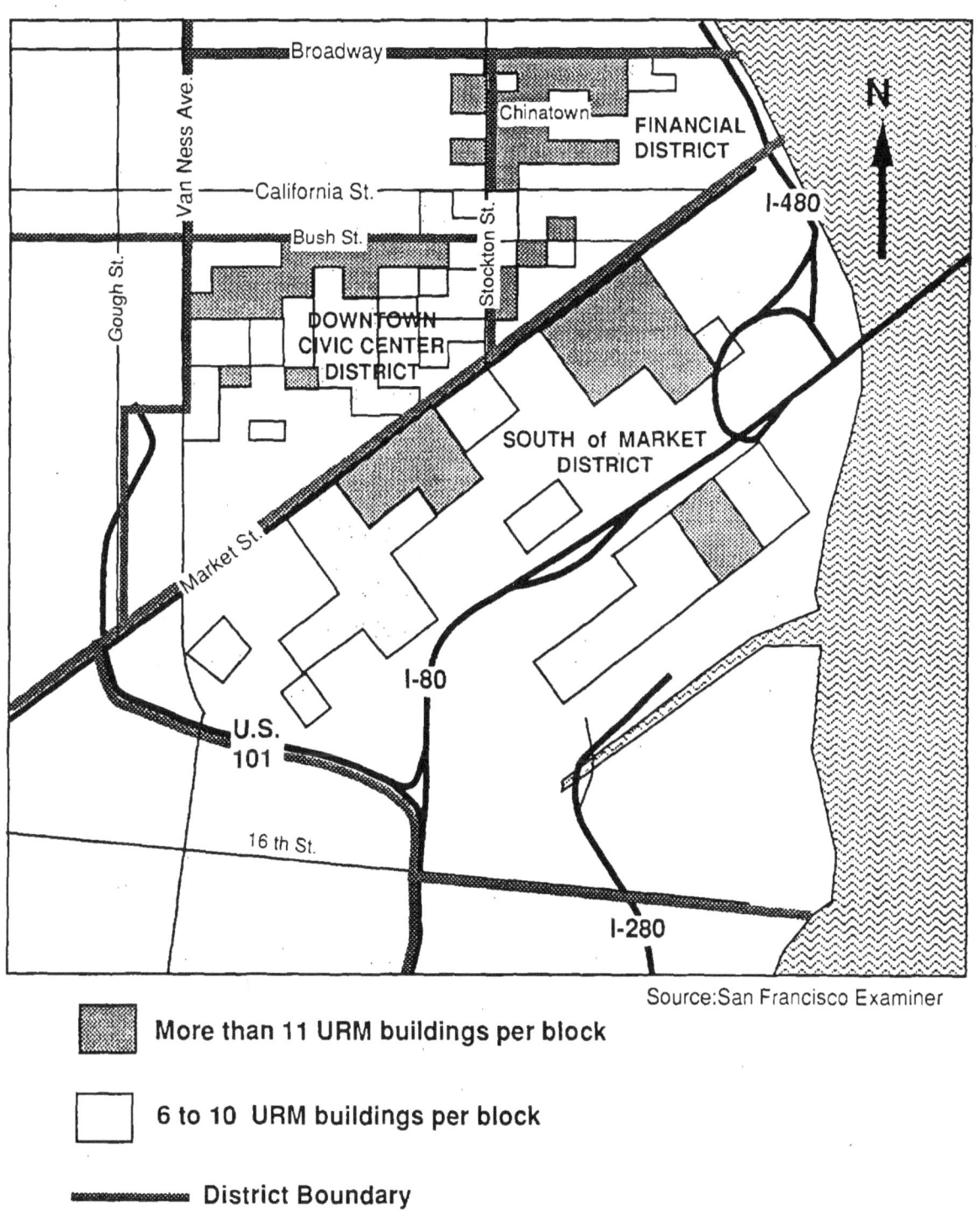

Figure 4.2.23 Map showing location of unreinforced masonry buildings within the Financial, South of Market, and Civic Center Districts.

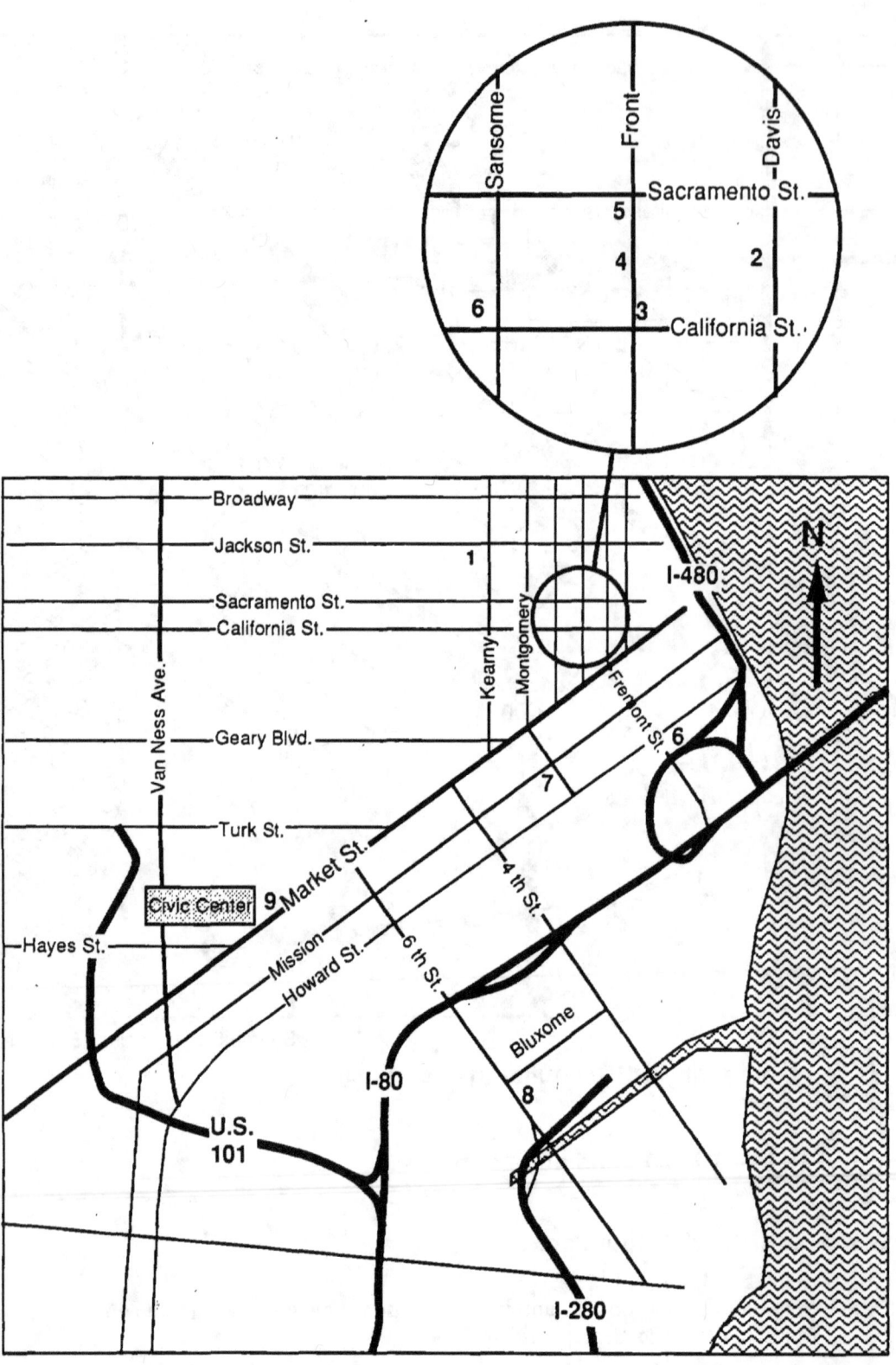

Figure 4.2.24   Location of structures within the Financial, South of Market, and Civic Center Districts discussed in the report.

Figure 4.2.25   Example of damage to unreinforced masonry building in the Chinatown area (location #1).

Figure 4.2.26   (a) Sidewalk showing distortions due to differential settlements, and (b) close-up view of intersection of sidewalk with retaining wall showing magnitude of differential movement.

Figure 4.2.27 (a) Severely damaged Marine Building at corner of Front St. and California St.; (b) Close-up view of the northwest corner showing severity of cracking.

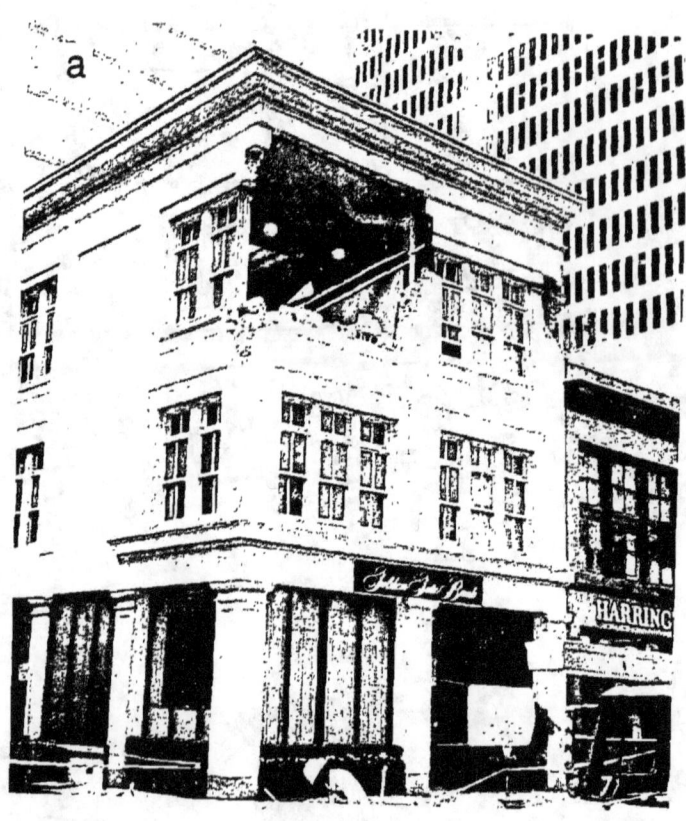

Figure 4.2.28   (a) Damage to the southeastern corner of the Golden State Bank Building; (b) Close-up view of the northeastern corner; damage was likely caused by pounding against the adjacent building.

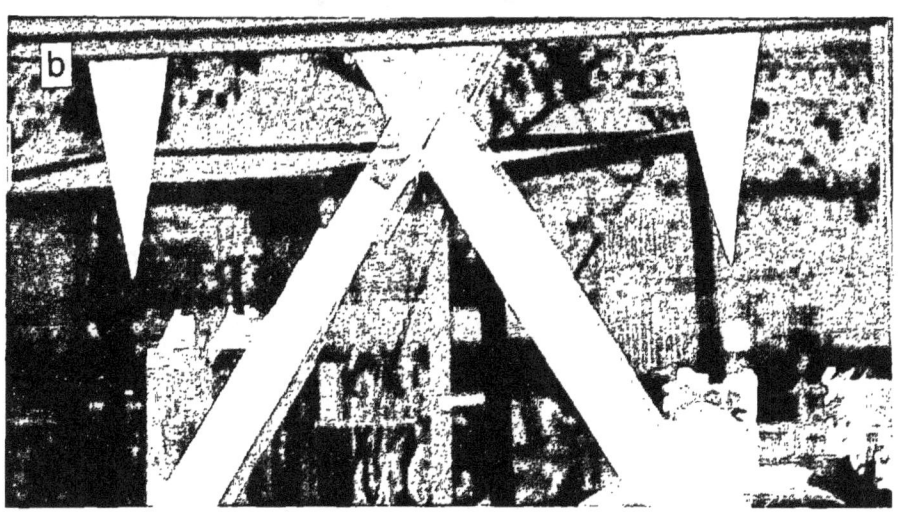

Figure 4.2.29   (a) The historic DeBernardi warehouse building showing the bracing added during seismic retrofitting; (b) close-up view of the bracing showing damage caused by earthquake.

Figure 4.2.30   Damage to the stone facing of the Bank of California building.

Figure 4.2.31   Aerial view of the south of Market District, looking toward the southwest.

Figure 4.2.32   Example of damage to masonry cladding of Wells Fargo Bank building (location #7).

Figure 4.2.33 (a) Reinforced concrete, flat-slab building which sustained severe damage to the exterior walls (location #6); (b) close-up view of damage to spandrels.

b

Figure 4.2.34   (a) Damage to upper story of unreinforced masonry buildir
                 (b) damage to the southwestern wall which resulted in th

4-31

Figure 4.2.35 Elevator counterweight jumped out of its track and collided with the cab in the Old Federal Building (location #9).

4.3 City of Oakland

According to newspaper reports[3] the city of Oakland suffered about $1.3 billion in damage. Two days after the earthquake it was estimated[4] that 1300 homes had been damaged, 141 of them seriously and 10 had to be demolished. Over 100 commercial structures were reported damaged, nine of which were total losses. In addition, four public buildings were closed, including City Hall.

Figure 4.3.1 is map of downtown Oakland which includes the area observed during the inspection. According to newspaper reports, at least five seriously damaged buildings were within the vicinity of 20th Street and Broadway.

City Hall was reported to have sustained extensive damage, however, no damage was observed to the exterior stone facade. Apparently, the damage occurred primarily to the interior, and it was reported that about $30 million would be needed to restore and upgrade the structure.

The damaged observed in the area inspected was confined primarily to steel-frame buildings with brick masonry cladding and to URM buildings. The Dalziel apartment building (location #1) shown in figure 4.3.2(a) had extensive cracking to its masonry facade. As can be seen figure 4.3.2(b), numerous diagonal cracks formed in the piers between the windows. The Oakland Hotel (location #6) shown in figure 4.3.3(a), which served as low-income housing, was also severely damaged. It was reported[5] that this building had been retrofitted by anchoring the masonry walls to the steel frame so that they would not fall in the event of an earthquake. As can be seen in the detailed photograph shown in figure 4.3.3(b), there was severe cracking of the masonry infill in the west wing and some bricks fell. The east wing of the building was not observed to have the same severity of cracking. Apparently the structural frame was not damaged as it is reported that the building is still occupied. A reinforced concrete block masonry building being constructed opposite the Oakland Hotel (see fig. 4.3.3(a)) was not damaged.

Figure 4.3.4 shows the three-story Clay Building (location #2) which had a serious failure of its unreinforced masonry walls. On the corner opposite to the Clay Building there was a two-story URM

---

[3]San Francisco Examiner, October 24, 1989

[4]The Tribune (Oakland), October 19, 1989

[5]Stephen Mahin, presentation at EERI-NRC-NCEER Congressional Briefing on the Loma Prieta Earthquake, Nov. 30, 1989, Washington, D.C.

building (location #3) which was apparently built as a produce market in 1917. As is shown in figure 4.3.5, there was failure of the parapet as well as a portion of the infilled wall. The building occupied the entire block, and the eastern portion, which was being renovated, did not appear to have been damaged. Another example of a URM-building failure (location #5) is shown in figure 4.3.6. The collapse of the outer wall crushed three vehicles parked in the adjacent lot. The high-rise steel frame structure, seen in the background of figure 4.3.6, being constructed at 12th Street and Broadway, suffered damage at the top. It was reported[6] that some steel members and the construction elevator fell to the ground. Fortunately there were only some minor injuries from what could have been a serious accident.

Along Broadway and Franklin Streets, several major unreinforced masonry buildings sustained severe damage. There was damage to infill walls of steel-framed buildings, and there was spalling of masonry veneers due to pounding of buildings.

Damage also occurred to some modern buildings. Figure 4.3.7 shows the Trans Pacific Centre at 11th Street and Broadway (location #4). The building had to be evacuated not because of structural damage, but because of ruptured sprinkler lines, broken windows, and fallen ceiling tiles. The 16-story telecommunications building at 20th and Franklin Streets (location #7) suffered damage. The structural system consists of a steel frame with reinforced concrete shear walls. As is shown in figure 4.3.8, extensive damage occurred to the shear walls as well as other concrete structural members.

In summary, the downtown area of Oakland suffered significant damage. Steel-framed buildings with masonry cladding and unreinforced masonry buildings were affected. In addition, damage was sustained by relatively new buildings. It will be of value to study why these new buildings were damaged, so that it can be determined whether changes to design practices are needed.

---

[6]San Francisco Examiner, October 23, 1989

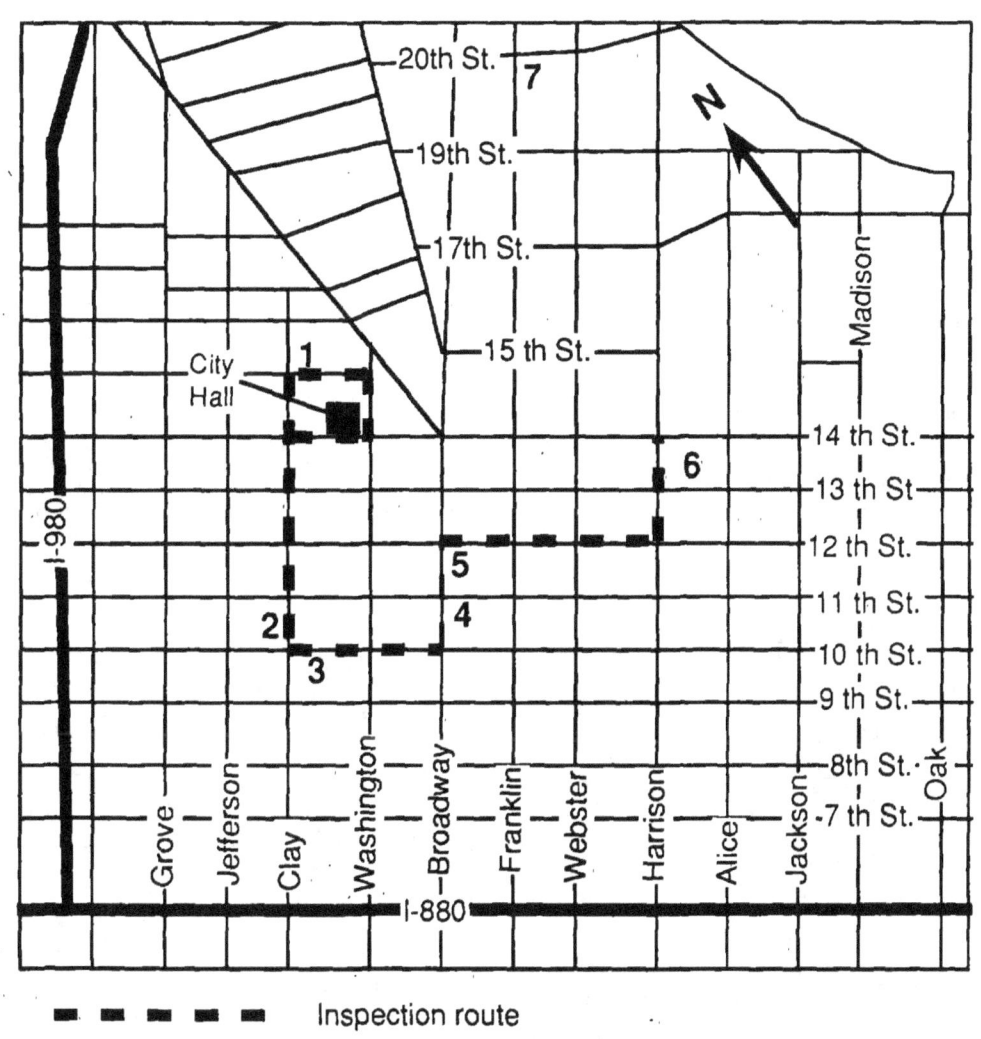

Figure 4.3.1   Downtown Oakland showing inspection route and buildings referenced in report.

Figure 4.3.2   Dalziel apartment building: (a) overall appearance and (b) close-up view of cracking in masonry piers (location #1).

4-36

a

b

Figure 4.3.3   Oakland Hotel: (a) View of west wing and (b) close-up view of damaged masonry infill
(location #6).

Figure 4.3.4   Damage to the Clay Building, an unreinforced masonry structure (location #2).

Figure 4.3.5   Extensive damage occurred to a two-story unreinforced masonry building built in 1917 (location #3).

Figure 4.3.6   Collapse of unreinforced masonry wall crushed vehicles in adjacent parking lot (location #5). In background is a steel-framed building under construction which sustained damage.

Figure 4.3.7   Trans Pacific Centre Building which suffered extensive damage due to ruptured water pipes, broken windows, and fallen ceiling tile (location #4).

Shear Wall
Damage

Figure 4.3.8   Damage occurred to the shear walls of a 16-story telecommunications building (location #7).

4.4 Epicentral Region

The investigative team visited Los Gatos, Watsonville, and Santa Cruz, Hollister, and Moss Landing (see fig. 4.4.1). These communities, except for Hollister, are located within a 30-mile (50-km) radius of the epicenter and were subjected to strong ground shaking. Strong motion records indicate the peak horizontal and vertical accelerations ranged from 0.4 to 0.5 g, as compared to 0.64 g at the epicenter. The majority of structures in this region are unreinforced masonry commercial buildings ranging from one to three stories in height and wood-framed dwellings. The patterns of observed damage were similar to what has been observed in previous earthquakes having similar ground shaking intensities. These include: collapse of masonry chimneys at the roof line, houses sheared off of their foundations, and partial or total collapse of unreinforced masonry walls.

In Los Gatos, about 400 out of 11,000 houses were damaged. Figures 4.4.2 (a) and (b) show examples of damage to wood-framed houses which shifted off of their foundations. The shifting was usually as a result. of the failure of the supporting perimeter walls. Figure 4.4.3 illustrates how a house, such as those which failed, is supported. The concrete footings support a short perimeter wall, known as a "cripple stud wall," which supports the frame of the house. The cripple stud walls are typically built using 2-by-4 studs and wooden boards as sheeting. When the ground moved during the earthquake, the cripple stud walls were unable to resist the induced horizontal forces. This caused the walls to sway until they could no longer support the weight of the house. The house crashed to the ground and secondary damage resulted from the impact. The same type of damage was also observed to houses in Watsonville.

The communities in the epicentral area have a concentration of old URM buildings in their central commercial districts. Extensive damage occurred in these areas. There were numerous parapet failures, which in many cases caused extensive damage to adjoining buildings. In addition, many buildings suffered extreme damage due to inadequate lateral resistance as illustrated by the building in figure 4.4.4 (a). .With many openings in the first story, masonry-clad, wood-framed structures, such as this, swayed excessively causing inadequately anchored brick veneers to fall. Along Main Street in Watsonville, many of the storefront windows were destroyed as shown in figure 4.4.4(b). The large openings in the first story of most buildings lead to low lateral strength and the excessive deformations during the shaking lead to glass failures.

Several historic masonry structures were severely damaged in Watsonville. The building shown in figure 4.4.5, built in 1893, had extensive failure of the parapet. The falling brick killed a woman in front of the bakery shown on the right side of the photo. Historic St. Patrick's Church, shown in figure 4.4.6, was also damaged. The church, constructed in 1903, had major failures of the exterior walls, and the steeple developed several large diagonal cracks. The hazard posed by the damaged steeple caused local officials to block off the northern end of Main Street leading to the business district. It was observed that retrofitted or modern structures at the northern end of Main Street were not damaged.

In Santa Cruz, the most concentrated damage to commercial structures occurred in the Pacific Garden Mall. About one-third of the buildings suffered severe damage. Figure 4.4.7 is a map of downtown Santa Cruz showing the portion of Pacific Avenue comprising the outdoor shopping mall. Aerial photographs of the mall area, which were taken on October 19, 1989, are shown in figure 4.4.8. The approximate coverage of the photographs is indicated on the map in figure 4.4.7.

At the center of figure 4.4.8(a) there is a two-story masonry structure at the corner of Pacific Avenue and Water Street (location #1). Figure 4.4.9 shows the appearance of the structure at street level. It was designed about 15 years ago according to the 1973 Uniform Building Code, and it survived without any sign of structural damage. Adjacent to this modern building is an older unreinforced masonry building, which is seen on the left side of figure 4.4.9. Although the facade shows a small amount of damage, the roof of the building collapsed and killed two persons.

Another roof collapse in the mall caused the death of one person. This failure occurred to the department store on the corner of Pacific Avenue and Cathcart Street, and can be seen in figure 4.4.8(c). The roof failure was caused by the collapse of the top story masonry wall of the adjacent building. This type of damage was observed at several other stores within the mall.

One of the historic structures severely damaged is the Cooper House located on the corner of Pacific Avenue and Cooper Streets (location #2). The unreinforced masonry building was built in the 1880's as the county courthouse. The building was reported to have survived the 1906 San Francisco earthquake[7], but it was extensively damaged during the Loma Prieta earthquake. As shown in figure 4.4.10, portions of exterior walls collapsed and there were extensive diagonal cracks throughout the exterior walls. The damage was so severe that the building subsequently was demolished.

A seven-story building is seen near the center of figure 4.4.8(b) (location #3). This reinforced concrete building, which was reported to have built in the 1920's, was severely damaged. The street level view in

---

[7]San Francisco Examiner, October 27, 1989

4-42

figure 4.4.11(a) shows that there were many wall openings in the second story. The close-up view in figure 4.4.11(b) shows some of the severe diagonal cracking which formed in the walls between the windows.

The city of Moss Landing, located on Monterey Bay, experienced soil liquefaction at many sites. Serious structural damage occurred to the State Marine Laboratory. As shown in figure 4.4.12, lateral spreading of the soil caused extensive cracking of the structure.

In summary, extensive damage was caused by the severe ground shaking in the epicentral region. Houses fell off of their foundations as a result of cripple stud wall failures. Unreinforced masonry walls cracked and collapsed. In many cases wall failures lead to roof failures in adjacent structures. Older steel and reinforced concrete framed structures were damaged. Modern structures and old structures that had been retrofitted suffered minor or no damage.

4.5 Summary

Damaged buildings were observed within San Francisco, Oakland, and the epicentral region. In San Francisco, damage was concentrated in the Marina and South of Market Districts. Amplification of ground motion by deep soil deposits appears to be a primary factor in explaining the distribution of damage. In the Marina District, the most extensive damage occurred to four-story apartment buildings having soft first stories and located at street corners. In other Districts of San Francisco and in Oakland, damage occurred primarily to unreinforced masonry buildings and to older steel-framed buildings with masonry infills. In the epicentral region, most of the damage occurred to unreinforced masonry buildings and to wood-framed houses with cripple stud walls. These observations show that, even within a region of the United States having the highest seismic risk, many seismically inadequate structures exist.

The Loma Prieta earthquake offered opportunities to examine the adequacy of various strengthening methods that have been used in the San Francisco Bay area. The investigation revealed many examples of strengthened structures that performed well, but there were also some cases of poor performance. In-depth analyses should be made to determine the performance of repaired structures to obtain basic information needed to prepare standards for strengthening seismically vulnerable buildings.

Even though the Loma Prieta earthquake was less severe than the "design" earthquake, some modern structures suffered significant damage. In-depth analyses of the reasons for these failures should be performed to determine if the failures were due to inadequacies in current standards.

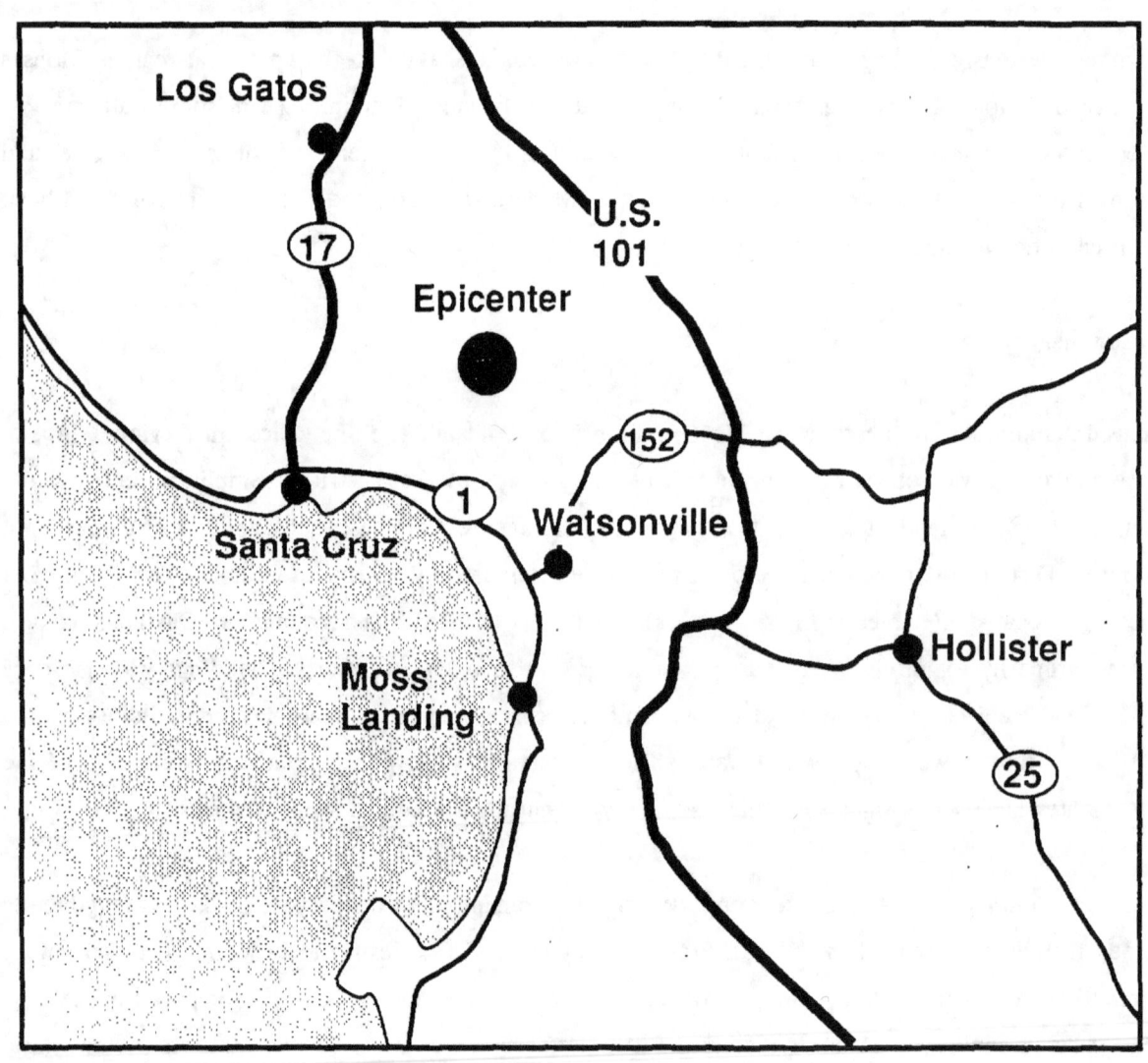

Figure 4.4.1   Cities visited within the epicentral region.

Figure 4.4.2   Examples of failures of houses in Los Gatos: (a) large house suffered large distortion and (b) a small house was rocked off of its foundation.

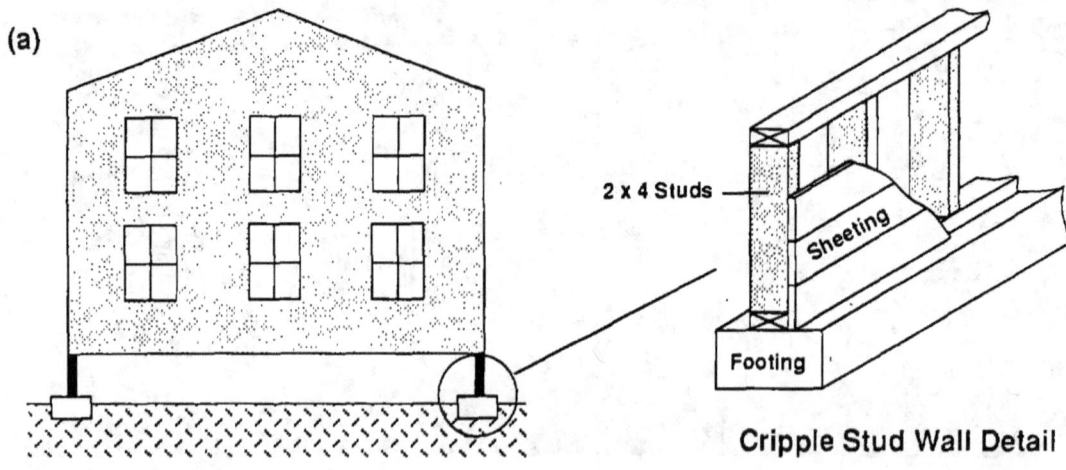

(a)

2 x 4 Studs

Sheeting

Footing

Cripple Stud Wall Detail

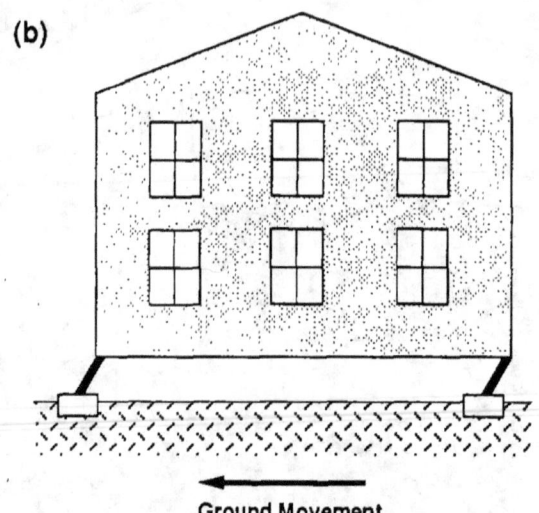

(b)

Ground Movement

Figure 4.4.3   Schematic of failure caused by inadequately braced cripple stud walls: (a) construction of cripple stud wall and (b) failure mechanism.

Figure 4.4.4   (a) Failure of wood-framed building with masonry walls and multiple opening in first story (Los Gatos); (b) typical damage to parapets and storefront windows (Watsonville).

Figure 4.4.5   Falling brick from this old masonry building in Watsonville caused one death.

Figure 4.4.6   St. Patrick's Church in Watsonville was severely damaged.

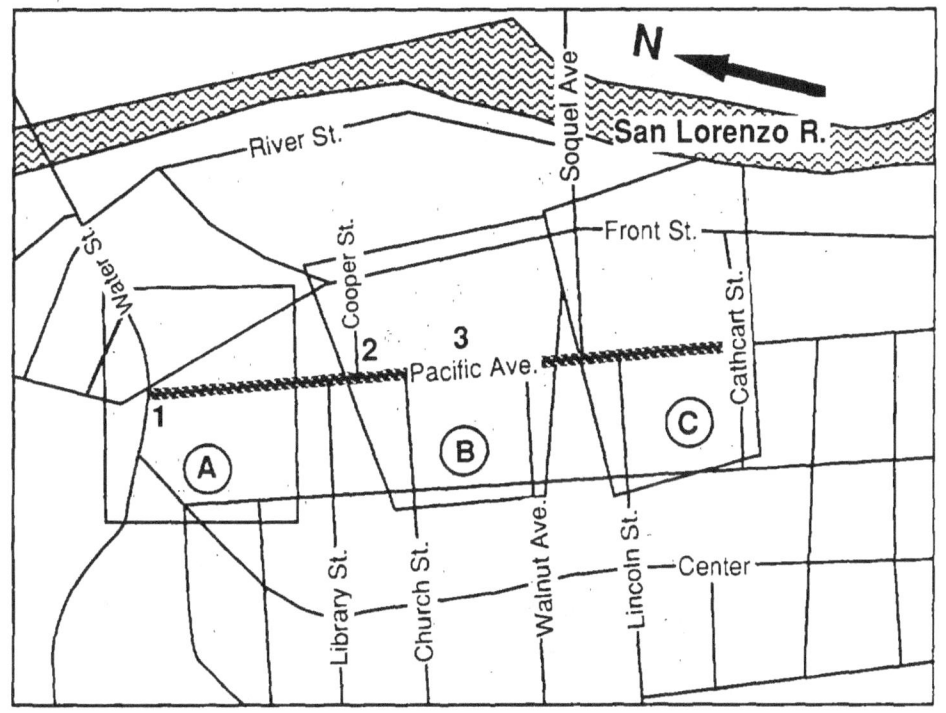

Figure 4.4.7   Map of Santa Cruz showing location of Pacific Garden Mall and areas covered by aerial photographs.

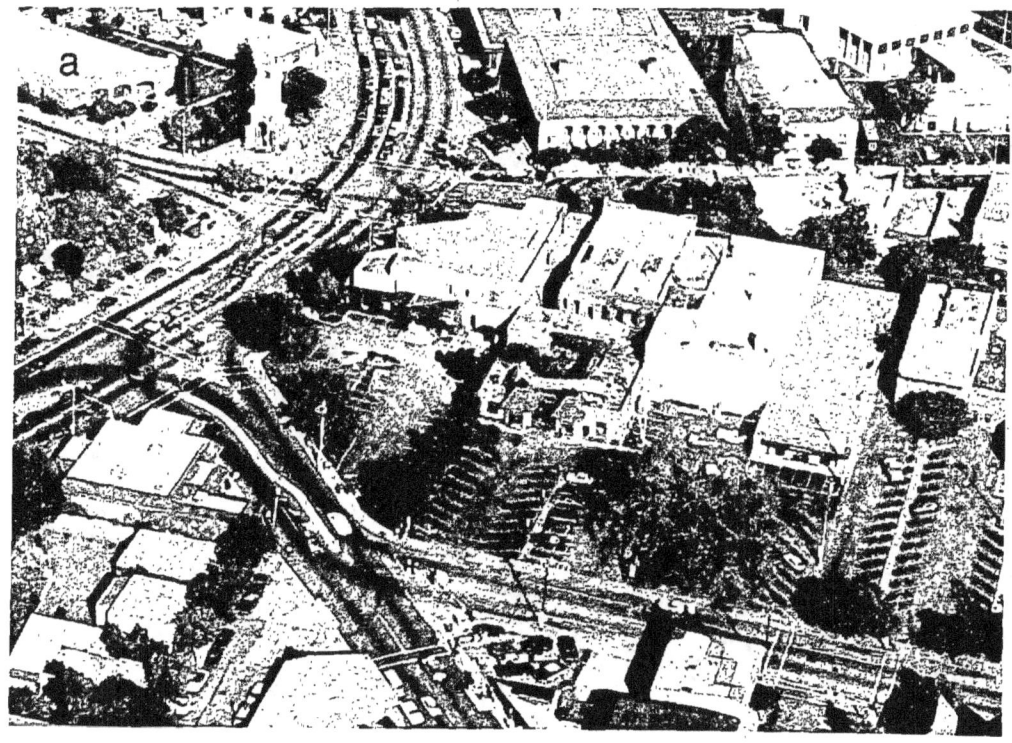

Figure 4.4.8   Aerial views of the Pacific Garden Mall: (a) northern portion.

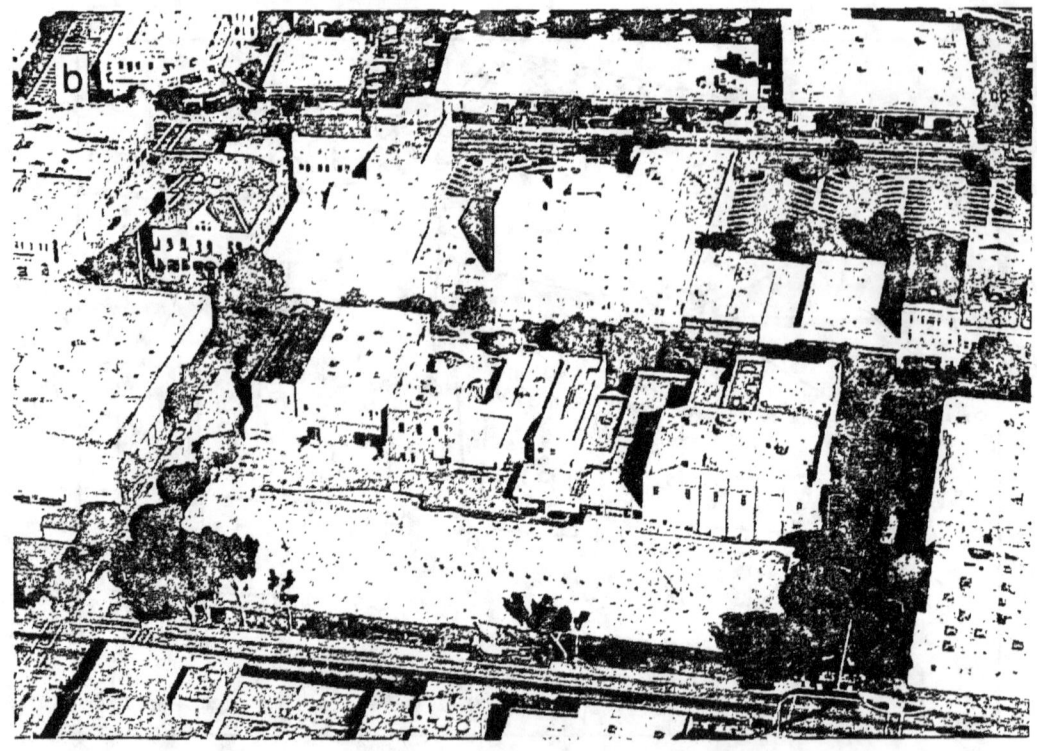

Figure 4.4.8 *(Cont'd)*   Aerial views of the Pacific Garden Mall: (b) central portion, and (c) southern portion.

Figure 4.4.9   Modern reinforced masonry structure which was undamaged; building on the left suffered roof failure causing two deaths (location #1).

Figure 4.4.10   Historic Cooper House in Santa Cruz was severely damaged and had to be demolished (location #2).

Figure 4.4.11   (a) Seven-story, reinforced concrete building suffered severe cracking; (b) Close-up view of damage to second-story walls.

Figure 4.4.12   Damage to Marine Laboratory in Moss Landing as a result of soil liquefaction.

5. PERFORMANCE OF BRIDGE AND HIGHWAY STRUCTURES

by William C. Stone, James D. Cooper, and Nicholas J. Carino

5.1 Introduction

The main highway network in the San Francisco Bay region sustained serious damage at several locations. The most notable is the damage to and collapse of the long, double decked viaduct sections of freeway in the San Francisco and Oakland areas. Except for the collapse of a single link span of the double-deck section of the San Francisco-Oakland Bay Bridge, most bridges in the area of the San Francisco Bay survived the earthquake with relatively minor damage. Most bridges and viaducts had been strengthened in the California Department of Transportation (Caltrans) Phase I seismic retrofit program which included identification of structures that are vulnerable to excessive displacements in the longitudinal direction and have the potential to have spans collapse. Typically, these structures have narrow hinge seats or discontinuities in the superstructure across piers or abutments and were constructed prior to 1971. Cables or bars were placed across these joints, tying the elements of the superstructure together.

This chapter describes damage to the Bay Bridge, and to I-880 (Nimitz Freeway) and other double-deck elevated highway structures. The results of preliminary analyses to determine the most likely causes of the collapse of I-880 are presented below.

5.2 Historical Development of Seismic Criteria

Until relatively recent times, almost all consideration of earthquake forces on structures and relevant code considerations have been concentrated in building construction as opposed to bridge and highway construction. The 1906 San Francisco, California earthquake, which caused an estimated $50 million of property damage, and a subsequent $350 million in fire damage was considered ill fortune (CSSC 1988). The city was rebuilt in almost identical fashion and remained vulnerable to earthquakes. The 1925 Santa Barbara, California earthquake caused several million dollars in damage and provided the impetus to consider adoption of earthquake design provisions in building codes. In 1927, the simple Newtonian concept of lateral earthquake force being proportional to mass was incorporated in the Uniform Building Code. The Long Beach, California earthquake of 1933 caused at least $50 million in damage and once again emphasized the need for more stringent earthquake design requirements. Since then, continual improvements have been made in the various U.S. codes.

The first requirement for the inclusion of seismic loading in the design of highway bridges in the United States was presented in the AASHO, American Association of State Highway Officials (now American Association of State Highway and Transportation Officials, AASHTO) 1958 and 1959 Interim to the 1957 Specifications (AASHO 1958-1959). These specifications remained unchanged until the 1975 Interim Specifications. In 1971 the AASHTO Bridge Committee prepared a proposal for a new earthquake criteria. Prior to adoption, the San Fernando, California earthquake (February, 1971) occurred and demonstrated that the proposed revisions were inadequate.

The 12th edition (1977) of the AASHTO "Standard Specifications for Highway Bridges" (AASHTO 1977) presented a new approach for designing highway bridges to withstand earthquake forces. Article 1.2.20 of the Specification requires, "In regions where earthquakes may be anticipated, structures shall be designed to resist earthquake motions by considering the relationship of the site to active faults, the seismic response of the soils at the site, and the dynamic response characteristics of the total structure." The specification is generally based on the 1973 Earthquake Design Criteria for Bridges by the State of California. The California criteria were developed for California conditions and subsequently modified to allow for their use in other areas of the United States where possibly damaging earthquakes can occur. The impact of the application of the specification, particularly in regions outside California, on design complexity, design and construction costs, and construction complexity was unknown at the time of adoption.

Consequently, the Federal Highway Administration initiated a study entitled "Bridge Seismic Design Guidelines" in 1977 to: (1) evaluate then current criteria used for seismic design; (2) review recent seismic research findings for potential use in a new specification; (3) develop new and improved seismic design guidelines; and (4) evaluate the impact of the guides on construction and cost. The guidelines were completed in 1979 and adopted by AASHTO as a Guide Specification in 1983.

5.3 Current Seismic Design Criteria

A basic premise in developing the current AASHTO bridge seismic design guide specification was that the provisions should be applicable to all parts of the country. Therefore, for purposes of design, guidelines were developed for four seismic performance categories (SPC) to which bridges are assigned based on the seismicity of the area in which the site is located and the importance of the bridge. Bridges are classified according to their relative importance - either as essential or nonessential. Essential bridges are determined based on their social/survival and security/defense classification. Essential bridges are those that must keep functioning during and after an earthquake.

The Seismic Performance Category defines the differing degrees of complexity and sophistication of seismic analysis and design which are specified. Four categories are defined. The highest level includes those bridges designed for the highest level of seismic performance with particular attention to methods of analysis, design, and quality assurance. The next level includes those bridges for which a slightly lower level of seismic performance is required, and allows slightly greater potential for damage than for the highest level. The next level requires a minimum of analysis and draws specific attention to support design details. Bridges in the lowest category require no seismic analysis but attention is provided to certain design details for superstructure support. The majority of bridges in the country fall into the second lowest seismic performance category. Most bridges in California fall into the two highest seismic performance categories.

The primary basis for development of the seismic design guidelines for bridges is to minimize the hazard to life and provide the capability for bridges to survive during and after an earthquake with essential bridges to remain functional. To meet this philosophy, certain principles were followed:

Small-to-moderate earthquakes should be resisted within the elastic range of the structural components without damage. Realistic seismic ground motion intensities should be used in the design procedure. Exposure to shaking from large earthquakes should not cause collapse of all or part of the bridges. And where possible, damage that does occur should be readily detectable and accessible for evaluation and repair.

In assessing bridge failures of past earthquakes in Alaska, California, and Japan, many of the "loss of span" type failures are attributed in part to relative displacement effects. Relative displacements arise from out of phase motion of different parts of a bridge, from lateral displacement and/or rotation of the foundations and differential displacements at abutments. Therefore in developing the guidelines, the design displacements were considered to be just as important as design forces. This represented a significant change in bridge design philosophy. For higher performance category bridges, requirements for ties between noncontinuous segments of a bridge are specified in addition to minimum bearing support lengths at abutments, columns and hinge seats.

The methodology used in the AASHTO Guide Specification is in part a "force design" approach but also addresses the relative displacement problem. The design methodology varies in complexity as the SPC increases from lowest to highest. Three additional concepts are included in the Guide Specification. First, minimum requirements are specified for bearing support lengths of girders at abutments, columns, and hinge seats to account for some of the important relative displacement effects that cannot be calculated by current state-of-the-art methods. Second, member design forces are calculated to account for the directional uncertainty of earthquake motions and the simultaneous occurrence of earthquake forces in two perpendicular horizontal directions. Third, design requirements and forces for foundations are intended to minimize damage since most damage that might occur will not be readily detectable. The selection of ground motion intensities to be used with the seismic design provisions was carefully reviewed by the Applied Technology Council (ATC 1978). Considerable study and effort had recently been made to develop seismic risk maps and associated design spectra for the "Tentative Provisions for the Development of Seismic Regulations for Buildings (ATC-3-06)." The maps are based on an appraisal of expected ground motion intensities, the probability that the design ground shaking will be exceeded is approximately the same in all parts of the United States, and frequency of occurrence of earthquakes in various regions of the country. It is possible that the design earthquake ground shaking might be exceeded, although the probability of this happening is quite small, about 10 percent in 50 years.

The AASHTO Guide Specifications provide for two methods of analysis which vary according to the refinement in the mathematical idealization. They are the single-mode spectral analysis method and the multi-mode spectral analysis method. All methods assume simultaneous support excitation.

5.4 Approach for Improved Seismic Response

The highway network is a vast system which forms vital and essential links between cities and towns across the United States. The interstate system of highways extends approximately 41,000 miles (66,000 km) and has about 47,000 bridges in the network. Added to that is another 89,000 bridges on the primary system. The exposure of the network of roads and bridges to seismic hazards varies greatly across the country. Bridges, grade separation, and elevated highway structure form critical links in this network and are most susceptible to seismically induced damage. They also represent the greatest economic risk if destroyed or damaged.

Two approaches are being taken to improve the seismic resistance of highway bridges. The first is to design and construct new highway bridges for seismic resistance. This requires considerable time, but is economically reasonable, and is being pursued. Design guidelines are being upgraded as more knowledge is gained about the response of specialized transportation structures to seismic activity. These new design guidelines can be applied to new construction as older bridges are removed from service because they are either structurally unsound or functionally obsolete. The second approach involves identifying those existing bridges which are important to the network and are susceptible to significant damage or collapse in the event of an earthquake. Those structures can be strengthened to enhance their response to seismic activity. This approach, however, requires significant expenditures and can prove economically difficult. A balanced approach is needed to reduce earthquake hazards. Design and construction of new structures should use available, cost effective design standards.

5.5 Introduction to Viaducts and Bridge Performance

Following the Loma Prieta earthquake Caltrans engineers conducted preliminary inspections of more than 1500 bridge structures in the area affected by the earthquake and determined that some 73 bridges had suffered minor damage of varying degrees, that five major viaducts and five other bridges suffered significant structural damage, and that major or partial collapses occurred at three sites. Figure 5.5.1 depicts the locations of the five damaged viaducts and the collapsed span of the Bay Bridge, indicated by shaded circles, and the I-880 collapse by the shaded oval. From previous discussion of the geotechnical aspects of the earthquake in Chapter 3, it can be appreciated readily that there is a strong correlation between the location of damage and the presence of deep underlying deposits of natural or man-made overburden. The three major collapse sites at I-880, the Bay Bridge, and Struve Slough, are of particular interest and will be discussed first. Of these, the first two were visible symbols of the Loma Prieta earthquake with I-880, in particular, capturing the attention of the national media for days following the quake as efforts to free trapped motorists continued. Other viaduct failures included the *Southern Freeway* [I-280] just to the east of Highway 101; I-280 at the China Basin distribution structure; The *Central Freeway* [Highway 101] in downtown San Francisco; the *Embarcadero Freeway* [I-480] at Mission Street in San Francisco; and I-980 just to the east of I-880 in Oakland. None of these viaducts collapsed. They did, however, suffer sufficient damage that all are still closed and have required the installation of significant timber shoring to insure stability until a proper retrofit can be effected. Damage to structures at these sites is described in sections 5.9 through 5.11.

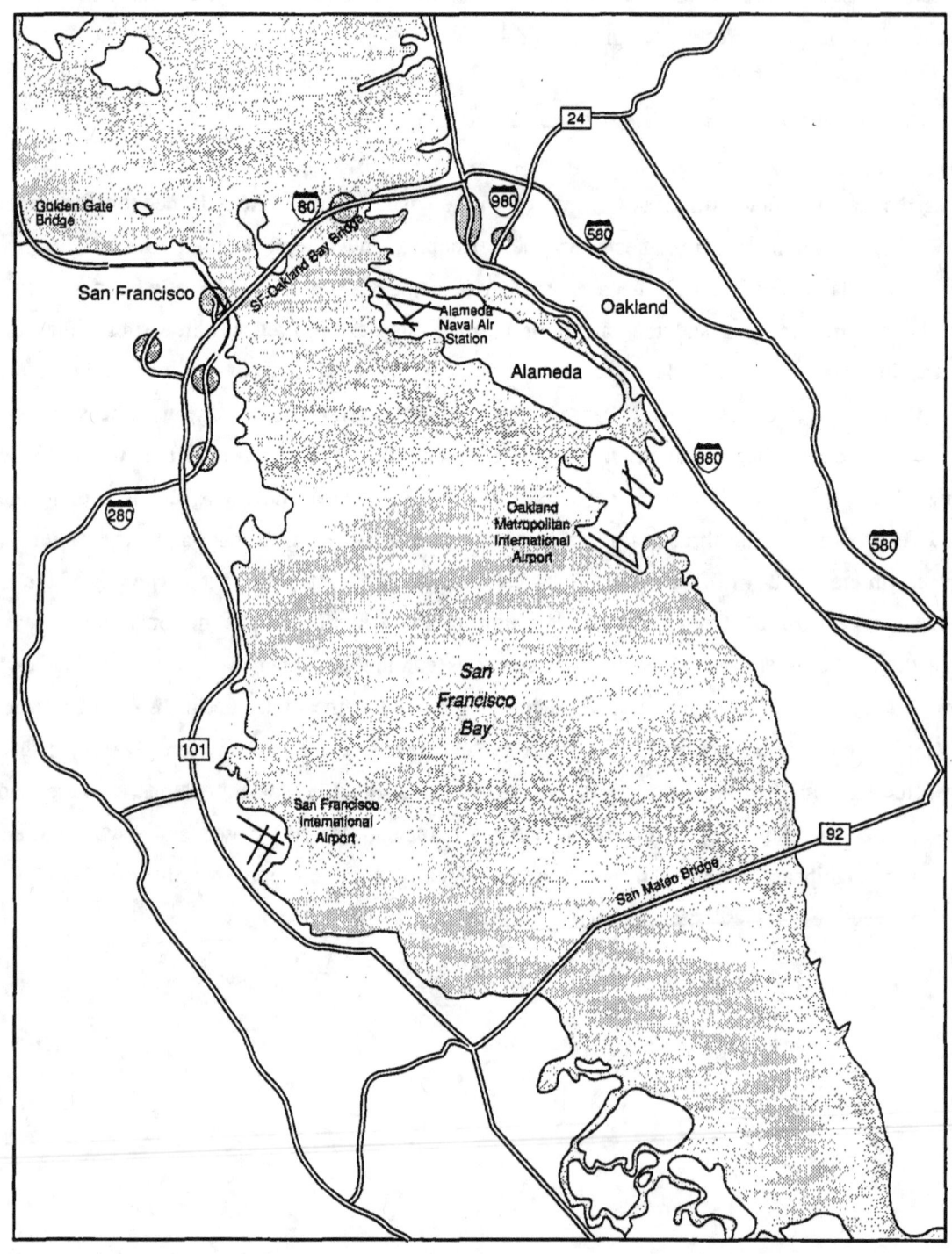

Figure 5.5.1   General location of bridge and viaduct damage in the Bay area as a result of the Loma
Prieta earthquake.

5.6 The I-880 Collapse

Interstate 880, also known as the Nimitz Freeway, is a primary north-south oriented 8-lane highway connecting San Jose with Interstates 580 and 80, adjacent to the east end of the San Francisco-Oakland Bay Bridge. Generally, I-880 is a ground level freeway with the exception of a 2 mile (3 km) elevated segment which is oriented approximately north-south and is bounded by 7th Street on the south and 34th Street on the north in Oakland (see fig. 5.6.1). The configuration of the elevated portion, known as the *Cypress Structure*, consisted of a bi-level system with four lanes of north-bound traffic on the first level, approximately 25 feet (8 m) above ground level, and four lanes of south-bound traffic on the upper level, approximately 50 feet (15 m) above ground level. Surface level traffic paralleled the Cypress Structure on both sides with underpasses at the major cross streets. Design work for this section was begun in 1951 and construction was completed in 1957. It is to be noted that the AASHTO design specifications for highway structures for this period (AASHTO, 1953) make no reference to design requirements for resisting lateral loads. However, the Caltrans Bridge Department design supplement for earthquake loads (Caltrans, 1949) did require bridge structures to resist earthquake loads of 0.06 times the weight of the structure for bridges on pile foundations as used for the elevated portion of I-880.

The structural configuration of the Cypress Structure consists of a series of 124 reinforced concrete transverse bents which support longitudinal cellular box girders that carry the road deck. The box girders vary from 71 to 90 feet (22 to 27 m) in length by 55 feet (17 m) wide and are integrally cast flush with the tops of the bent girders as shown in figure 5.6.2. The road deck has a relatively uniform weight of approximately 8 tons per foot (230 kN/m) along the longitudinal direction, which can be used to determine vertical and inertially induced loads to the various bents.

5.6.1 Description of Structure

There were 11 distinctively different bent configurations used on the Cypress Structure, but only three primary types were present in the majority of the collapsed section, which extended from the first expansion joint north of Bent 63 at 18th Street to just short of Bent 113 at 34th Street. The total length of the collapsed section was 3970 feet (1210 m), contrary to the 1.5 mile (2.4 km) figure commonly quoted in the media following the quake. The three predominant bent configurations are shown in figures 5.6.2 through 5.6.4 and are labelled as Type 1, 2, and 3 bents. A fourth type, which was similar to the Type 3 bent but with an additional support column for the first level and prestressing for the upper bent girder, is shown in figure 5.6.5. A fifth variant, similar to a Type 2 bent, but with a

Table 5.6.1 Bent Configurations for the Collapsed Portion of I-880

Bent	Type	Bent	Type	Bent	Type	Bent	Type	Bent	Type
63	1	73	5	83	1	93	1	103	1
64	1	74	5	84	1	94	1	104	1
65	1	75	2	85	1	95	4	105	1
66	1	76	2	86	1	96	4	106	1
67	1	77	2	87	1	97	4	107	1
68	1	78	2	88	1	98	4	108	1
69	1	79	2	89	1	99	1	109	6†
70	3	80	2	90	1	100	1	110	6†
71	2	81	1	91	1	101	1	111	6†
72	2	82	1	92	1	102	1	112	7Φ

† Bottom portal frame detail is similar to Type 4 bent; Top portal frame details are similar to Type 1 bents. The roadway deck for the lower bent gradually decreases in height above the surface from Bent 109 to Bent 111.

Φ This consists of a single portal frame supporting the upper roadway with hinged connections between the column bases and the pile caps and a moment resisting connection between the beams and the transverse girder. The lower roadway is supported a few feet above the surface by another transverse girder with moment resisting connections to the columns.

cantilevered detail for the lower level girder, is shown in figure 5.6.6. A summary of bent types within the collapsed section is presented in table 5.1.

There are several characteristics common to most bents for the Cypress Structure. In all cases the lower portion of each bent, comprising two vertical support columns and a horizontal (some were superelevated) connecting girder, was designed to achieve a moment resisting connection between the columns and girder. The columns generally measured 72 inches (1.83 m) deep by 48 inches (1.22 m) wide and were heavily reinforced with 44-#18 Grade 40 longitudinal reinforcing bars. Contrasting this massive axial reinforcement, #4 bar rectangular ties with 90-degree hooked ends were provided on 12 inch (310 mm) centers as lateral confinement. The columns were supported by 36 to 54 inch (0.91 to 1.52 m) thick reinforced pile caps which in turn were cast on top of driven pile foundations. The pile tip penetration depths varied from 16 feet (5 m) at Bent 63 (the southernmost limit of the collapse) to a maximum of 55 feet (17 m) for Bents 72 through 78. The majority of those from Bent 88 through the northern limit of the collapse had depths of 40 to 45 feet (12 to 14 m). The connection between the columns and the pile caps was designed as a rectangular depressed shear key, generally measuring 18 inches (460 mm) long by 36 inches (910 mm) wide and containing 4-#10 dowel bars which formed a 10 inch (250 mm) square at the center of the key. The remainder of the joint was filled with a half-inch (13 mm) layer of expansion joint material. For all intents and purposes this detail acted as a hinge. Several bents, notably

95-98 which are skewed on a 29-degree angle at Grand Avenue to accommodate railroad tracks, have longer spans which dictated the use of a third central column as shown in figure 5.6.6. The lower cross girders generally had dimensions of 48 inches (1.22 m) in width with a depth varying from 96 to 114 inches (2.44 to 2.90 m). Typical reinforcement details are shown in figure 5.6.6, Section C-C'. The details of the upper bents are more varied. Type 1 bents, which comprised more than half of those in the collapsed section, were designed similarly to the lower bents, that is, moment resisting connections between the columns and cross girder, and pinned connections at the base of both columns. The upper columns were tapered from 48 inches in width at the top, to accommodate girder reinforcement, to 36 inches (910 mm) at the bottom with a constant 48 inch section depth. Like the bottom columns, these were heavily reinforced in the axial direction with 22-#18 bars, half that of the lower column, with #4 ties with 90-degree hooks on 12 inch (310 mm) centers. Of particular interest is the detail of the connection between these upper columns and the lower bent frame shown in figure 5.6.7. A 27 inch (680 mm) high pedestal, reinforced as shown in Section B-B' in figure 5.6.7, was used to accommodate placement of the shear key/hinge detail shown in Section A-A'. The 4-#10 dowel bars shown in the shear key detail extended 30 inches (760 mm) above and below the joint which, under normal circumstances, meets the development length requirements for this type of bar. It should be noted that the #4 stirrups used for lateral confinement of the lower bent columns, observed during the field investigation, stop at the bottom face of the lower bent girder, i.e. there was no specific confinement steel within the joint. The 14-#10 x 36-inch (910 mm) pedestal reinforcement bars shown in Section B-B' were embedded just 6 inches in the upper, outside corner of the lower bent beam-column joint, in the same area where some 16-#18 negative moment reinforcement bars for the lower bent girder splice to two rows of vertical #18 bars for the lower column. The congestion caused by this detail is evident just below Section B-B' in figure 5.6.7. Lacking substantial lateral confining reinforcement in the joint, it appears likely that any lateral loads transmitted across the pedestal (Section B-B') would be resisted only by the shear strength of the concrete and that negligible resistance to lateral motion would be contributed by the reinforcement contained within the pedestal. Calculations, presented below, of the loads to cause failure, which assume full development of the pedestal ties, can therefore be considered conservative.

The design of the Cypress Structure permitted a future access ramp for Grand Avenue to be added to the west side of the freeway. In order to accommodate the extended spans required of the upper bent girder, prestressing tendons were used in place of deformed steel reinforcement. These prestressing bars, which were unbonded, were designed to be extended and subsequently anchored to the west face of the girder following the addition of the ramp. The three-hinge detail associated with these prestressed bents is shown in figure 5.6.3. The two upper hinges were similar in detail to that shown in Section A-A' of figure 5.6.7. The presumed intent of this approach was to accommodate shortening of the upper deck

5-9

girder, apparently assumed at the time to be on the order of 2 to 3 inches (50 to 80 mm). Recent calculations by Caltrans engineers indicated a shortening of 5/8 inch (16 mm), but this is based on nearly 40 years of experience. At the time of design, the concept of prestressing was in its infancy and the use of a dual hinged column on one side of the bent to accommodate the presumed large displacements induced by prestressing is an understandable approach where gravity loads are the predominant force acting on the structure. With the three-hinge design, however, all lateral loads must be resisted by the right-hand (east side) column alone (see figs. 5.6.3 and 5.6.6) which is designed with continuous longitudinal reinforcement that extends upward from the lower bent column. The notable exception to this situation is for Type 5 bents where a cantilevered detail demands that the upper column steel be anchored only in the lower bent girder.

The specified working stress for the concrete was 1,250 psi (8.62 MPa). Cores taken after the earthquake from column sections by researchers from the University of California at Berkeley (EERC, 1989) indicated a compressive strength of 6,000 psi (41 MPa) and a modulus of 3.7 million psi (25.5 GPa). The reinforcement, except for prestressing bars, was Grade 40.

In 1977, as part of the Caltrans Phase I Seismic Retrofit Program, the Cypress Structure was equipped with cable restrainers at each transverse expansion joint between the longitudinal box girders. These expansion joints were spaced at approximately 240 feet (73 m) and were intended to reduce temperature induced stresses in the deck structure. There were, on the average, three bents between expansion joints which could be expected to act as a continuous unit along with the upper- and lower-deck box girders. In order to prevent earthquake-induced ground displacements from unseating one of these expansion joints, which would lead to immediate collapse of at least one span, a series of cables were used to anchor the ends of the mating box girders together. Figure 5.6.8 shows a typical detail in which three cable restrainer units were installed at each expansion joint. In order to prevent pullout of the cable assemblies under seismic loads, a set of reinforced concrete bolsters were cast to increase the thickness of the end diaphragms for the box girders. Seven 3/4 inch (19 mm) wire rope cables were wrapped around a metal drum on one side to form a horseshoe-shaped cable bundle. The ends of the cables were swaged into two 7-cable anchor blocks located on one side of the expansion joint. It may be appreciated that the presence of these restrainers, in addition to preventing the unwanted dropping of a deck segment, also effectively creates a longitudinal hinge at each expansion joint, across which both vertical and horizontal structural loads can be transmitted.

5.6.2 Description of Collapse by Motorists

It was fortunate that the third game of the World Series of baseball, between the San Francisco Giants and the Oakland A's, was about to be played in San Francisco at the time of the earthquake. It has been reported by California state transportation officials that traffic on I-880 was extremely light as a result of many people having left work early to watch the game on television or at the stadium. Furthermore, due to road construction south of the Cypress Structure, a substantial amount of north-bound traffic was detoured through alternate ground-level roads[1]. When the earthquake occurred, a 3970-foot (1210-m) section of the double-decked Cypress Structure collapsed, killing 42 motorists, most of whom were travelling north-bound on the lower level and were crushed by the upper deck. Useful accounts of the collapse, by eyewitnesses who were in a position to ascertain the dynamic behavior of the structure, are scarce. One pedestrian near 18th Street observed, "It was like a big, giant, long ocean wave, and behind each wave a portion of the freeway collapsed. As the top level crashed down on the cars below, shearing cleanly at 18th street, cars shot off the sides of the [upper] freeway, crashing and flipping into the street."[2] One survivor who was on the upper deck travelling south said that, "there was a distinct initial [sideways] jolt as the earthquake first struck. I thought one of my tires had gone flat. My first thought was to get off the freeway as quickly as possible, so I sped up. Approximately 20 seconds later the second wave hit and behind me [in the mirror] I could see concrete dust plumes shooting into the air."[3] This particular witness was one of the last to make it past 18th Street ahead of the collapse. The same witness also made the poignant remark that in retrospect he noticed that others were making all efforts to stop their cars and that lane changes were being made involuntarily. Furthermore, it was suggested that many of those travelling north-bound intentionally stopped beneath girder bents, under the false assumption that these, like the doorways of buildings which purportedly offer greater safety in the event of an earthquake, would provide safety from falling objects. Several survivors indicated that sufficient time was available prior to the collapse that motorists were able to stop their cars and, in some cases, even get out. Unfortunately, and as the clustering of car locations outlined in paint on the upper deck by recovery personnel attests, parking beneath the bents was likely the worst choice, as there was no clearance when the girders fell.

---

[1]Governor's Board of Inquiry Meeting, State of California: "The 1989 Loma Prieta Earthquake," December 13-14, 1989, Hyatt Regency International Hotel, Oakland, CA.

[2]San Francisco Examiner, October 18, 1989 Special Edition.

[3]Governor's Board of Inquiry Meeting, State of California: "The 1989 Loma Prieta Earthquake," December 13-14, 1989, Hyatt Regency International Hotel, Oakland, CA.

5.6.3 Summary of Aerial Photos

The second day after the earthquake an aerial reconnaissance of the I-880 collapse was carried out via helicopter by the team. A set of close-up oblique aerial photos of the collapsed portion of the Cypress Structure is presented in figures 5.6.9 through 5.6.22. Figure 5.6.9 shows an overall view looking south from Bent 113. The northern extent of the collapse is visible in figure 5.6.10 with Bent 113 remaining intact at left center. Beginning at Bent 106 (fig. 5.6.11) and extending through Bent 104 (fig. 5.6.12), both upper and lower levels of the freeway collapsed to ground level. From Bent 104 through Bent 98, only the upper deck collapsed. Figures 5.6.13 through 5.6.15 show the anomalous span between Bents 96 and 97 which remained intact following the earthquake. In viewing these figures, it should be kept in mind that Bents 95 through 98 were all Type 4 bents and that Bents 96 and 97, specifically, were skewed to the primary axis of the bridge by 29 degrees to accommodate the railroad tracks visible in figure 5.6.14; Bents 95 and 98 were not skewed. Furthermore, expansion joints exist immediately north of Bents 95 and 98.

Various collapse sequences have been proposed centering on span 96-97. One theory assumes that span 96-97 served as the initiation point, with two progressive collapse waves propagating to the north to Bent 113 and simultaneously to the south to Bent 62. Another scenario involves span 96-97 serving as the arrester, with simultaneous collapse waves propagating towards it from Bent 113 on the north and from a point somewhere in the prestressed section between Bents 71 and 80 to the south. The southern collapse section would, consequently, have also propagated south to Bent 62. Yet another theory holds that the lateral accelerations experienced by Bents 96 and 97 were insufficient to cause the shearing failures seen at Type 1 and 2 bents and that all of these latter bents essentially failed nearly simultaneously. Unfortunately, available eyewitness descriptions of the collapse are not precise enough to validate these theories, or to suggest others. However, the observation by several survivors that the entire structure was moving up and down as though "giant waves" were travelling down the structure, and the fact that the upper deck came to rest squarely on top of the lower deck (implying nearly simultaneous failure of east and west upper bent columns) are of particular interest.

Figures 5.6.16 through 5.6.18 show a uniform section between Bents 94 and 80 in which the upper deck has collapsed directly on top of the lower deck. All of the bents in this section were Type 1 and exhibited a distinctive failure mode in which both upper bent columns sheared at their base from the supporting pedestals and splayed outward as the weight of the upper deck carried the bent down to the lower level girder where the collapse was generally arrested. Beginning at Bent 80 and extending south to Bent 71 (figs. 5.6.18 and 5.6.19) all bents were of the three-hinged post-tensioned variety (Types 2 and

5-12

5), designed to be extended westward for the future construction of the Grand Avenue access ramps. These three-hinge bents exhibited two distinctively different collapse modes. The first, visible between Bents 74 and 80 in figures 5.6.18 and 5.6.19, involved the destruction of the eastern upper bent columns and the general rotation of the upper deck in a clockwise fashion (looking north), pivoting about the western two-hinged upper bent columns. In stark contrast, the western two-hinged columns were ejected from the structure for Bents 71 through 73. These column segments landed as much as 30 feet (9 m) from the bent face, as evidenced by 2 foot (600 mm) deep, 6 foot (1.8 m) diameter craters in the adjacent pavement where the column ends impacted. Bents 63 through 69 (figs. 5.6.20 through 5.6.22) were all Type 1 and exhibited failure similar to that described previously. The southern extent of the collapse can be clearly seen at the expansion joint just north of Bent 62.

5.6.4 Ground Details

Figure 5.6.23 shows a ground-level view looking northward from Bent 86 on the west side of the expressway. All of the bents visible in this photo were Type 1 which invariably exhibited a symmetrical failure with both upper columns shearing free at their base and being splayed outward as the upper deck fell. The timber posts visible beneath the lower deck were installed by Caltrans under each bent to insure that there was no subsequent settling of the structure during rescue operations. Further evidence that the upper deck fell nearly squarely on the lower deck with no significant sidesway is shown in figure 5.6.24 which is looking northward from atop Bent 80.

Figures 5.6.25 through 5.6.28 show four minor variations of Type 1 bent failure. All views are from the west side of the respective bents. At Bent 65 (fig. 5.6.25), it can be seen that the upper column support pedestal is still attached to the base of the column and that an inclined failure plane exists through the failed pedestal. Note that confining reinforcement in the vicinity of the lower girder/column joint is non-existent. As for most Type 1 bent failures, the upper columns remained tenuously attached to the upper bent girder. Bent 85 (fig. 5.6.26) shows a similar situation regarding the upper column support pedestal (beneath the numbers "85" in the figure). Here it is evident that the failure plane for the pedestal ran flush with the curved face formed by the lower bent girder negative moment steel. It is also evident that the seismic loads, in combination with a lack of confining steel in the upper beam/column joint, were sufficient to induce an explosive rupture of concrete at the top of the column, breaking it free from the upper girder steel seen at the top center of the photo. It should be emphasized, and it will become clear in subsequent discussion, that such compressive failures did not initiate the collapse of the bent, despite the lack of lateral confining steel in the upper girder/column joint. At Bent 90, the upper column apparently sheared through the 4-#10 dowel bars at the center of the shear key and was propelled outward with sufficient force to separate the column top from the upper bent girder. The upper bent column support pedestal can still be seen projecting above the lower column.

Figure 5.6.28 shows a final variation of a Type 1 bent failure. This particular column, at Bent 94, carried a pipe through its center which drained the upper deck. Given a lack of significant confining reinforcement (note the thin #4 ties which appear as wires compared with the massive #18 axial reinforcement), the presence of this pipe likely served to create the fracture path which split the column.

Figure 5.6.29 shows a closeup of a Type 2 bent failure in which the eastern half of a series of three-hinged prestressed bents collapsed, due to shearing failure at the base of the east column, leading to a rigid body rotation of the upper deck about the western, two-hinged columns. As can be seen, the western column shear keys did perform as hinges even under rotations sufficient to cause compressive spalling on the interior face of the columns (fig. 5.6.30). Most of the upper bent girders fractured due to impact-induced bending stresses. This in turn yielded, and subsequently fractured most of the post-tensioning bars which, because they were unbonded, were partially expelled from the girder due to rebound from the release of stored elastic energy, as sown in figure 5.6.31. It is of some significance that Bent 78, the innermost frame in figure 5.6.32, was skewed at an angle of 16 degrees. This difference, although subtle, may be part of the explanation for why this particular section did not fail completely. This performance is to be directly contrasted with Bent 72 (see figs. 5.6.33 and 5.6.34) in which the western two-hinged columns were ejected from the structure. Of particular note in figure 5.6.33 are the bent #10 bars projecting both from the top of the lower bent column as well as the bottom face of the upper bent girder. These represented the only continuous reinforcement through the upper and lower shear keys. Figure 5.6.35 leaves no doubt that lateral confining steel was insufficient to prevent localized fracture of the concrete and the subsequent pullout of these dowels. A closeup of the top of the Bent 71 upper two-hinge column in figure 5.6.35 shows a detail of the still intact shear key, 4-#10 dowel bars, and, in this particular instance, a central drainage pipe. In this case the dowel bars remained intact within the column and pulled out, instead, from the upper girder joint.

Figures 5.6.36 and 5.6.37 show details of the span between Bents 96 and 97, the only one to remain completely intact between Bents 62 and 113. There are several obvious differences which could account for this. The Type 4 bent, which includes Bents 95-98, contains an additional central column in the lower bent which would serve to limit lateral sway at the first deck level. More importantly, the reinforcing steel at the base of the upper bent columns is continuous with the lower columns, eliminating the pedestal/hinge detail that appears to have contributed to widespread failure in Type 1 bents. Figure 5.6.37 indicates that, despite severe flexurally induced cracking at the lower column/girder joint, the upper and lower columns remained intact. These structural differences contributed to increase structural stiffness and thus decrease the natural period of vibration. Determination of whether the differences in vibrational characteristics between bents is of vital significance in understanding the overall collapse is beyond the scope of this report. However, it would appear that, due to the long length of the structure with respect to the propagation speed of the disturbance (it has been estimated that a lag time of several seconds existed between the time when the surface waves hit the southern end of the Cypress Structure and when they arrived at its northern end), such variations in structural vibrational characteristics, as well as those for the underlying soil at each particular bent, may need to be considered for an accurate dynamic model of the structure.

The section of expressway between Bents 104 and 106 (fig. 5.6.38) contains the only portion of the Cypress Structure to have exhibited complete failure in both upper and lower decks. These were Type 1 bents in an area where the lower road deck was beginning its descent to the northern distribution structure. Beyond Bent 106 both upper and lower decks were superelevated on the east side. Other than these minor differences, there were no particularly distinguishing characteristics which would have made these bents more susceptible to failure. It has been suggested (EERI, 1989) that greater accelerations may have been experienced towards the northern end of the structure due to the presence of Bay Mud deposits, which are deepest towards the northern end of the collapsed section and would have led to soil amplification. This argument is unconvincing in light of geotechnical data subsequently made available (CDMG, 1989b). The remaining possibilities include construction defects and/or resonance of the entire Cypress Structure which could have led to higher forces in this particular area, as a result of random coincidence of modes, than would be expected using the simple Newtonian lateral force approach discussed below. In any event, there was vastly different performance of the lower bent columns to the north of Bent 104, as exhibited, for example, at Bents 105 and 108 shown in figures 5.6.39 and 5.6.40. Bent 108, in particular, exhibited the only gross shear failure of a lower column seen in the entire Cypress Structure.

Figure 5.6.41 shows a view looking south from Bent 114 at the northern extent of the collapse. Significant changes in bent configuration begin to take place at Bent 113. The lower deck is supported nearly at ground level, while the upper deck is supported on outrigger beams cast integrally with their supporting columns. No hinges, except at the foundation level, are present in these bents. This change in stiffness at the commencement of the northern distribution structure was certainly a factor as to why the collapse either initiated or terminated at this location. Similar changes in structural configuration exist at the southern limit of the collapse where the presence of access ramps led to stiffer bents.

5-15

5.6.5 Observations on Contributing Causes of Collapse

There is no site-specific acceleration record for the Cypress Structure. However, initial reports from the California Department of Conservation, Division of Mines and Geology (CDMG, 1989a), and from the U.S. Geological Survey provide strong motion records from the Oakland Outer Harbor Wharf (1.5 miles (2.4 km) to the west); at the base of a two-story office building in Oakland (1.5 miles to the southeast); and from the base of another two-story building in Emeryville (1 mile (1.6 km) to the north). Acceleration records from these three sites had peak horizontal accelerations of 0.29g, 0.26g, and 0.26g, respectively. In a second report on the geotechnical aspects of the earthquake by the California Department of Conservation, Division of Mines and Geology (CDMG, 1989-b) it is observed that:

> "The strong motion data from the Oakland area does indicate that amplified levels of motion occurred at the Cypress Structure. However, the amplification effect occurs throughout the flat lying portions of Oakland, not just in a localized zone near the Cypress Structure.... Whatever factor is causing the increased shaking levels in Oakland extends throughout the flat lying areas, and is not limited to areas of bay mud."

On the basis of these findings it may be concluded that the Cypress Structure was subjected to horizontal accelerations of between 0.26g to 0.29g. Acceleration records from these sites taken in perpendicular directions do not differ greatly, indicating that the orientation of the Cypress Structure was not of critical importance in its subsequent response to the earthquake. Response spectra for the Oakland Wharf site (CDMG, 1989-b) indicate peak structural accelerations of 1g for a structure with a natural period of vibration of 1.5 seconds at 2% damping. In order to estimate the natural period of the Cypress Structure, a series of finite element computer models were constructed for Type 1 and Type 2 bents. The models included a single bent of the specified type which included the inertial mass and stiffness contributions of an 80 foot (24 m) section of the deck box girders as well as those for the bent girders and columns. The results of these analyses, based upon uncracked section properties derived from the as-built drawings, are presented in figures 5.6.42 and 5.6.43. The results indicate first and second mode frequencies for Type 1 bents of 2.5 Hz and 6.4 Hz, respectively; for Type 2 bents the first and second mode frequencies were 2.0 Hz and 6.3 Hz, respectively. The values for the Type 1 bent compare extremely favorably with first and second mode frequencies of 2.5 Hz and 6.5 Hz, respectively, measured by University of California at Berkeley researchers during a full scale test of Bents 45, 46, and 47 following the earthquake[4]. On the

---

[4]Governor's Board of Inquiry Meeting, State of California: "The 1989 Loma Prieta Earthquake," December 13-14, 1989, Hyatt Regency International Hotel, Oakland, CA.

basis of these analyses, and the response spectra for the Oakland Outer Harbor Wharf station, it can be determined that for 2% damping (as determined from the Berkeley tests) both Type 1 and Type 2 bents in the Cypress Structure experienced first mode equivalent accelerations of 0.35g.

Following the Uniform Building Code (UBC, 1988) assumption of an inverted triangular distribution for the effective lateral load due to the earthquake applied to each deck level, and taking into account that the weight of each level is approximately equal, and that the upper roadway is approximately twice the height above the ground as the lower level, the elastic force at the upper level will be twice that at the lower level. Thus two-thirds of the total base shear force is effectively applied to the upper level bent and one-third to the lower bent. These forces were subsequently used as input for static finite element analyses of bent Types 1, 2, and 5, in which the three predominant types of failure were observed. Vertical inertial loads were applied as a uniform acceleration of 1.06g, based on the vertical peak acceleration components at the seismic stations previously mentioned.

For lightly reinforced concrete sections, plots of linear elastic tensile stress trajectories are good indicators of where cracks will initiate and the likely paths they will follow under a decreasing-strength failure situation. The results, presented in figures 5.6.44 through 5.6.46, both as contours of maximum principal tensile stress and as tensor plots of the principal stresses, indicate that the column support pedestal for the upper columns in Type 1 bents is highly stressed and that crack initiation will occur beneath the shear key with the crack pattern as shown in figure 5.6.44(d). Crack initiation in the concrete was assumed to occur at a tensile stress of 460 psi (3.17 MPa), based upon the ACI tensile strength formula (ACI, 1989) for a compressive strength of 6,000 psi (42 MPa). The stresses shown in figures 5.6.44 through 5.6.46 are a result of both the lateral seismic load as well as outward shearing forces associated with the portal frame reactions at the shear key due to vertical loads on the upper bent. This latter contribution accounts for more than half the load required to shear the column support pedestal for a Type 1 bent, which is determined to be 333 kips (1480 kN) for concrete having $f'_c = 6000$ psi and is directly dependent upon the maximum vertical acceleration seen by the structure. The calculated lateral base acceleration required to achieve a shearing load of 333 kips at the pedestal, by modifying Priestley et al. (Priestley, 1989) to account for the measured concrete strength, is 0.2g. With the cracking of the right column support pedestal, it can be seen that the upper left-hand beam/column joint is subjected to large tensile stresses due to bending which would lead to crack initiation. While there is considerable positive moment steel in the upper bent girder at this location, no transverse reinforcement was noted during the field inspection. This condition could be expected to contribute to a brittle, explosive failure mechanism following shearing of the left lower pedestal as the bent was rocked in the opposite direction on the reverse cycle. Based on this reasoning, it has been hypothesized by some investigators that the Type 1 upper bents could have been destroyed during just one complete cycle of loading at maximum acceleration (Priestley, 1989; EERI, 1989).

Static load tests carried out on Bents 45-47 by the University of California at Berkeley[5] indicated failure initiation in Type 1 bents to take place at a lateral load of 465 kips (2070 kN) per bent, with the lateral load being applied to the top deck of the upper bent. Utilizing the UBC load distribution approach previously described, this leads to an equivalent base shear of approximately 700 kips (3120 kN) which equates, for a typical bent and 80 feet (24 m) of deck, to a base acceleration of 0.25g.

An equally serious situation exists for Type 2 bents, as shown in figure 5.6.45. Cracking is expected at the joint between the upper and lower columns along the diagonal path shown. Likewise, flexural cracking is indicated at the interior corner of the *lower* bent beam/column joint. Due to the increased cross section of the upper columns, the collapse load is expected to be higher than for the Type 1 bents. The calculated collapse load, following Priestley et al. (Priestley, 1989) and modified for a concrete compressive strength of 6000 psi, indicates failure at a shear force of 451 kips (2010 kN), or 38% higher than that for a Type 1 bent. The calculated collapse acceleration for Type 2 columns is 0.25g; no corresponding experimental data are available.

Figure 5.6.46 shows the stress distribution at the critical joint between the upper bent column and the cantilevered portion of the lower bent girder for Bent 74. Although it is indicated that a vertical crack will initiate under the given loads at the interior corner of this joint, this would be insufficient to cause failure given the massive amount of negative moment steel from the lower bent girder at this location. Field inspection described in the report by Bertero et al. (Bertero, 1989) indicates that the negative moment steel did not extend sufficiently far into the joint to be effective. It is hypothesized that a shear failure occurred at this location immediately following the formation of the tensile crack shown at the interior corner. The formation of this crack, based upon a linear scaling of the applied lateral loads, could initiate at a lateral acceleration as small as 0.1g.

The above discussion is graphically illustrated in figures 5.6.47 through 5.6.49 which indicate the proposed failure initiation sequence for the three predominant types of bent failures observed at the Cypress Structure and depict the state observed in the field after the collapse.

---

[5]Governor's Board of Inquiry Meeting, State of California: "The 1989 Loma Prieta Earthquake," December 13-14, 1989, Hyatt Regency International Hotel, Oakland, CA.

It is interesting to note that the calculated column shear resistance reported by Priestley et al. (Priestley, 1989) for Type 4 bents (see fig. 5.6.5), when modified to account for the measured compressive strength of the concrete, comes to 398 kips (1770 kN). Accounting for portal frame reaction shear at the column bases for the upper bent, the lateral base acceleration required to achieve failure is 0.38g, i.e., greater than the expected acceleration from the response spectra reported by CDMG (CDMG, 1989b). These frames, as can be seen in figure 5.6.37, suffered significant damage, but remained standing.

The analyses described thus far assumed that each bent and its tributary sections of the box girder deck respond to the earthquake in a manner which is independent and decoupled from the transient response of the adjacent bents. The analyses also assumed a failure mechanism triggered by the effects of lateral loading. Two pieces of evidence are worth considering. First, the failure was essentially vertical. It is unlikely that such uniform vertical collapse would have resulted solely from the effects of lateral loading. Second, eyewitness reports indicated the presence of "giant waves" rolling down the length of the elevated structure. Taking these two points into account, dynamic modal analyses of a 9-span segment of the Cypress Structure were carried out. The results indicate that the 9-span long structure had a lateral vibrational period of 9 seconds, well beyond the period of peak lateral accelerations based upon the response spectra of the record from the Oakland Outer Harbor Wharf site. However, the vertical mode of vibration (see fig. 5.6.50) had a period of about 0.16 seconds (6.2 Hz) which is remarkably close to the predominant period of the vertical acceleration of the record for the area. Structural amplification in this mode could account for three disparate aspects of the I-880 collapse: 1) it accounts for the observations made by witnesses; 2) structural amplification in this mode would lead to large vertical forces acting upon the bents. It is important to recall that more than half the shearing load to cause failure in a Type 1 bent was due to portal frame horizontal reactions which are a result of vertical loading. A significant increase in the vertical reaction forces, as a result of resonance in the mode shown in figure 5.6.50, would also lead to failure of the bents, but with the important exception that the failure would necessarily be symmetric; 3) the lower and upper road decks do not necessarily vibrate in phase, nor with the same amplitude (see fig. 5.6.50). For those places where the decks vibrate in phase, the reaction forces could be much greater. This helps to explain the variations in failure which were observed along the length of the collapsed section, particularly towards the northern end where both decks collapsed.

The above analyses, which are of a preliminary nature, explain the possible causes for the I-880 collapse. It is concluded that simple lateral load analysis would not be adequate to describe completely the seismic response of the Cypress Structure and that the dynamic behavior of the entire structural system needs to be considered in order to predict correctly the modes of failure.

5.6.6 Summary

1. While the precise dynamic behavior of the Cypress Structure prior to its collapse remains to be explained, it may be concluded that at least three different failure mechanisms existed whose ultimate resistance could be expected to be substantially exceeded during the earthquake. Type 1 bents were shown experimentally to fail at 0.25g lateral acceleration, significantly lower than the anticipated 0.35g acceleration predicted for the site based on available response spectra. The inability to resist the applied lateral load for all bents which collapsed can be directly traced to a lack of sufficient confining steel within the critical joint details. It should, however, be appreciated that the calculated, and measured, resistances of the bents to lateral load substantially exceeded the AASHO design criteria under which the bridge was designed in 1951.

2. The Cypress Structure was non-redundant. Once one of the upper bent columns for a particular bent failed, the full load would be transferred to the remaining support, leading to an explosive failure consistent with that observed at the site following the earthquake.

3. The lower bent columns and girders appeared, in general, not to be a factor in the collapse.

4. It is believed that inconsistencies and questions remain which cannot be answered by the simple lateral loads models employed in this preliminary study. Further detailed work should be carried out involving transient dynamic, inelastic modeling of the Cypress Structure as a whole.

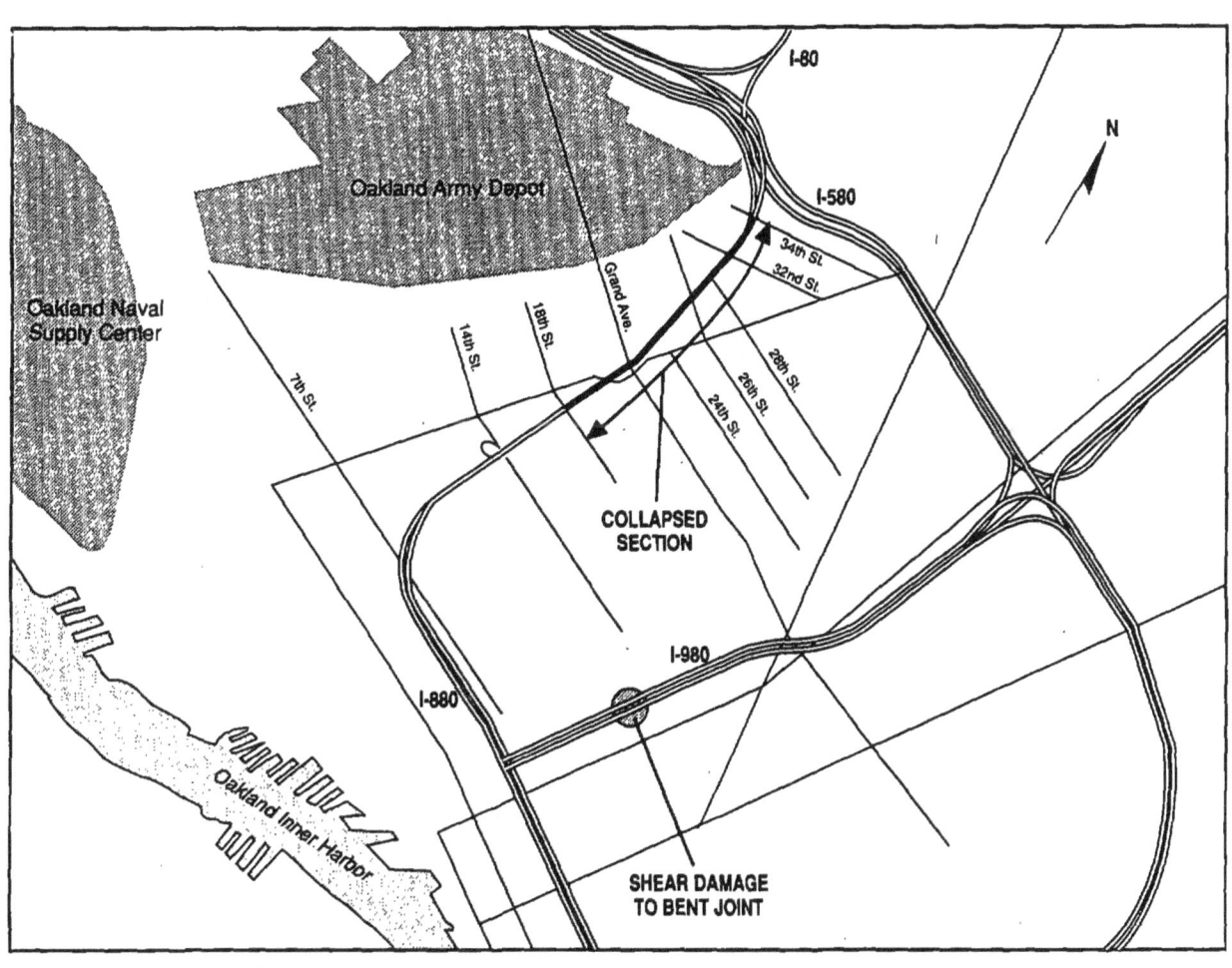

Figure 5.6.1   Map of northwest Oakland depicting the location of the collapse of I-880 and bent damage to I-980.

TYPE 1 BENT: I-880

[Bents 64-69; 82-94; 100-106]

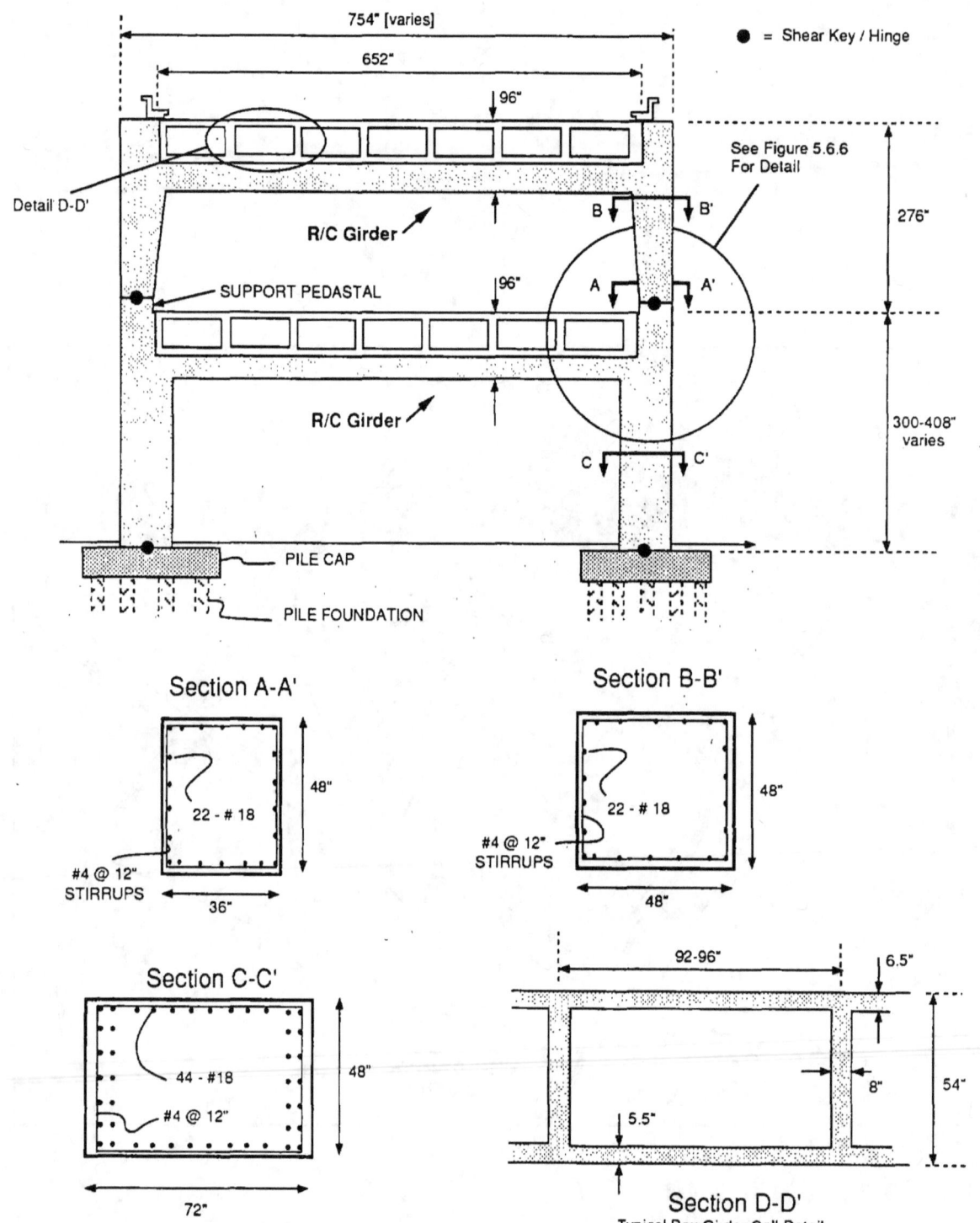

Figure 5.6.2   Structural configuration of Type 1 bents used on the elevated section of I-880.

TYPE 2 BENT: I-880

[Bent 71,72, 75-80]

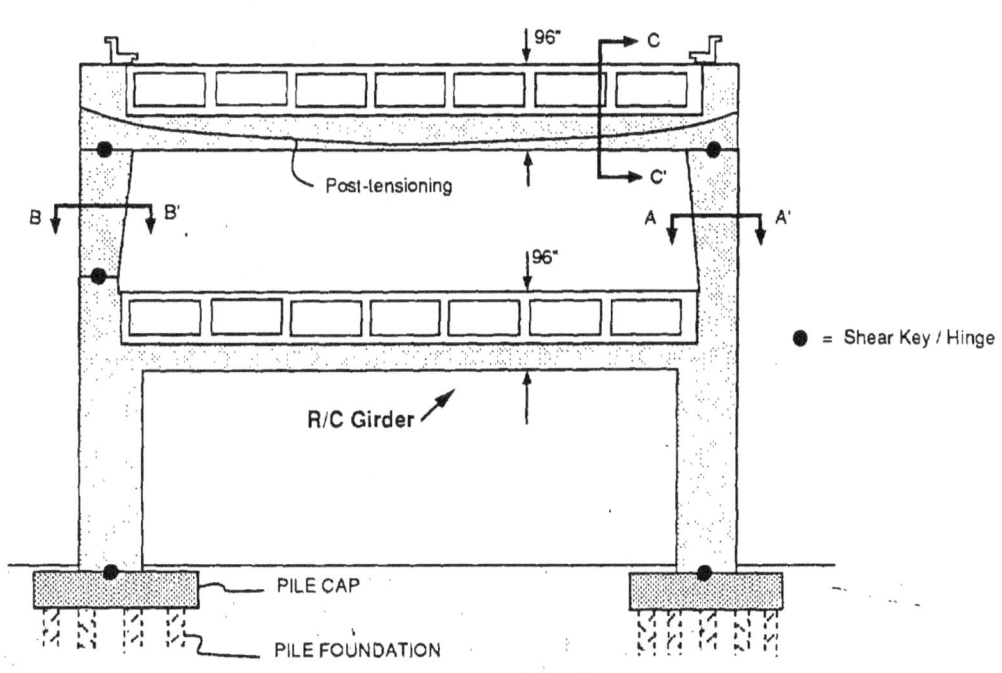

Post-tensioning

96"

96"

R/C Girder

● = Shear Key / Hinge

PILE CAP

PILE FOUNDATION

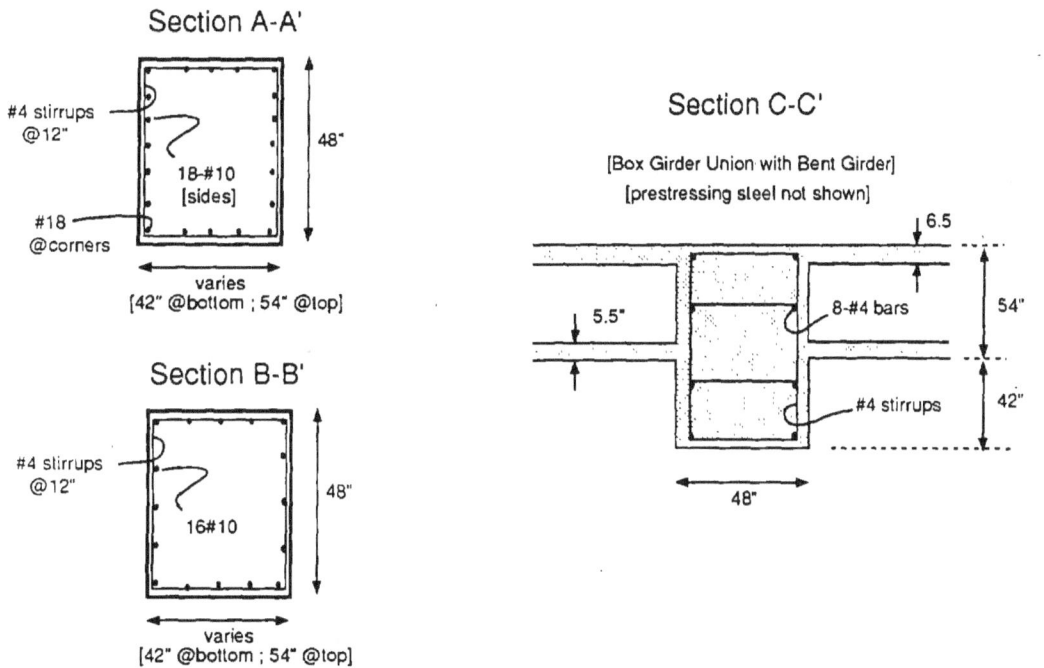

Section A-A'

#4 stirrups
@12"

18-#10
[sides]

#18
@corners

48"

varies
[42" @bottom ; 54" @top]

Section B-B'

#4 stirrups
@12"

16#10

48"

varies
[42" @bottom ; 54" @top]

Section C-C'

[Box Girder Union with Bent Girder]
[prestressing steel not shown]

6.5

5.5"

8-#4 bars

54"

#4 stirrups

42"

48"

Figure 5.6.3   Structural configuration of Type 2 bents used on the elevated section of I-880.

TYPE 3 BENT: I-880

[Bent 70]

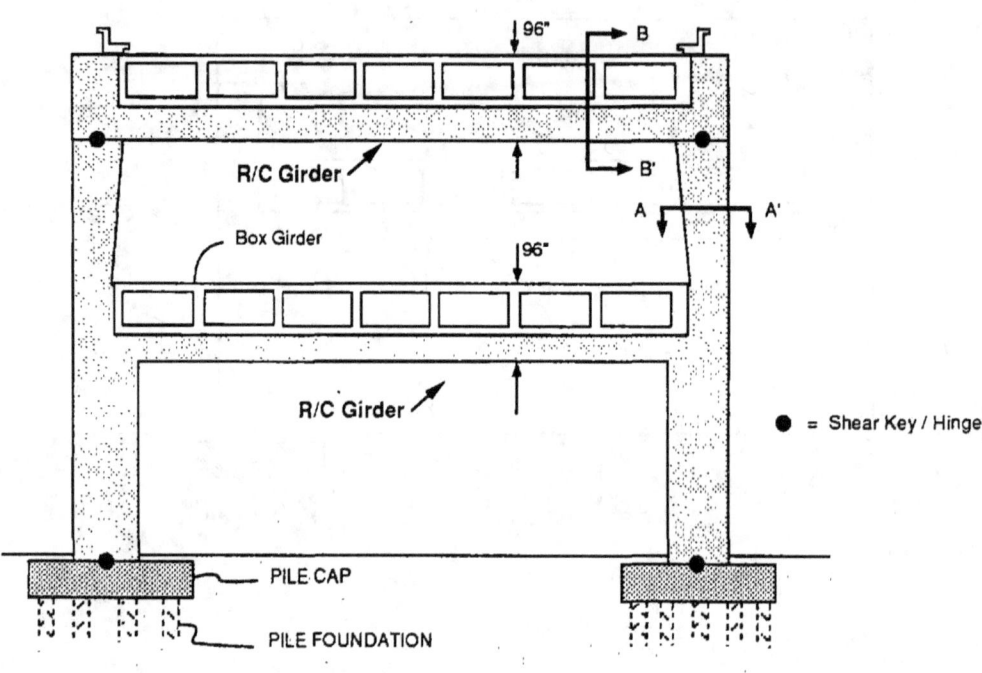

● = Shear Key / Hinge

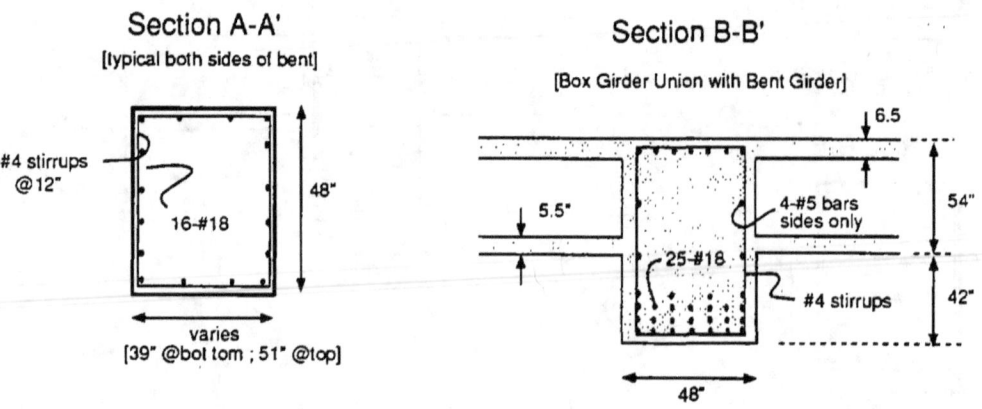

Figure 5.6.4   Structural configuration of Type 3 bents used on the elevated section of I-880.

TYPE 4 BENT: I-880

[BENT 95-98]

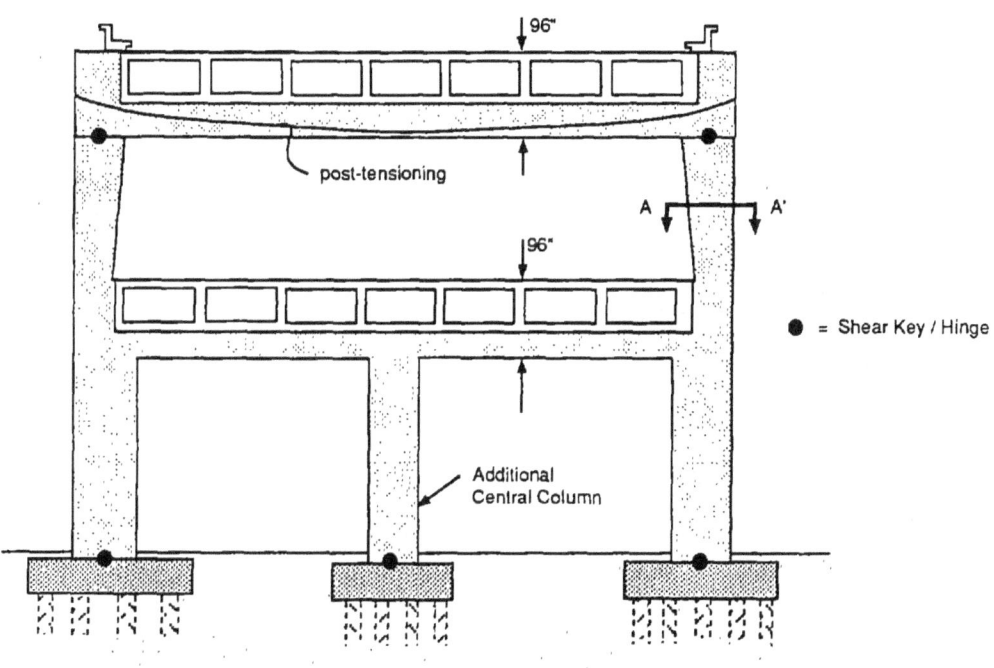

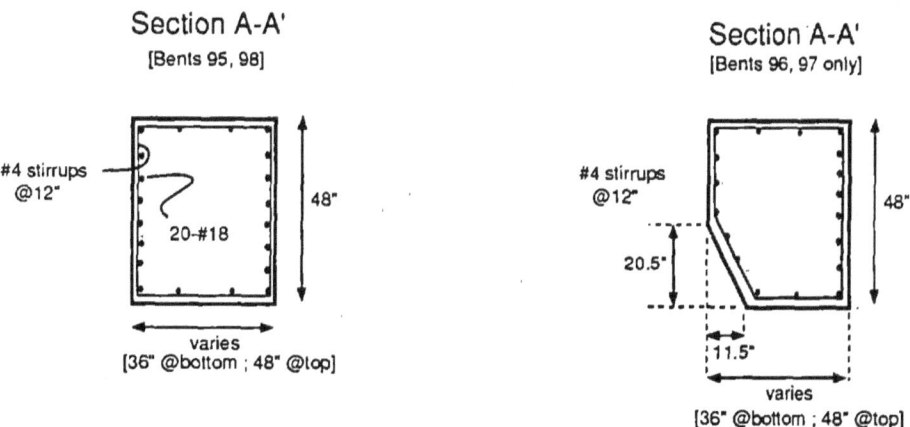

Figure 5.6.5   Structural configuration of Type 4 bents used on the elevated section of I-880.

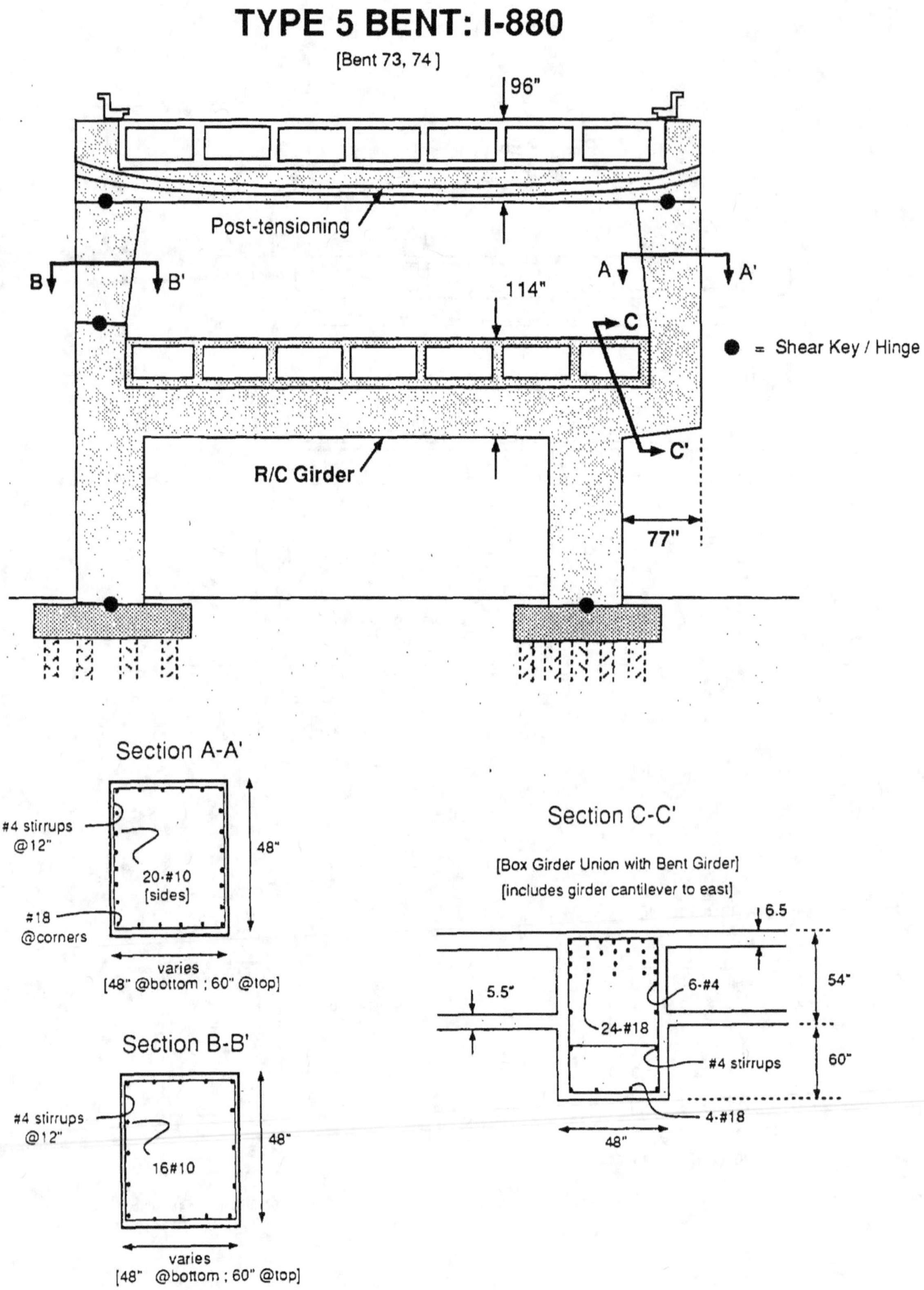

TYPE 5 BENT: I-880

[Bent 73, 74]

Figure 5.6.6 Structural configuration of Type 5 bents used on the elevated section of I-880.

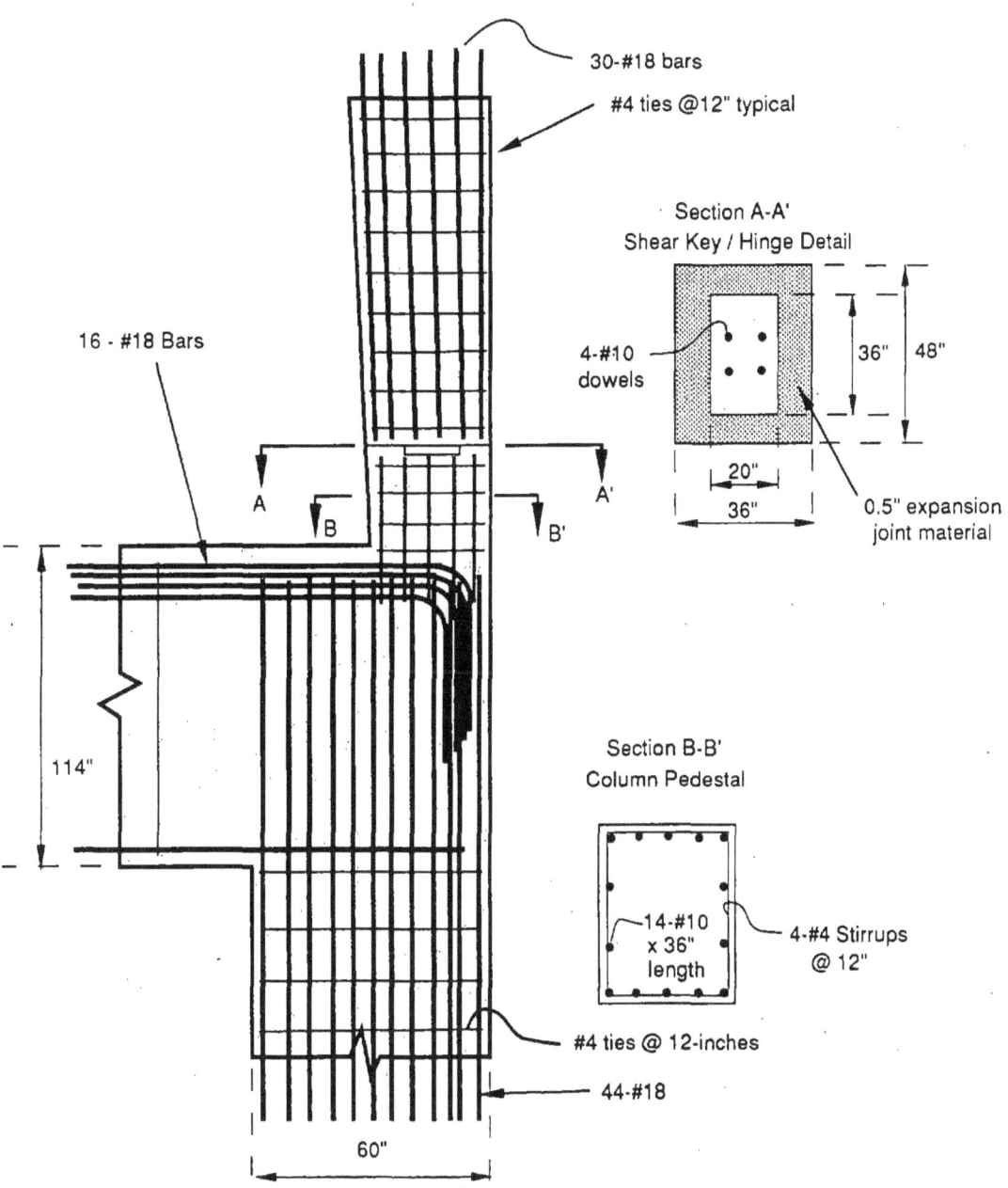

30-#18 bars

#4 ties @12" typical

16 - #18 Bars

114"

60"

Section A-A'
Shear Key / Hinge Detail

4-#10
dowels

36"   48"

20"

36"

0.5" expansion
joint material

Section B-B'
Column Pedestal

14-#10
x 36"
length

4-#4 Stirrups
@ 12"

#4 ties @ 12-inches

44-#18

A   A'

B   B'

Figure 5.6.7   Reinforcement detail at the connection between the upper and lower portal
frames for the Type 1 bents used in Cypress Structure, I-880.

Seismic Retrofit for I-880 : Cypress Structure

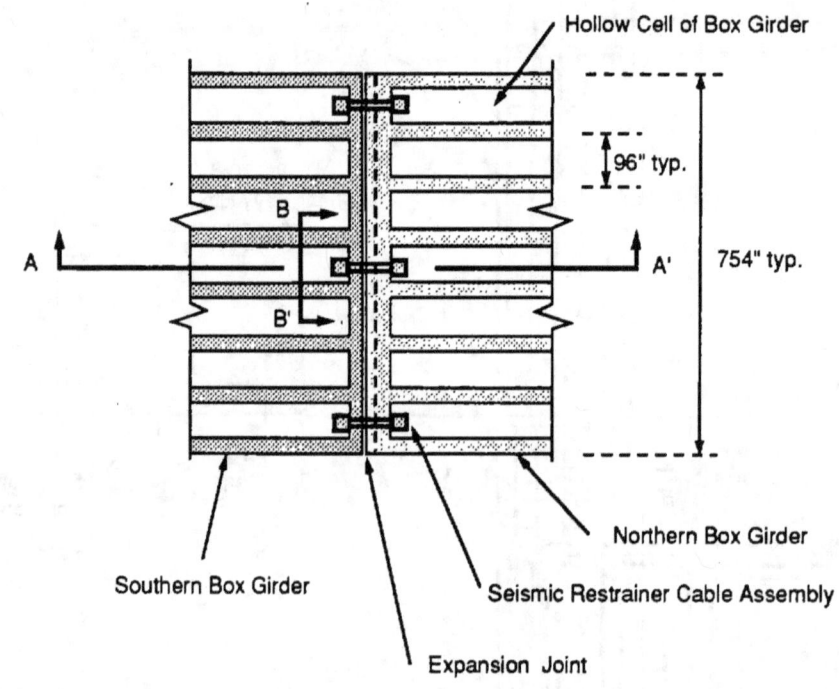

Hollow Cell of Box Girder

96" typ.

754" typ.

A ——→ A'

B →
B' →

Southern Box Girder

Northern Box Girder

Seismic Restrainer Cable Assembly

Expansion Joint

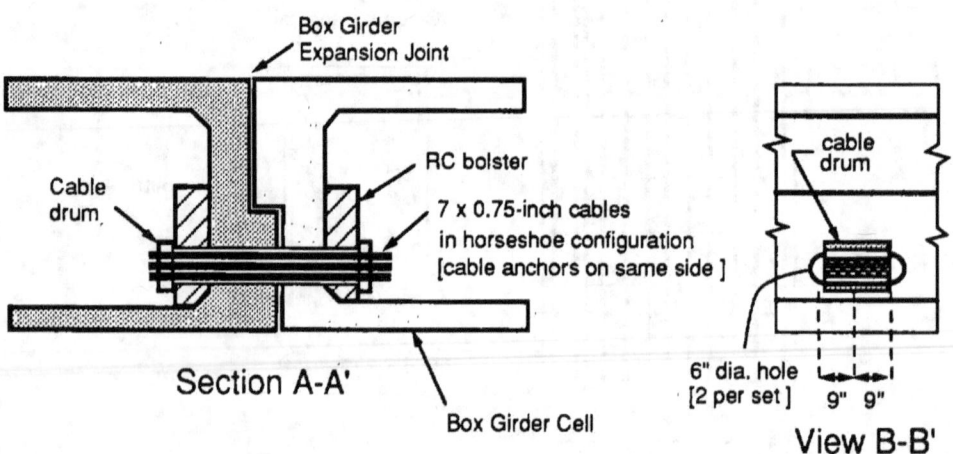

Box Girder
Expansion Joint

RC bolster

7 x 0.75-inch cables
in horseshoe configuration
[cable anchors on same side]

Cable
drum

Section A-A'

Box Girder Cell

cable
drum

6" dia. hole
[2 per set]   9" 9"

View B-B'

Figure 5.6.8   Detail of the Caltrans Phase I Retrofit implemented at the box girder expansion joints for Cypress Structure, I-880.

Figure 5.6.9   Aerial photo of Cypress Structure looking south from the northern
limit of the collapse at 34th Street in Oakland.

Figure 5.6.10   Aerial photo looking east to the northern limit of the collapsed portion of Cypress Structure between Bents 110-113.

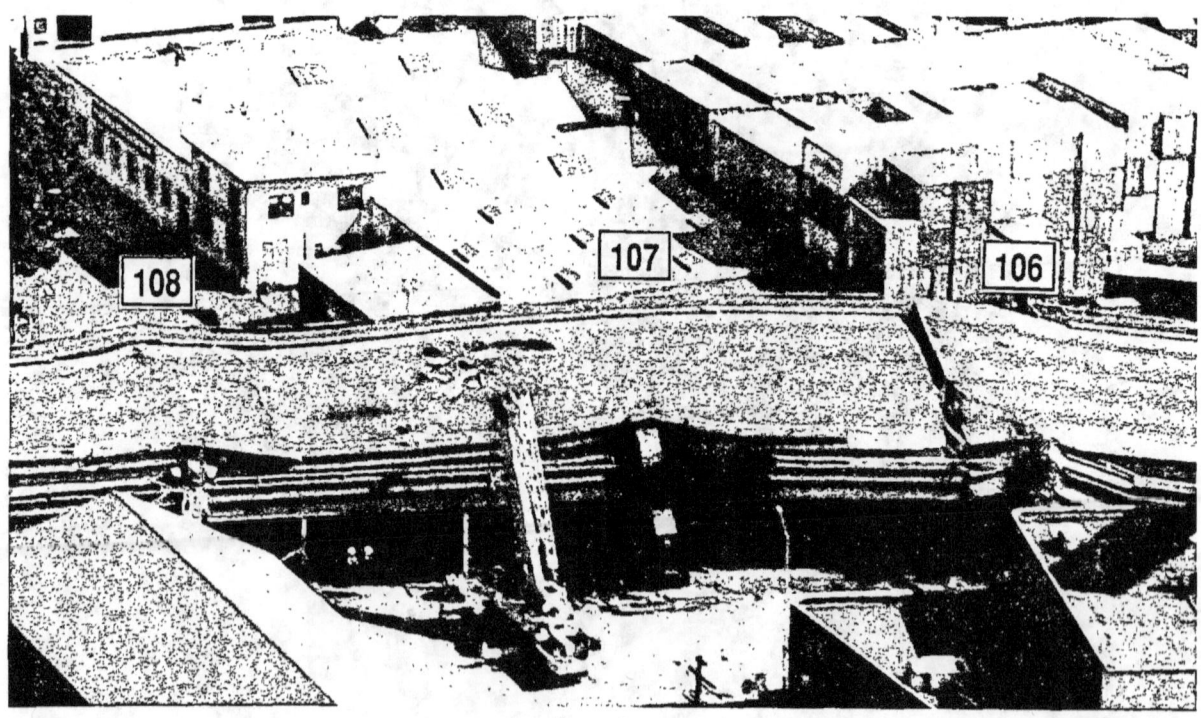

Figure 5.6.11   Aerial photo looking east to the collapsed portion of Cypress Structure between Bents 106-108.

Figure 5.6.12   Aerial photo looking east to the collapsed portion of Cypress Structure between Bents 104-106.

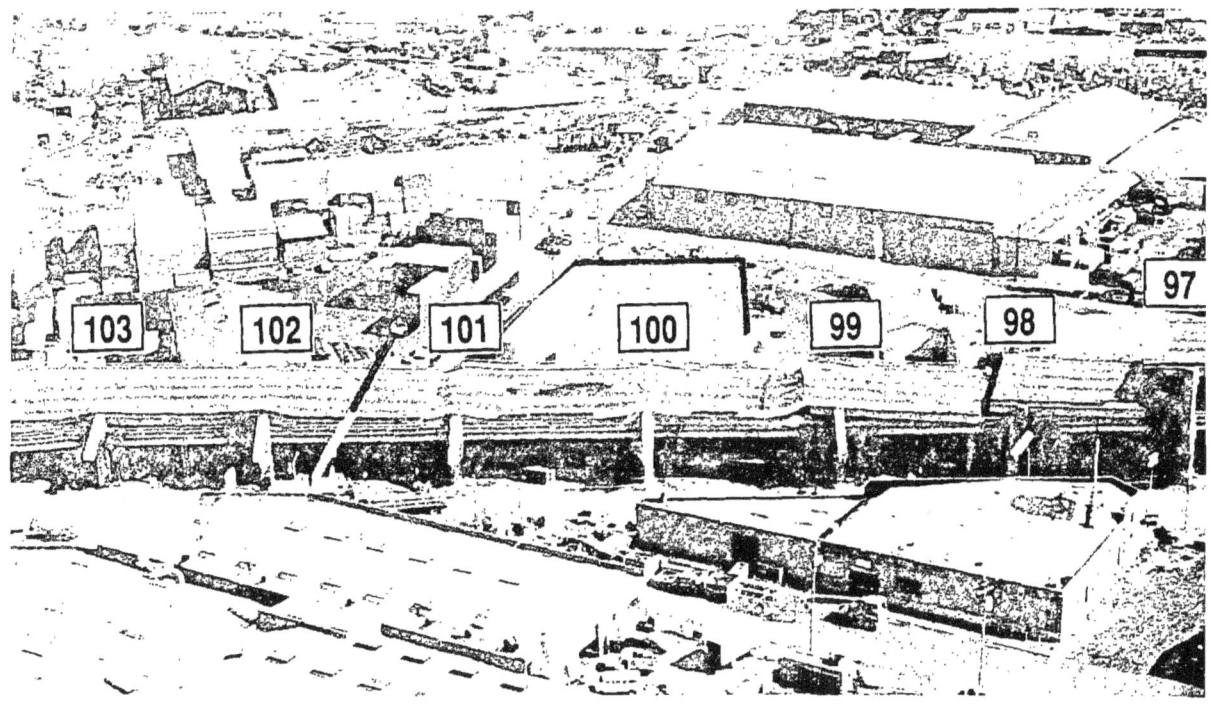

Figure 5.6.13   Aerial photo looking east to the collapsed portion of Cypress Structure between Bents 97-104.

Figure 5.6.14   Aerial photo looking east to the collapsed portion of Cypress Structure between Bents 94-100.

Figure 5.6.15   Aerial photo looking west to the collapsed portion of Cypress Structure between Bents 94-100.

Figure 5.6.16   Aerial photo looking east to the collapsed portion of Cypress Structure between Bents 86-94.

Figure 5.6.17   Aerial photo looking east to the collapsed portion of Cypress Structure between Bents 83-90.

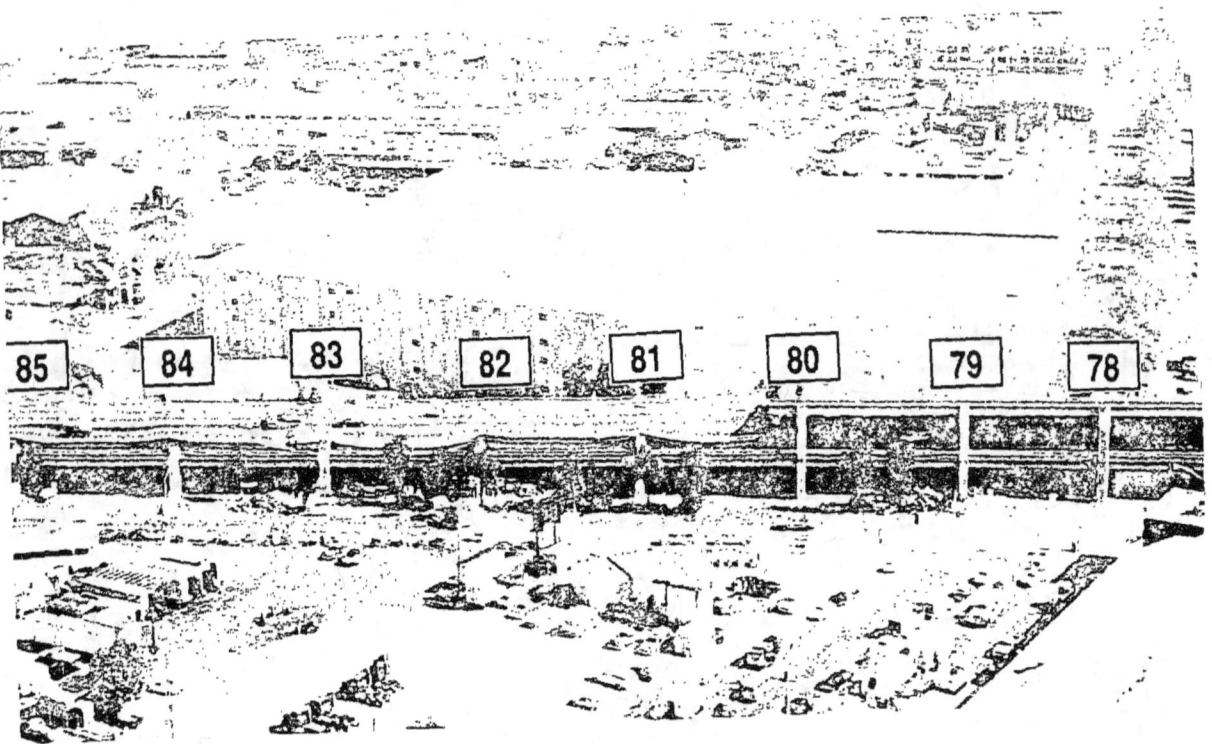

Figure 5.6.18   Aerial photo looking east to the collapsed portion of Cypress Structure between Bents 78-85.

Figure 5.6.19   Aerial photo looking east to the collapsed portion of Cypress Structure between Bents 71-78.

Figure 5.6.20   Aerial photo looking east to the collapsed portion of Cypress Structure between Bents 66-72.

Figure 5.6.21   Aerial photo looking east to the collapsed portion of Cypress Structure between Bents 62-68.

Figure 5.6.22   Aerial photo looking east to the southern limit of the collapsed portion of Cypress Structure between Bents 62-64.

Figure 5.6.23   View of the west side of Cypress Structure looking north between Bents 86-92. These were all Type 1 bents which demonstrate the uniformity of the collapse mechanism.

Figure 5.6.24   View of the upper deck of Cypress Structure looking north of Bent 80. This photo illustrates the negligible lateral displacement of the upper deck relative to the lower deck during the collapse.

Figure 5.6.25

A view of the west side of Bent 65 of Cypress Structure illustrating the predominant failure mode for a Type 1 bent. The upper frame columns sheared through the support pedestal which connected them to the lower frame. In most cases the upper columns remained connected to the upper deck as shown.

Figure 5.6.26

Failure of the west side of Bent 85. In this particular case a portion of the sheared support pedestal is still attached to the base of the upper column. The top of the column failed explosively and separated from the upper frame girder.

Figure 5.6.27

Failure of the west side of Bent 90. In this case the supporting pedestal for the upper columns was completely disintegrated; only the interior face of axial reinforcement that was present in the pedestal remains imbedded in the lower column. It can be seen that the failure plane followed the face of the curved negative moment steel from the lower frame girder.

Figure 5.6.28

Failure of the west side of Bent 94. The presence of a central pipe, used to drain the upper deck, permitted a fracture plane to develop through the center of the column. The eastern half of the column disintegrated under compressive load while the western half spalled off.

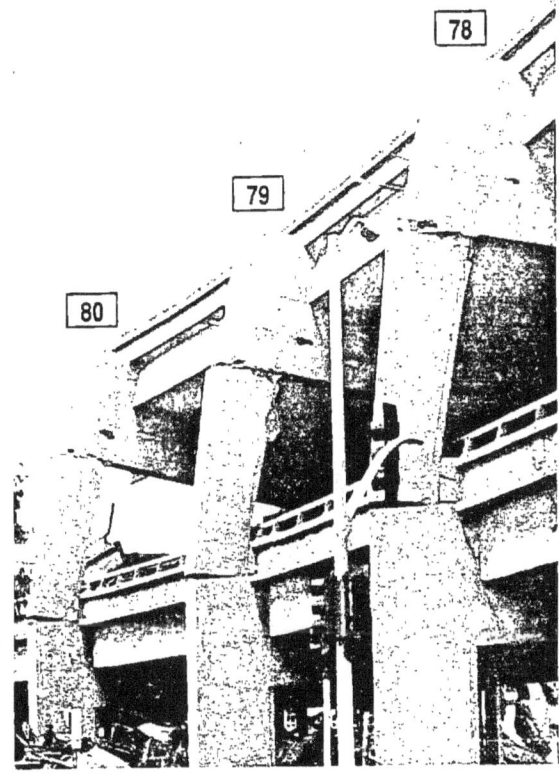

Figure 5.6.29

A view looking north at the west side of Bents 78-80. These were all Type 2 bents which included prestressing of the upper girders. This particular mode of failure, in which only the east columns of the upper frames failed, is noted as a Type A Failure in subsequent discussions. Type A Failures occurred in Bents 74 through 80 (see figs. 5.6.18 and 5.6.19).

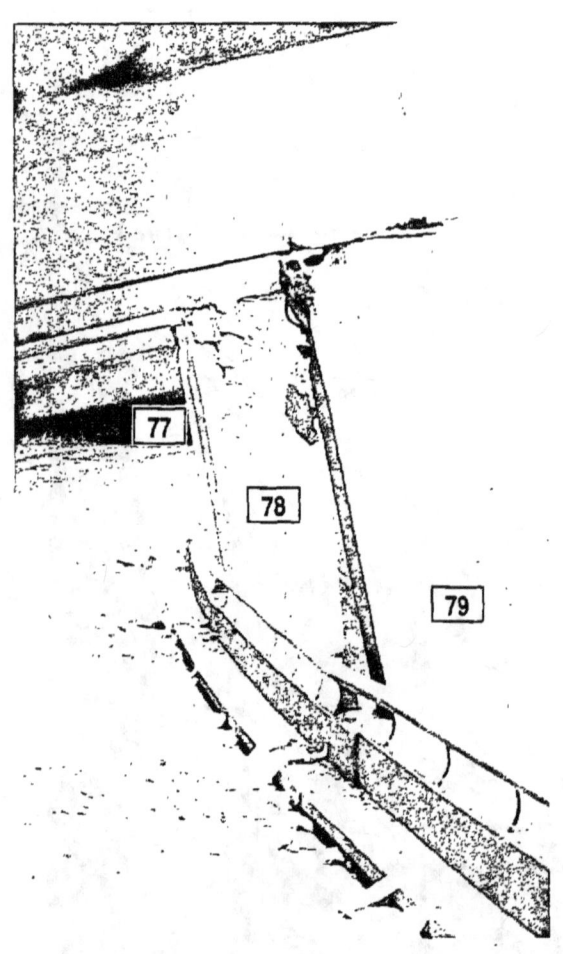

Figure 5.6.30

A close-up view looking south from Bent 80 at the west side of the upper portion of Cypress Structure. Note compression spalling along the interior face of the tops of the columns.

Figure 5.6.31

Due to excessive flexural displacements in the upper frame girder, most of the post-tensioning tendons yielded and then fractured. The tendons were unbonded, to permit extension of the top girder at a later date as part of a planned access ramp. The stored elastic energy drove the tendons from their ducts, as shown here at Bents 74, 75, and 76 on the east side of Cypress Structure.

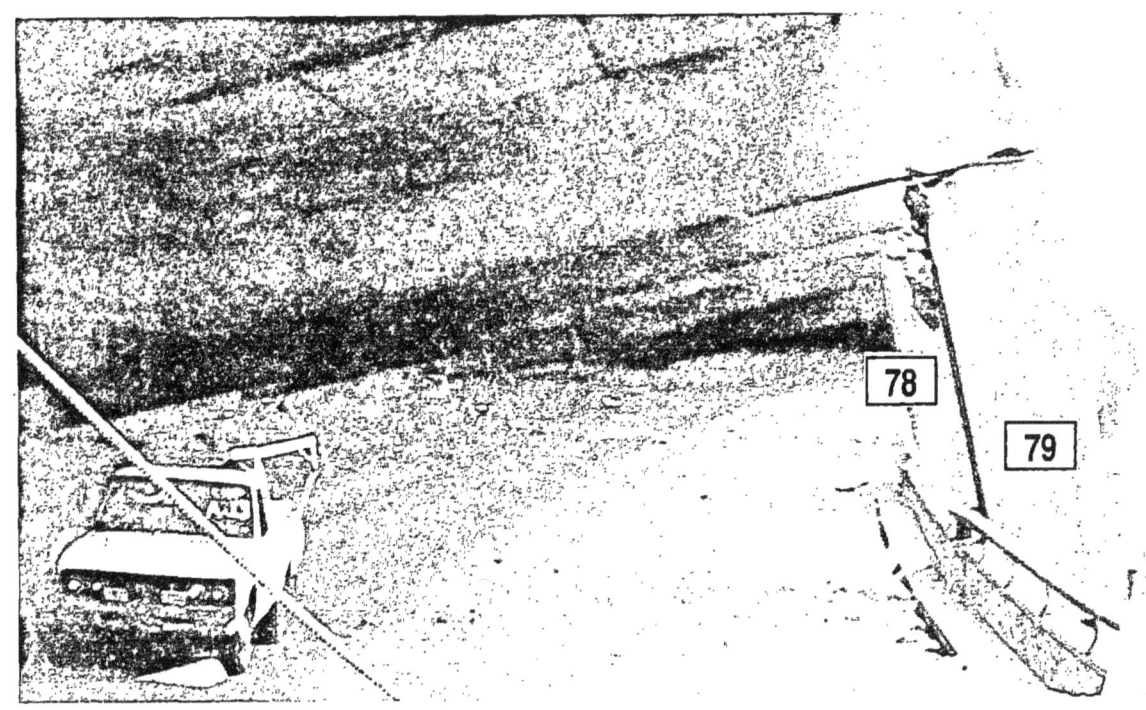

Figure 5.6.32   There was, apparently, a belief among motorists that it was safer to stop beneath the bent girders, as shown here, looking south from Bent 80.

Figure 5.6.33

A close-up of the west side of Bent 72 shows the second, or Type B, variation of failure observed for Type 2 bents. In this case the entire double-hinged upper frame column segment has been ejected from the structure. The 4-#10 bars which passed through the upper and lower shear keys may be seen projecting from the base of the upper girder and the top of the lower column.

Figure 5.6.34   Detail of the base of the two-hinged column that was ejected from the west side of Bent 72. The 4-#10 dowel bars which passed through the center of the shear key have been pulled free.

Figure 5.6.35   Detail of the bottom of the two-hinged column that was ejected from the west side of Bent 71 showing central pipe used to drain the upper road deck and the 4-#10 dowel bars used to transfer shear across the hinge.

Figure 5.6.36   View looking west towards Bents 96 and 97 which supported the only segment of the upper deck to remain standing between Bents 62 and 113.

Figure 5.6.37

Detail of the west side of Bent 97 showing extensive shear cracking at the interior beam/column joint for the lower frame and compression spalling at the upper beam/column joint. Axial reinforcement for the upper frame columns was continuous with the lower frame columns on both east and west sides. This, and the larger cross section, helps to explain why these Type 4 bents did not collapse.

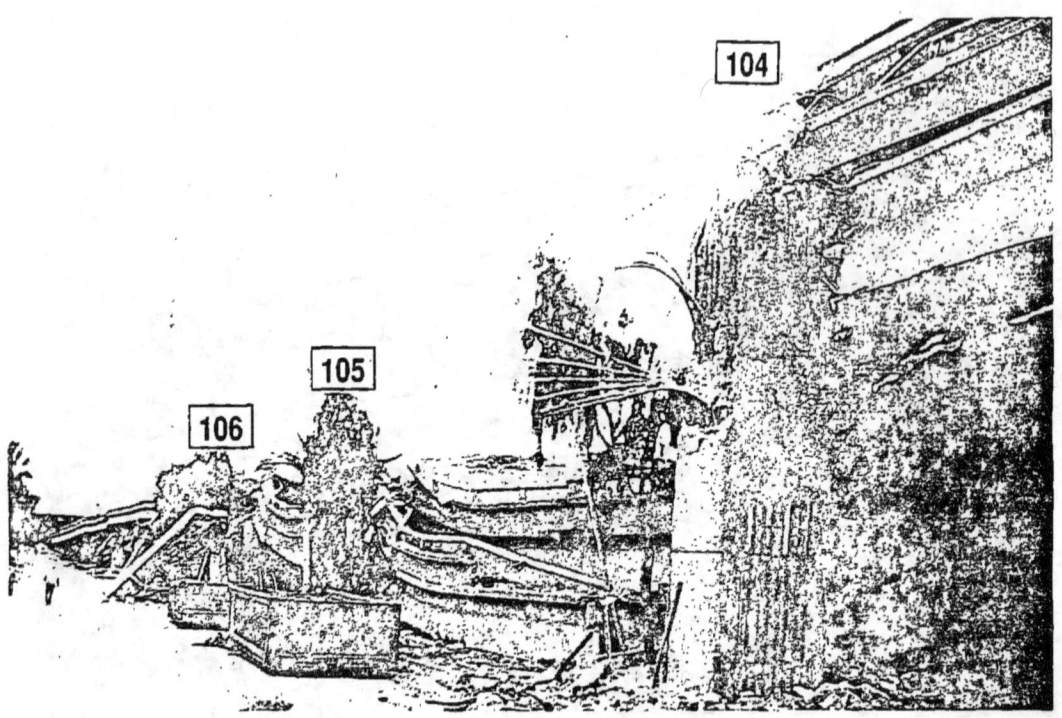

Figure 5.6.38 . The section of Cypress Structure between Bents 104 and 106 was the only location in which both upper and lower bent frames failed.

Figure 5.6.39

Close-up of the west side of Bent 105 looking south, illustrating complete shear failure of the lower bent beam/column connection.

Figure 5.6.40

Close-up view of the east side of Bent 108 looking north. This was the last Type 1 bent prior to the northern limit of the collapse at Bent 113. In addition to the common failure of the pedestal supporting the upper frame column, the column of the lower frame sustained a total shear failure.

Figure 5.6.41   View looking south along the east side of Cypress Structure from Bent 115. The northern limit of the collapse extended to within six feet of Bent 113.

5-45

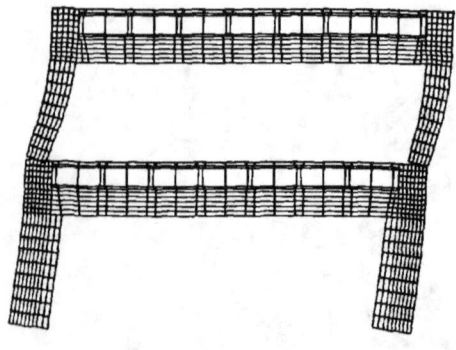

Mode 1: 2.5 Hz

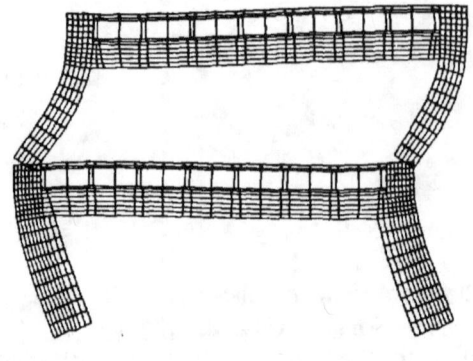

Mode 2: 6.4 Hz

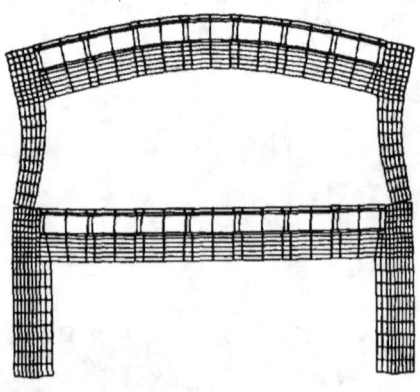

Mode 3: 9.8 Hz

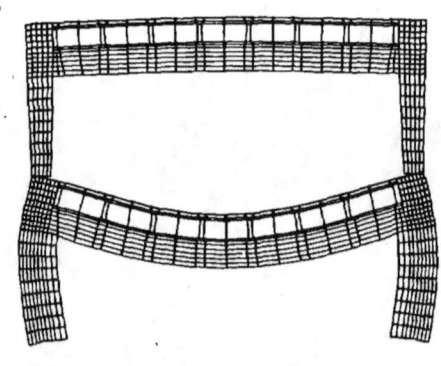

Mode 4: 12.8 Hz

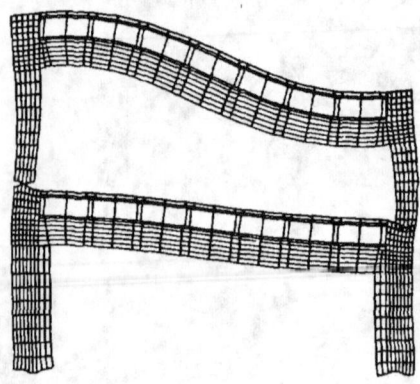

Mode 5: 23.4 Hz

Figure 5.6.42   Vibrational mode shapes for Type 1 bents used in the Cypress Structure, I-880.

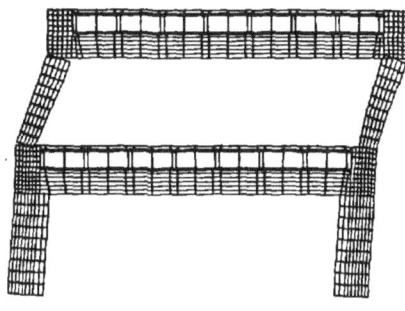

Mode 1: 2.0 Hz

Mode 2: 6.3 Hz

Mode 3: 9.2 Hz

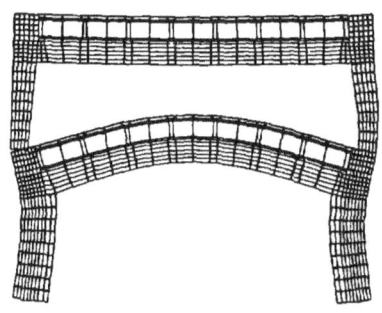

Mode 4: 13.1 Hz

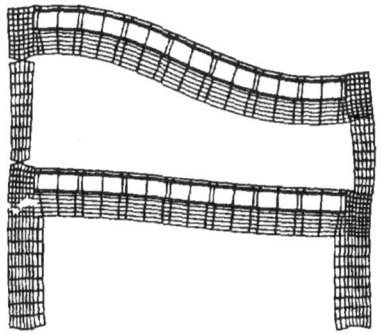

Mode 5: 23.3 Hz

Figure 5.6.43   Vibrational mode shapes for Type 2 bents used in the Cypress Structure, I-880.

TYPE 1 BENT: I-880

[Bents 64-69; 82-94; 100-106]

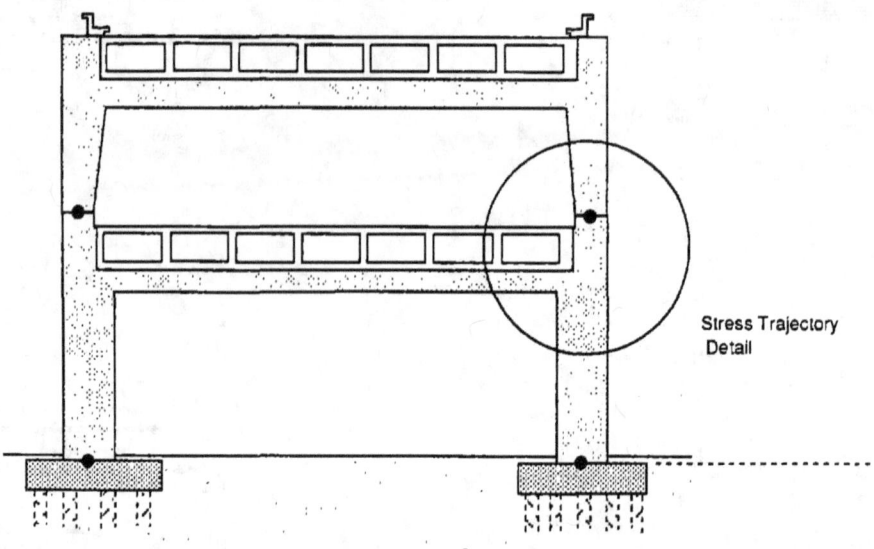

Figure 5.6.44(a)   Type 1 bent.

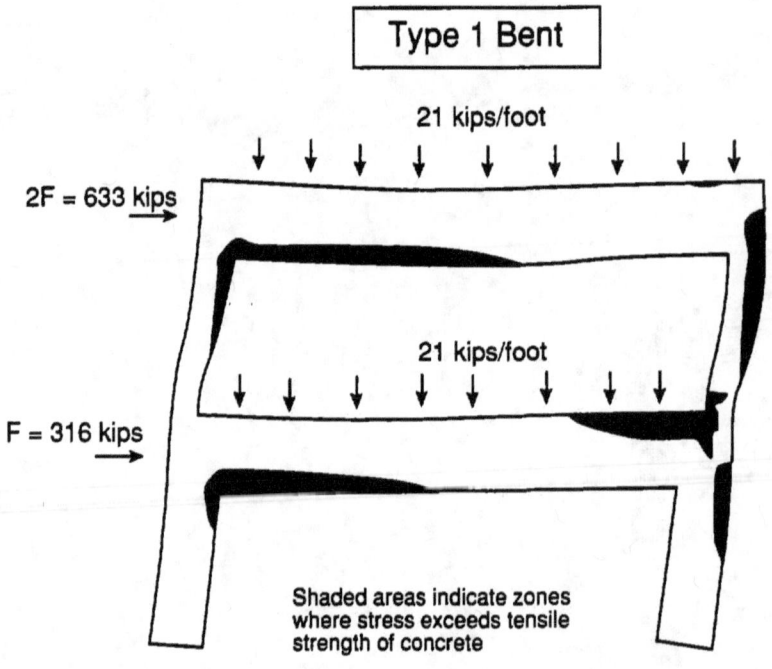

Figure 5.6.44(b)   Displaced shape of Type 1 bent under applied loads showing zones of principal tensile stress sufficient to induce cracking.

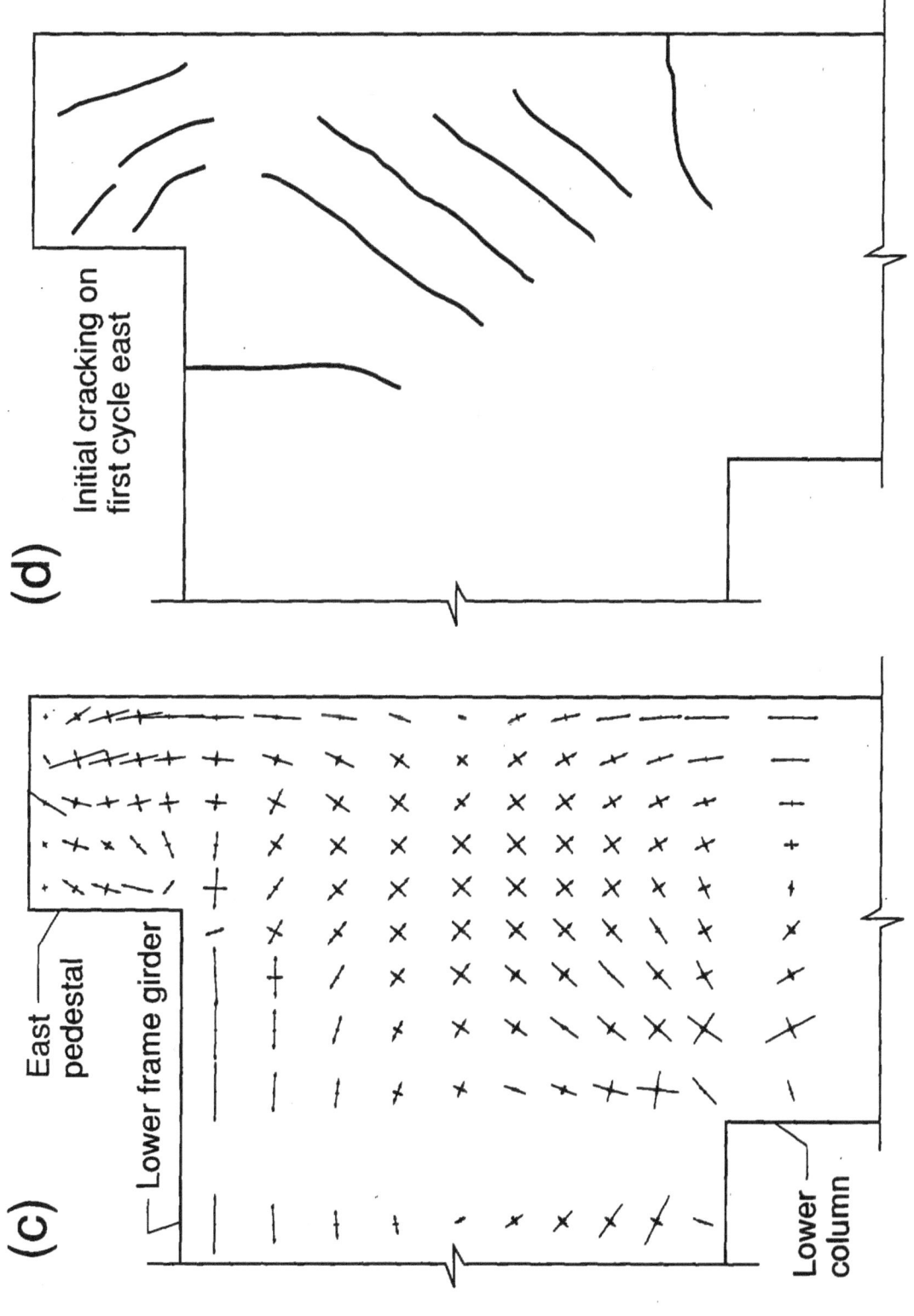

(d) Initial cracking on first cycle east

(c) East pedestal

Lower frame girder

Lower column

Figure 5.6.44 (c) Principal stress tensors for pedestal region in Type 1 bent. Scale 0.25 inch = 650 psi (6.3 mm = 4.5 MPa). (d) Predicted cracking during first half-cycle of lateral load.

TYPE 2 BENT: I-880

[Bent 71,72, 75-80]

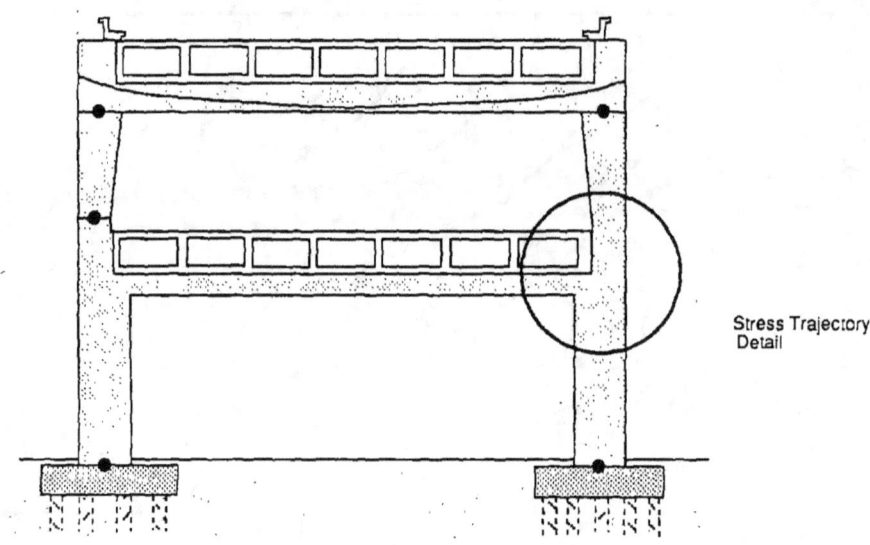

Stress Trajectory
Detail

Figure 5.6.45(a)   Type 2 bent.

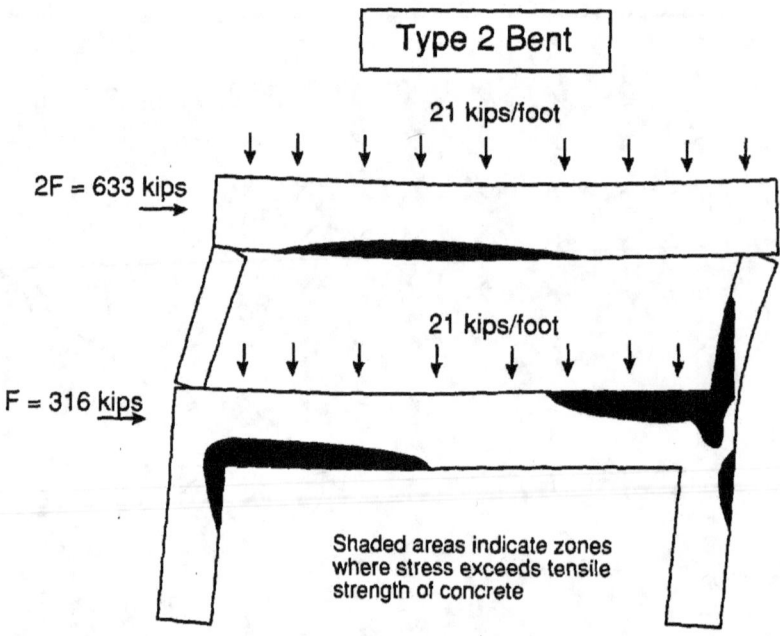

Figure 5.6.45(b)   Displaced shape of Type 2 bent under applied loads showing zones of principal tensile stress sufficient to induce cracking.

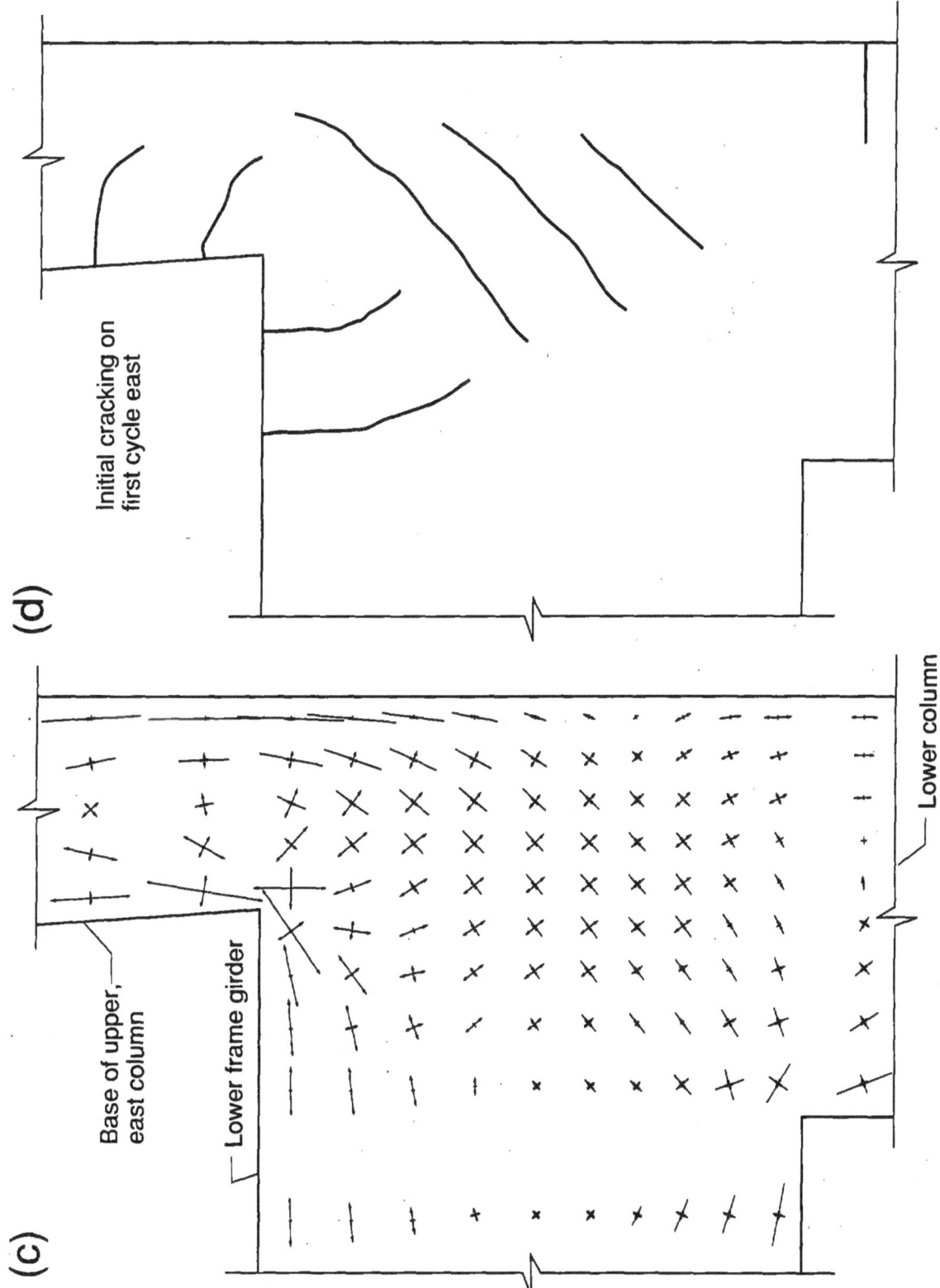

(c)

Base of upper, east column

Lower frame girder

Lower column

(d)

Initial cracking on first cycle east

Figure 5.6.45   (c) Principal stress tensors for pedestal region in Type 2 bent.   Scale 0.25 inch = 650 psi (6.3 mm = 4.5 MPa).
(d) Predicted cracking during first half-cycle of lateral load.

TYPE 5 BENT: I-880

[Bent 73, 74]

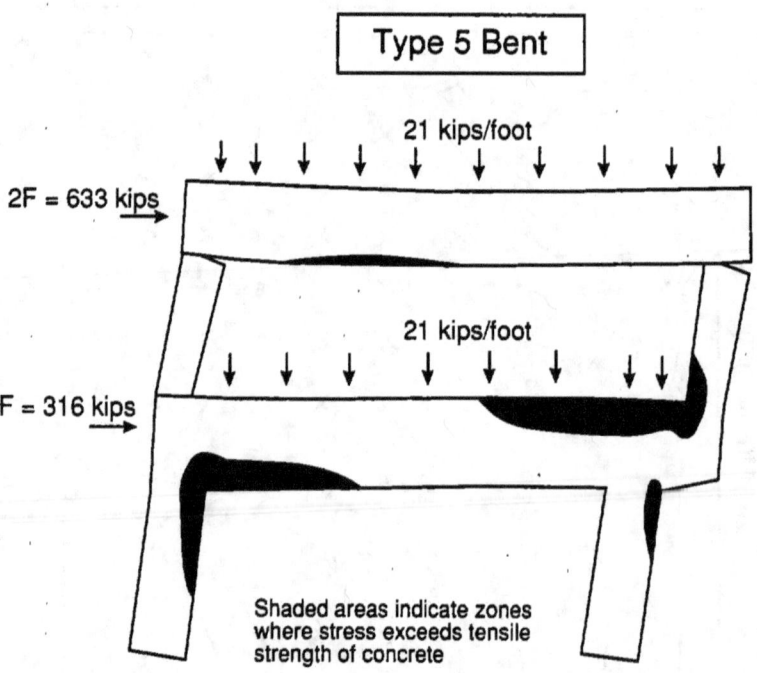

Figure 5.6.46(a) Type 5 bent.

Type 5 Bent

21 kips/foot

2F = 633 kips

21 kips/foot

F = 316 kips

Shaded areas indicate zones
where stress exceeds tensile
strength of concrete

Figure 5.6.46(b) Displaced shape of Type 5 bent under applied loads showing zones of principal tensile stress sufficient to induce cracking.

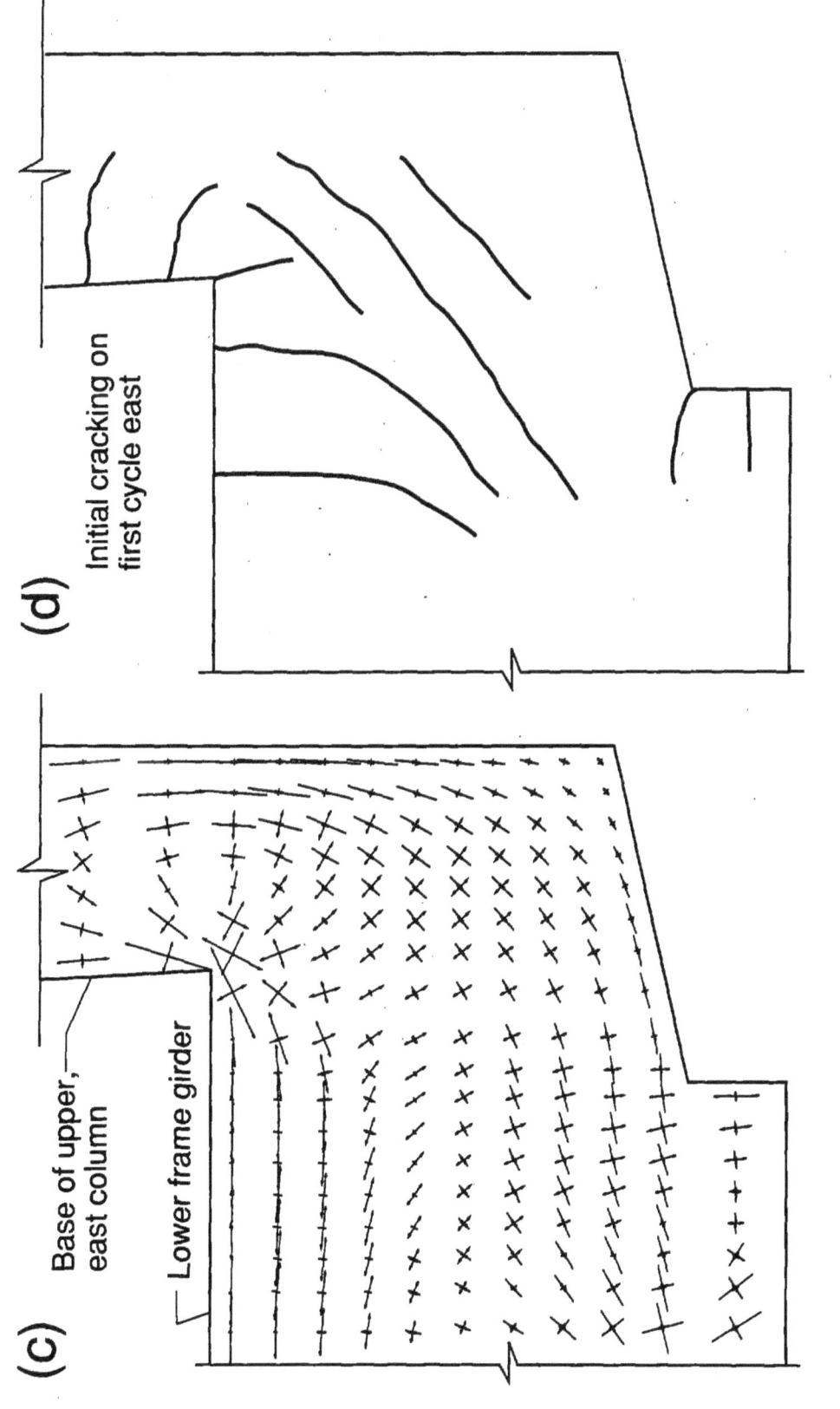

(c) Base of upper, east column

Lower frame girder

(d) Initial cracking on first cycle east

Figure 5.6.46 (c) Principal stress tensors for pedestal region in Type 5 bent. Scale 0.25 inch = 650 psi (6.3 mm = 4.5 MPa).
(d) Predicted cracking during first half-cycle of lateral load.

5-53

TYPE 1 BENT: I-880

[Bents 64-69, 82-94; 100-106]

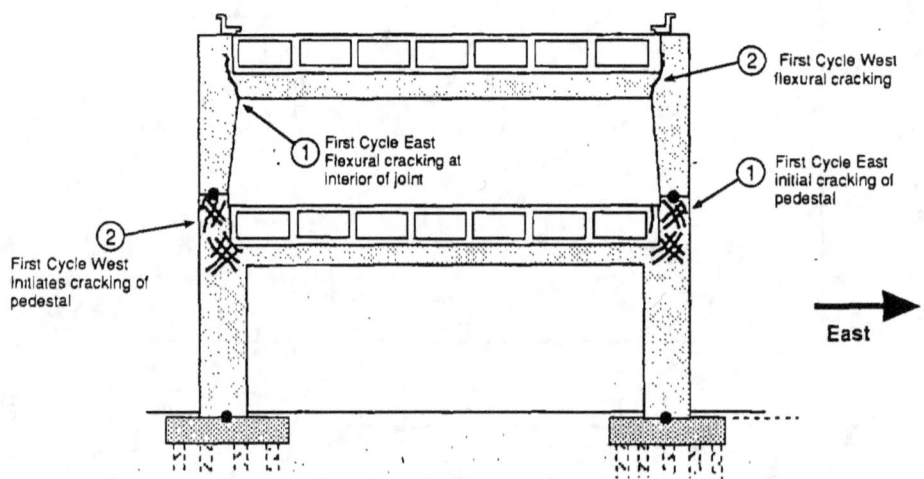

First Cycle West flexural cracking

First Cycle East Flexural cracking at interior of joint

First Cycle East initial cracking of pedestal

First Cycle West initiates cracking of pedestal

East

A: Crack Initiation Under Lateral Load

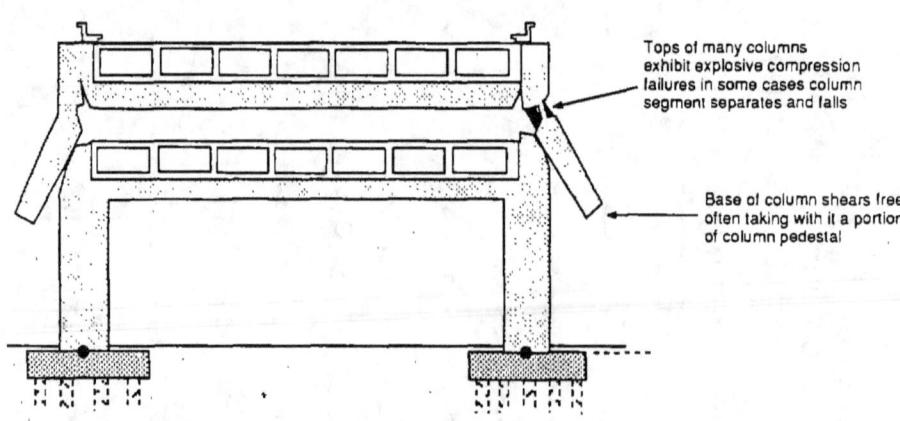

Tops of many columns exhibit explosive compression failures in some cases column segment separates and falls

Base of column shears free often taking with it a portion of column pedestal

B: Typical Failure Mode for Type 1 Bents

Figure 5.6.47   Top: Anticipated crack initiation sequence for Type 1 bents under lateral loading. Bottom: Observed failure mode for Type 1 bents at Cypress Structure.

TYPE 2 BENT: I-880

[Bent 71,72, 75-80]

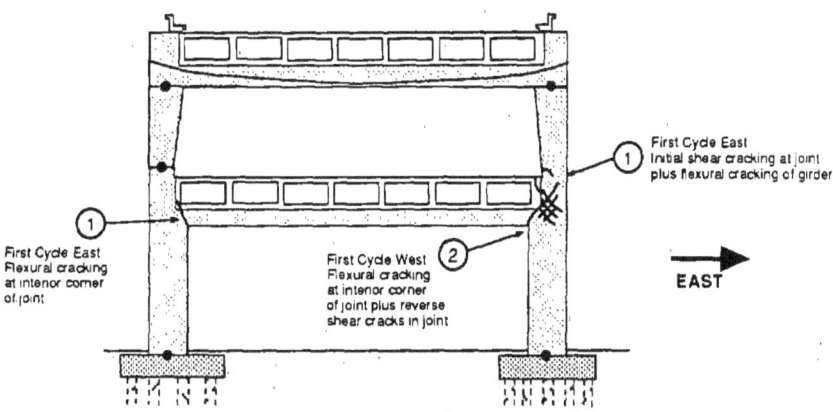

First Cycle East
Initial shear cracking at joint
plus flexural cracking of girder ①

① First Cycle East
Flexural cracking
at interior corner
of joint

First Cycle West
Flexural cracking
at interior corner
of joint plus reverse
shear cracks in joint ②

EAST →

Crack Initiation Under Lateral Load

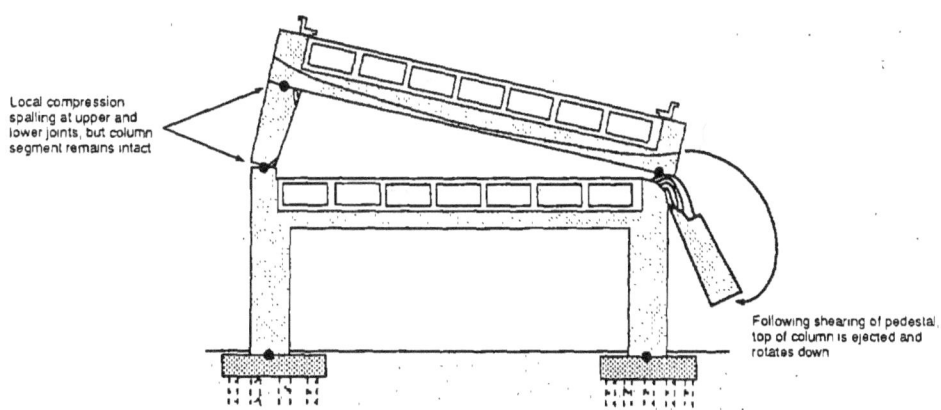

Local compression
spalling at upper and
lower joints, but column
segment remains intact

Following shearing of pedestal,
top of column is ejected and
rotates down

Failure Mode Type A

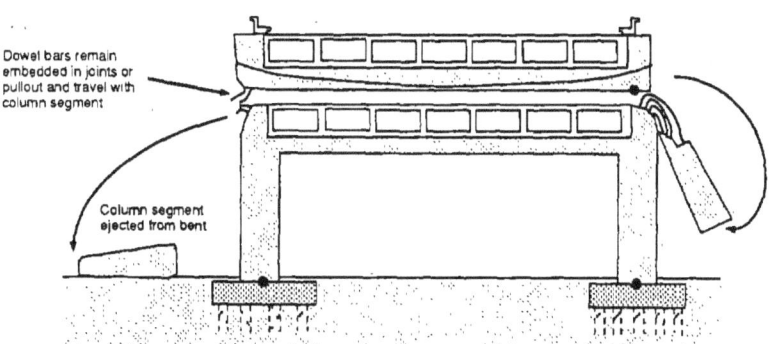

Dowel bars remain
embedded in joints or
pullout and travel with
column segment

Column segment
ejected from bent

Failure Mode Type B

Figure 5.6.48   Top: Anticipated crack initiation sequence for Type 2 bents under lateral loading.
Middle: Observed failure mode "A" for Type 2 bents at Cypress Structure.
Bottom: Observed failure mode "B" for Type 2 bents at Cypress Structure.

5-55

TYPE 5 BENT: I-880

[Bent 73, 74]

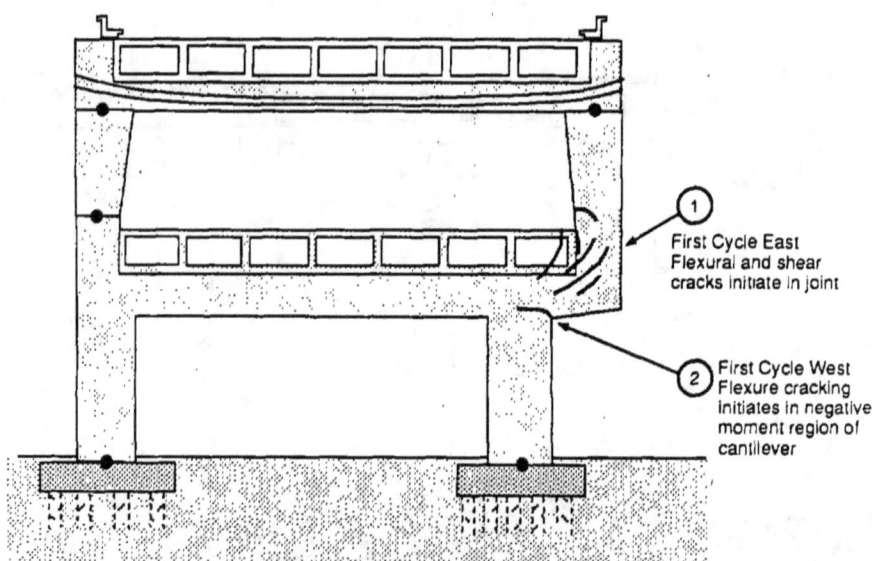

A: Crack Initiation Under Lateral Load

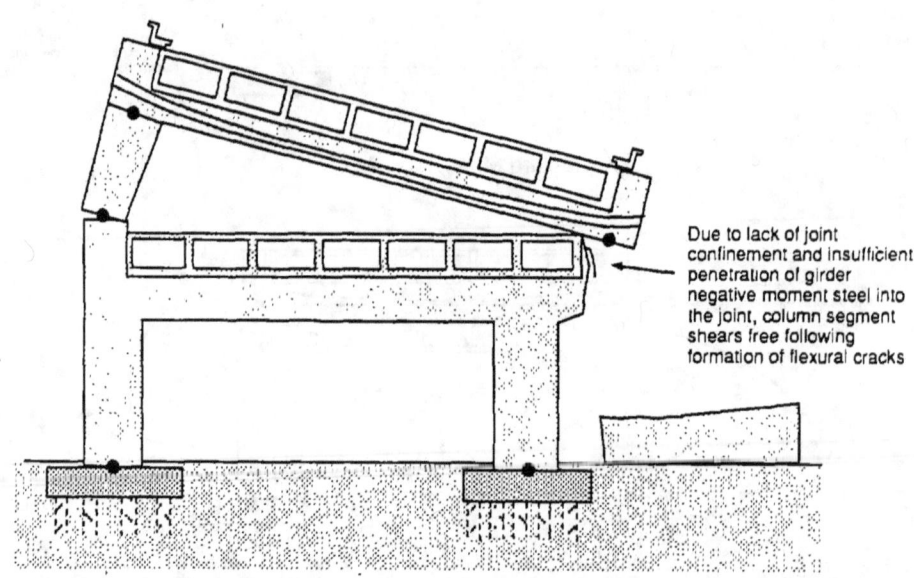

B: Observed Collapse Mode for Bent 74

Figure 5.6.49   Top: Anticipated crack initiation sequence for Type 5 bents under lateral loading. Bottom: Observed failure mode for Type 5 bents at Cypress Structure.

I-880: 3-SPAN UNIT

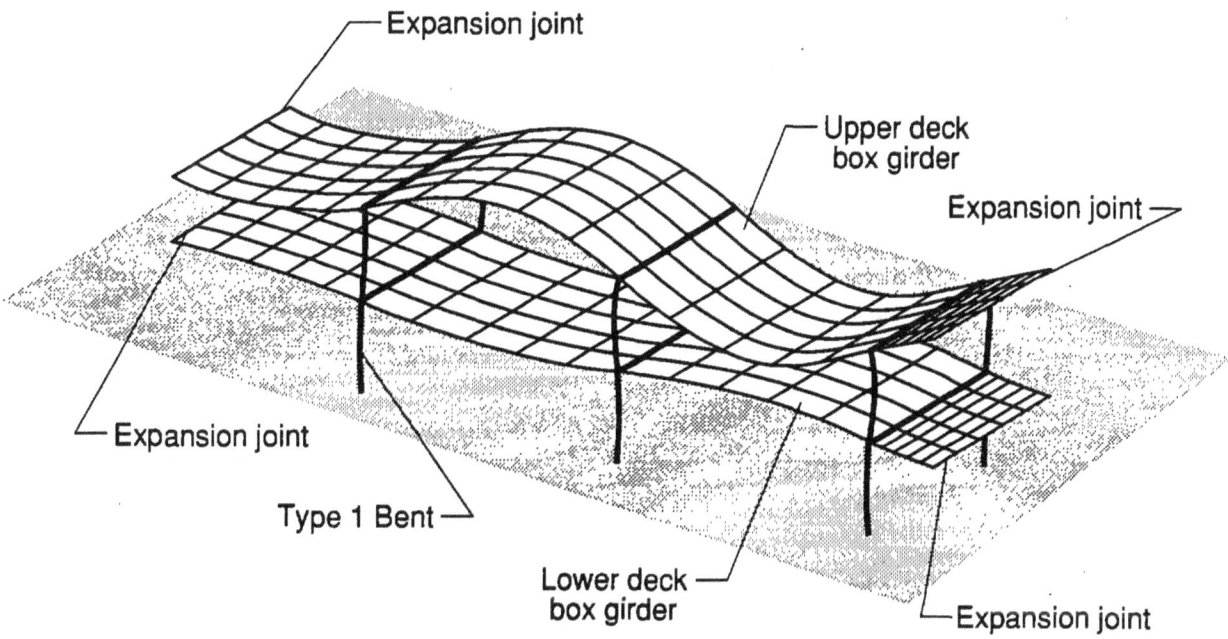

Figure 5.6.50   Vertical vibration mode shape for Cypress Structure. Period = 0.16 seconds (6.2 Hz). Boundary conditions at the ends of the spans were chosen such that the effective model included nine spans of the structure; only the central three are shown here for clarity with the termination points for the box girders occurring at the expansion joints.

5.7 Bay Bridge

The San Francisco-Oakland Bay Bridge is a part of Interstate 80 and is the largest engineered structure within the zone of influence of the earthquake. It is a key lifeline element which significantly affects traffic flow in the Bay area. The bridge spans 8.3 miles (13.3 km) and consists of a series of interconnected structural systems. The two longest spans each measure 2,310 feet (704 m) and are the central sections of the twin suspension bridges which comprise the west bay section from the San Francisco wharf to Yerba Buena Island on the east (see figs. 5.6.1 and 5.6.2). From the east end of the suspension spans the five-lane double-deck highway leads through the south end of Yerba Buena Island via the world's largest single bore tunnel and empties into the east bay segment which is comprised of a series 22 truss spans of various configurations which lead 1.75 miles (2.8 km) to Pier E23 in the Oakland mud flats, west of the toll house and administration building (see figs. 5.6.2 and 5.6.3.). The truss segments which support the roadway generally consist of upper and lower 54 foot (16 m) wide concrete decks supported by longitudinal girders resting on transverse plate girders. The transverse girders connect the deck systems to the two parallel trusses as shown in figure 5.6.6.

There was no apparent damage as a result of the earthquake to the west bay suspension bridges. First reports of the earthquake via the media, however, showed the dramatic collapse of the 50 foot (15 m) link spans at pier E-9 (see fig. 5.6.4), approximately halfway between Yerba Buena Island and the Oakland landing. Inspection revealed that both the upper and lower decks had simultaneously been pulled off their bearing seats as the truss east of pier E-9 moved, by Caltrans measurements, as much as 10 inches (250 mm) east during the first excursion of motion before returning 5 inches (130 mm) to the west, leaving a residual 5 inch (130 mm) eastward displacement. The western girder seats for the upper and lower bridge decks (see fig. 5.6.6) were simply supported configurations in which the bottom flange of the deck girders sat on a riveted angle bracket while two vertical angle brackets constrained movement of the girder web. The bearing seat was only 6 inches (150 mm) wide, so that when truss E9-E10 moved eastward both top and bottom decks slipped off their respective angle brackets and pivoted downward, landing as shown in figures 5.6.4 and 5.6.5. This mechanism is evident when viewing figures 5.6.7 and 5.6.8 which show closeup photos of the western bearing seats for the lower deck girders and the eastern hinge seat for the upper deck girders, respectively. There is practically no damage visible in figure 5.6.7 to the bearing seats, indicating that the girder flanges had cleared the edge quickly and fell away without any further impacting before the lower deck girders landed on a transformer station mounted on the utility deck on the north side of the bridge. The eastern deck girder supports for the link spans, which were in contrast bolted to the girder, were severely distorted (fig. 5.6.8) and in some cases torn loose. It has been suggested that were it not for the presence of the transformer station both spans would likely have torn free from the girder restraining bolts and fallen into pier E-9, causing far greater damage[6]. During the fall the upper deck cut through several power and communication lines and additionally severed a water main on the south side, but otherwise the damage was confined to the decks themselves.

A few comments are in order to understand the seismic displacements observed in the east bay trusses. Although there are 22 total spans involved, 16 of these are grouped into four structural units with regard to longitudinal (generally temperature induced) displacements. Figure 5.6.3 indicates that the first of these units consists of the 2420 foot (738 m) cantilevered truss section connecting pier E1, the final pier on Yerba Buena Island, to pier E-4. The E-1 detail is a fixed connection; the pier E-4 connection allows for expansion. Caltrans has reported indications (paint scrapings) which show that pier E-4 experienced as much as 12 inches (305 mm) of overall movement without damage to the unit. The expansion joint was designed to accommodate 24 inches (610 mm) of displacement at this particular location. Unit 2 consists of the five 509 foot (155 m) truss spans connecting pier E-4 to pier E-9. No damage was reported to this unit.

Pier E-9 is a four-column diagonally braced tower which was designed as a laterally stiff mid-point support for the east bay spans. Its two western column tops form the seats for the truss shoes of the 509 foot span from pier E-8 to pier E-9 and are bolted to these shoes. Likewise, the eastern column tops were connected to the western truss shoes of span E-9 to E-10. These shoes were connected to pier E-9 by means of 20 1 inch (25 mm) bolts each. During the earthquake Unit 3, which also includes span E-10 to E-11, moved eastward as previously described before returning some 5 inches (130 mm). All 40 bolts in the E-9 connecting shoes appeared to be failed in both tension and shear. This is explained by the fact that the shoe detail consists of a 12 inch (305 mm) pin connection between the truss and the shoe, with the centerline of the pin lying at a level 27 inches (690 mm) above the base of the shoe. Lateral displacements of Unit 3 to the east would therefore, in addition to applying substantial shearing forces to the 40 bolts, would also apply a significant overturning moment that would largely be resisted by the western-most bolts in tension. Fortunately the shoe seat was sufficiently broad that the shoe remained atop the seat. Caltrans reported that the northeast shoe had a permanent displacement of 5.5 inches (140 mm) east and 5/8 inch (16 mm) north following the quake; the southeast shoe moved 5 inches (130 mm) east and 1/2 inch (13 mm) north. These were subsequently forced back into place with a jacking load of 400 tons (3560 kN). It was reported that this load decreased as friction at the truss shoes was overcome

---

[6]Governor's Board of Inquiry Meeting, State of California: "The 1989 Loma Prieta Earthquake," December 13-14, 1989, Hyatt Regency International Hotel, Oakland, CA.

and that there was some elastic rebound from pier E-10[7]. Within 4 weeks of the quake, Caltrans had replaced the deck girders for the pier E-9 link spans, placed precast concrete panels between them, cast the composite deck, and reopened the bridge for traffic. The 40 1 inch (25 mm) bolts connecting the E-9/E-10 truss shoes to the eastern column tops of pier E-9 were replaced with high strength bolts. Whether this is to the advantage of the bridge during future earthquakes is subject to review. Opinions have been expressed by some[8] that the shearing of these bolts served as a fuse, isolating pier E-9 from otherwise large lateral loads which could have led to disastrous column buckling.

Subsequent detailed studies on a pier by pier basis carried out by Caltrans revealed no damage to the six 292 foot (89 m) trusses and their supporting piers which comprise Unit 4. However, all of the simply supported 292 foot (89 m) trusses east of pier E-17 had all 12 1 inch (25 mm) diameter retainer bolts broken at each shoe location. All north and south movements were restricted by keeper plates placed next to the bearing shoes and attached to the piers. The bolts which failed on these truss shoes also appeared to have been due to combined tension and shear. This shear failure permitted the various trusses between pier E-17 to E-23 to move somewhat independently. The expansion side of each truss was clamped by earthquake restrainers installed in 1975 as part of the Phase I retrofit program. The restrainers all sustained some form of damage but kept the expansion bearing in place. The final resting place of the north and south shoes are, according to Caltrans testimony to the Governor's Board of Inquiry, as follows:

    Pier E-17: no apparent movement
    Pier E-18: north shoe 3/4" (19 mm)west; south shoe 1/8" (3 mm) west
    Pier E-19: north shoe 1" (25 mm)west; south shoe 1.5" (38 mm) west
    Pier E-20: north shoe 2" (51 mm)west; south shoe 2" (51 mm) west
    Pier E-21: north shoe 2.25" (57 mm)west; south shoe 2 5/8" (67 mm) west
    Pier E-22: north shoe 5" (127 mm)west; south shoe 2.5 "(64 mm) west.

On the basis of these displacements, as well as paint scrapings on the truss supports, it was concluded that piers E-18 through E-22 moved as much as 10 inches (250 mm) in the east-west direction before coming to rest.

A final failure occurred in the span just east of the massive concrete structure at pier E-23. The rivets connecting the floor beam to the concrete pier were sheared off, permitting span E-23/E-24 to move

---

[7]Governor's Board of Inquiry Meeting, State of California: "The 1989 Loma Prieta Earthquake," December 13-14, 1989, Hyatt Regency International Hotel, Oakland, CA.

[8]Earthquake Engineering Research Institute, EERI 1989, EERI-NRC-NCEER Congressional Briefing, "Loma Prieta (Northern California) Earthquake," Senate Russell Office Building, Room 253, November 30, 1989.

eastward. The floor beam on the east side of pier E-23 moved, according to Caltrans measurements, 2.5 inches (640 mm) in both the north-south and east-west directions, with a residual displacement of 2 inches (51 mm) east and 1.5 inches (38 mm) north of its original position. The floor beam pulled the attached stringers to within one-quarter inch (6 mm) of the edge of the beam seats. The webs had already moved outside the guide angle (see Detail A, fig. 5.6.6). Had the displacement of the floor beam been a quarter inch further this span, which was similar to the link span at pier E-9, would also have collapsed. The construction of extended beam seats for this span contributed to the delay in the subsequent re-opening of the Bay Bridge. It is noted that between pier E-9 and pier E-23 there was a residual opening displacement following the quake.

Summary

1. Damage to the San Francisco-Oakland Bay Bridge was concentrated within three general areas. These included the collapse of the upper and lower link spans at pier E-9 and the shearing of the truss shoe retainer bolts for span E-9/E-10; the general shearing of truss shoe retainer bolts for spans between piers E-17 and E-23; and the near loss of span E-23/E-24.

2. In general, the entire structure performed remarkably well and what damage there was proved to be minor. It may be useful, however, to conduct a detailed investigation of the subsoil conditions, particularly beneath the east bay spans, characterize their dynamic properties, and then use this as a set of boundary conditions for a full three-dimensional transient dynamic analysis of the complete section from Yerba Buena Island to pier E-23 to arrive at anticipated maximum displacement demand at the truss shoe connections. These data would then permit better design of the shoe size, as well as the required strength of the restraining bolts.

Figure 5.7.1   View looking east from San Francisco to Yẽrba Buena Island showing the two main suspension spans for the Bay Bridge. No damage was detected in this section.

SAN FRANCISCO - OAKLAND BAY BRIDGE

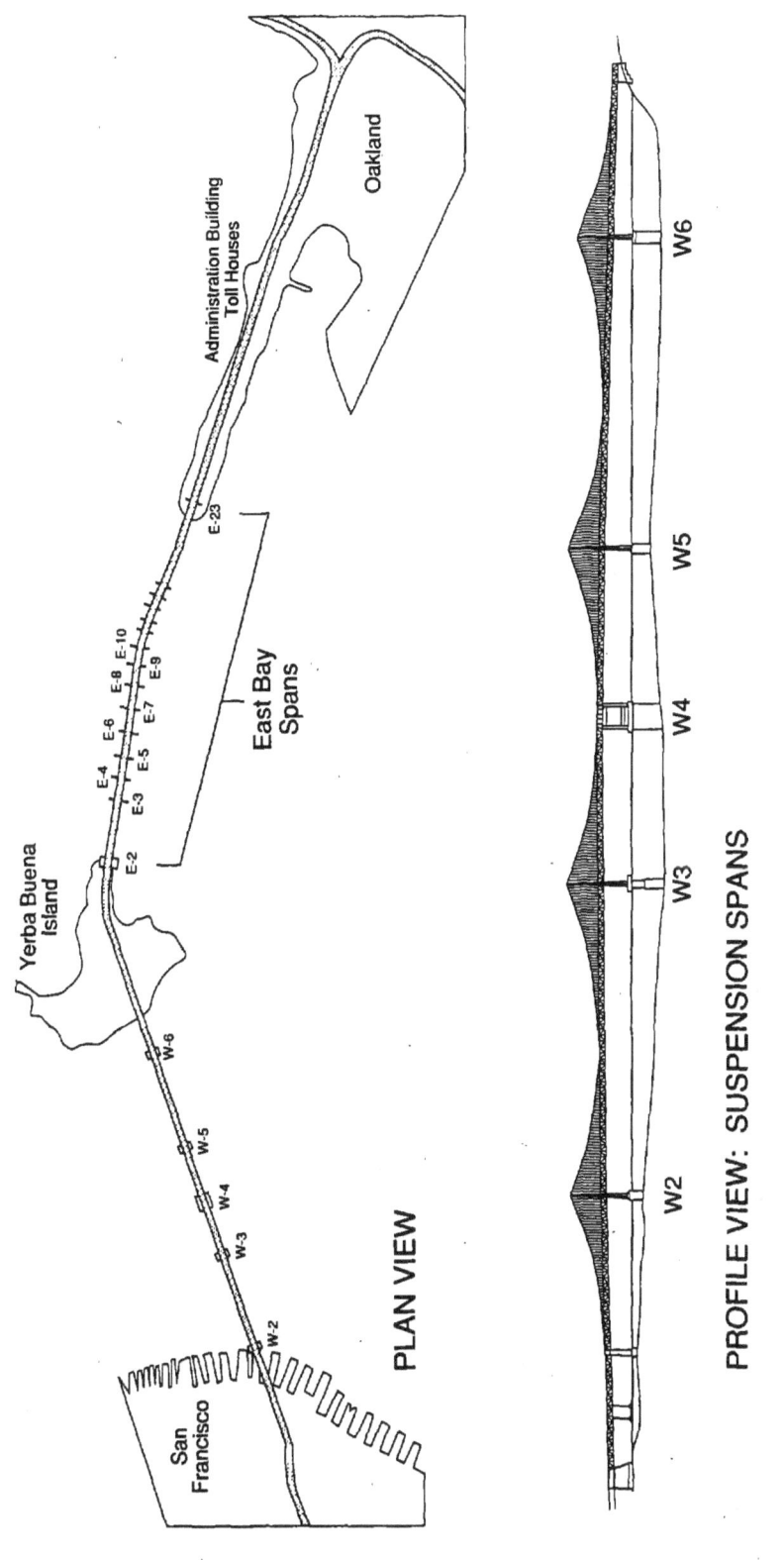

PLAN VIEW

PROFILE VIEW: SUSPENSION SPANS

PROFILE VIEW: CANTILEVER & TRUSS SPANS

Figure 5.7.2   Plan and profile views of the San Francisco-Oakland Bay Bridge. Damage, as well as significant residual displacement of structural elements, was confined to the section between Piers E-9 and E-23 in the east bay spans.

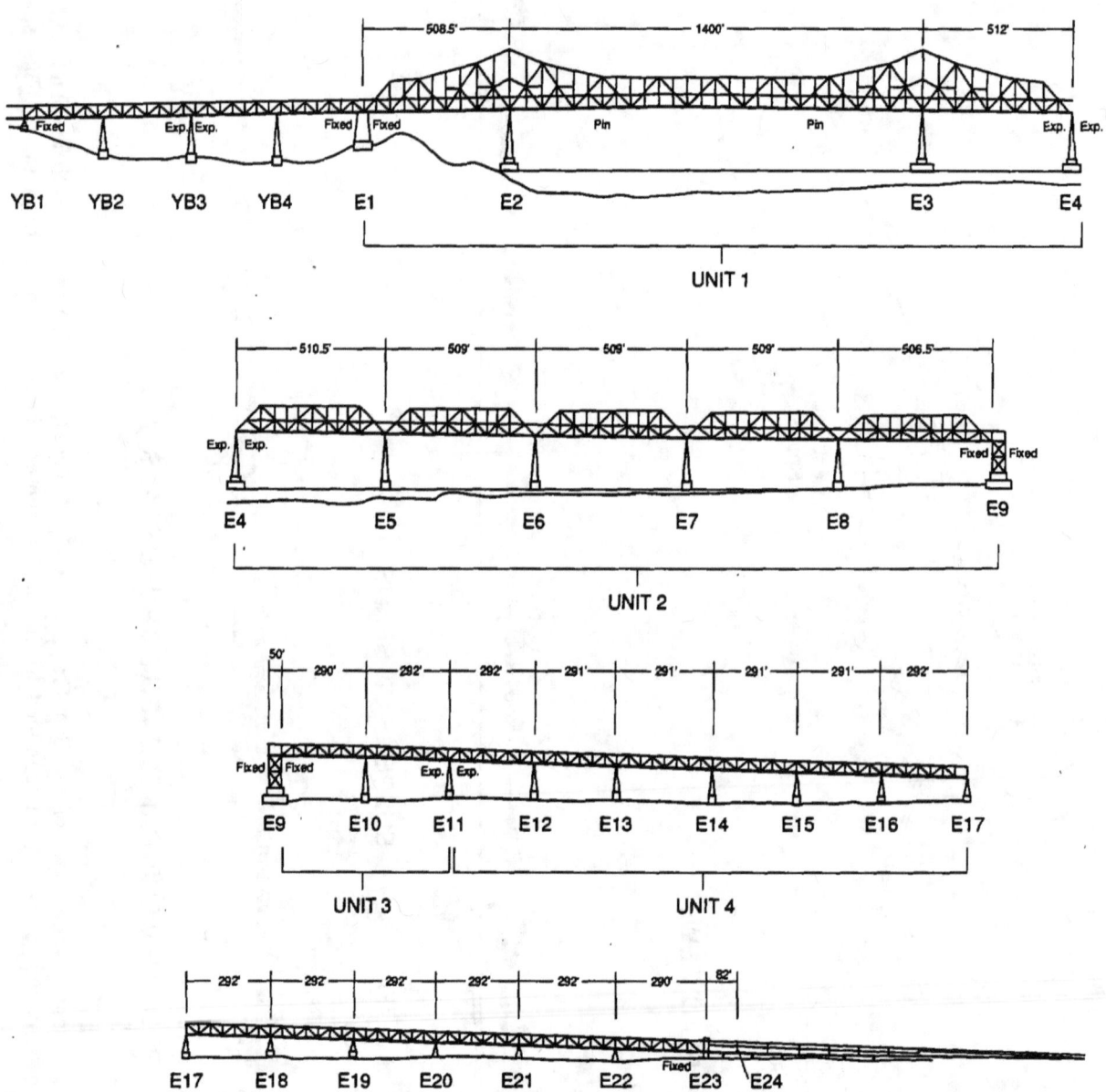

Figure 5.7.3   Detail of the east bay truss spans. Unit 3 was determined to have moved eastward as much as 10 inches, causing the collapse of the two deck segments at Pier E-9. Additional damage, generally involving the failure of retainer bolts, occurred between Piers E-17 and E-24.

Figure 5.7.4   Aerial photo looking north at Pier E-9 on October 19, 1989 showing the collapsed upper and lower 50 foot deck spans.

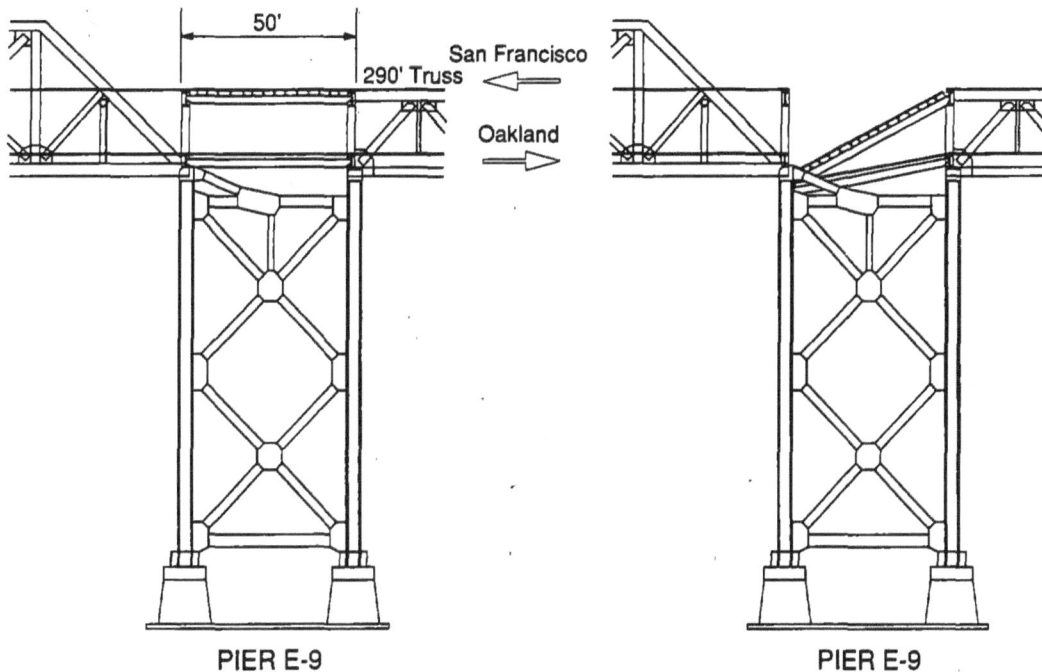

Figure 5.7.5   Schematic detail of Pier E-9 looking north. Evidence indicates that the 290 foot truss segment on the east side of the pier moved eastward, simultaneously unseating both Upper and lower deck segments.

San Francisco - Oakland Bay Bridge
[Typical Deck Cross Section at Pier E-9]

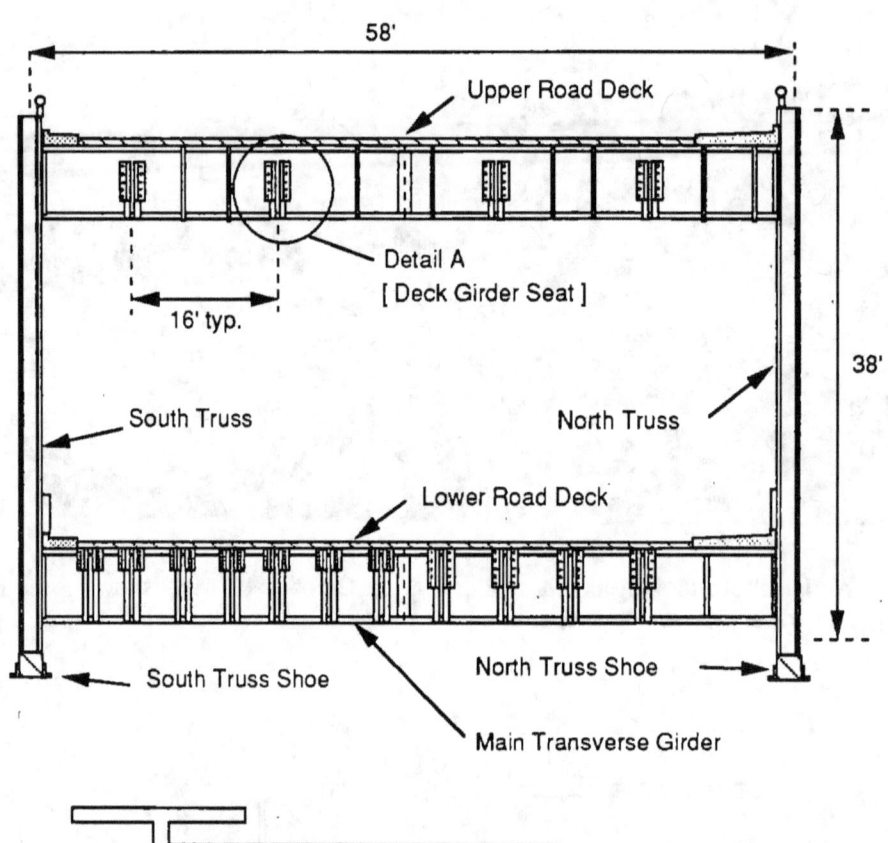

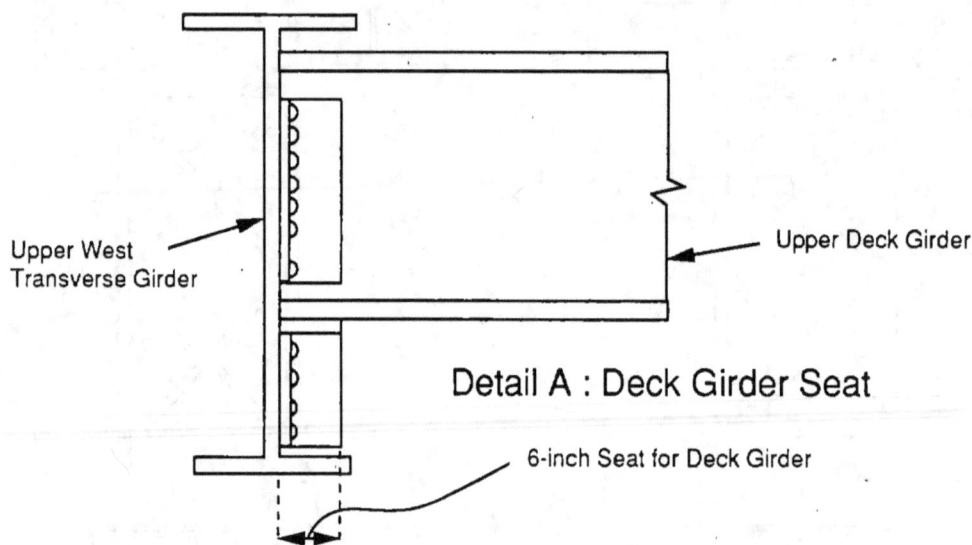

Detail A : Deck Girder Seat

Figure 5.7.6   Cross-sectional detail of the Bay Bridge at Pier E-9, showing upper and lower roadway transverse support girders and longitudinal deck girder seats.   The connection of the longitudinal girders to the transverse girders consisted of a simple bearing seat on the west side;   The eastern beam seat was bolted.

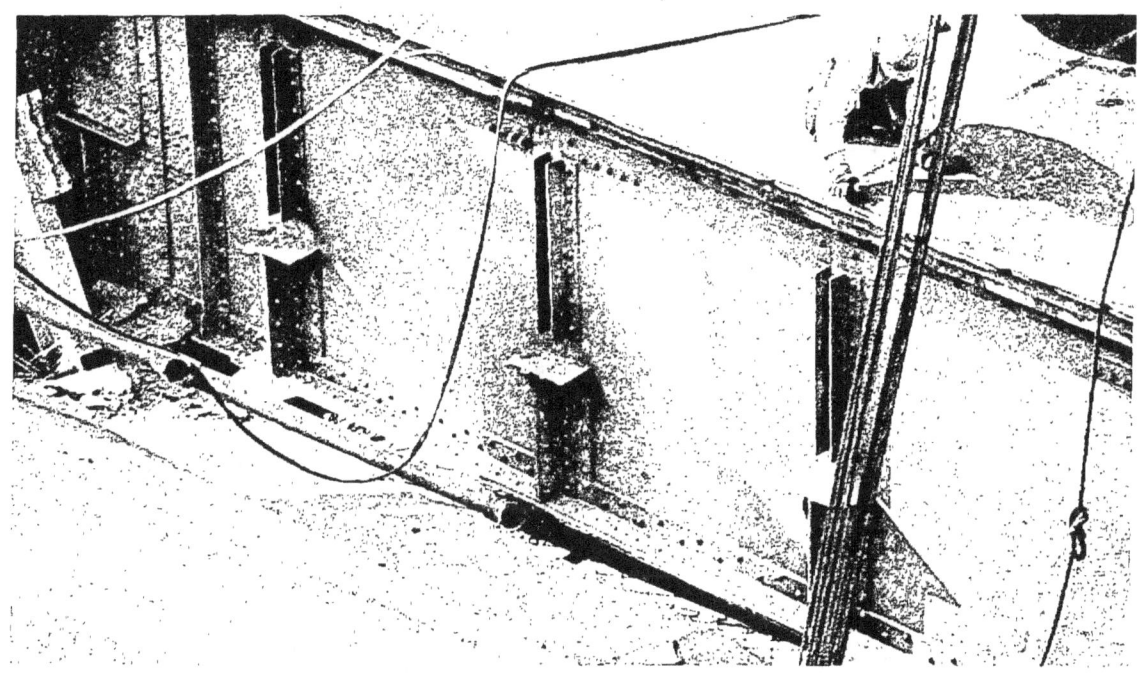

Figure 5.7.7   Close-up of the western girder seats for the lower road deck at Pier E-9.   Lack of
significant damage to these seats, and to those supporting the upper road deck, indicates
that both upper and lower segments moved eastward by an amount sufficient to permit
both to slide off the western seats and drop simultaneously.

Figure 5.7.8

Close-up of the eastern seat for the upper deck
girder showing distortion of bolted beam seat.

Figure 5.7.9   Close-up of the northeast shoe for the 290 foot truss between Pier E-9 and E-10. During the earthquake this truss moved eastward as much as 10 inches before returning to leave a 5.5-inch residual displacement to the east and 5/8-inch to the north.

5.8 Struve Slough Bridges

The team did not visit the Struve Slough bridges, located on state Highway 1 south of Watsonville, but this particular collapse has been described in detail elsewhere (Civil Engineering,1989). At the California Governor's Board of Inquiry meeting of December 14, 1989, Caltrans officials reported the following:

"The Struve Slough Bridges were a pair of reinforced concrete T-beam bridges built in 1964. The bridges are not unusual and were considered typical of bridges built at that time. Approximately 800 feet (244 m) long and 34 feet (10 m) wide, the structures were founded on pile extensions at each bent and on monolithic diaphragm abutments. The spans were 37 feet (11 m) long and the pile bents consisted of 4 driven piles each. The piles were about 80 feet (24 m) long and were driven full length and extended to the superstructure. Three expansion hinges were located in each bridge in spans 6, 11, and 16 on the west bridge and spans 6, 11, and 17 on the east bridge."

"Seismic retrofit consisting of the addition of cable restrainer units to each expansion hinge was added to the bridges in 1984. About 7 spans of the eastern structure and 10 spans of the western structure collapsed. Collapse was generally downward, however the western bridge moved transversely about 2 feet (610 mm). The structure shows little evidence of significant forces [being transmitted] to the abutments or superstructure. The hinges showed no evidence of banging and the abutments did not indicate that any movement took place there. The approach fills settled about 3 inches (75 mm)."

"The hinge restrainers performed well and held the structure together in spite of the large downward movement. Some evidence existed at the site that auto traffic had crossed the bridge during or immediately after the event. The pile extensions under the structure were lightly confined with #3 wire at about 12 inch (305 mm) pitch and failed primarily at the top. Some piles apparently also failed some distance below the ground surface. The soil displacement at the base of several of the piles was in several directions up to a maximum of 18 inches (460 mm). The eastern structure dropped about 5 feet (1.52 m) onto damaged pile extensions. The western structure dropped to the ground surface about 8 to 10 feet below (2.44 to 3.05 m). A few of the piles on the western bridge separated from the bent, displaced, and punched through the deck slab as the superstructure fell to the ground (see fig. 5.8.1)."

Figure 5.8.1   View looking north of State Highway 1 crossing Struve Slough, approximately 1 mile south of Watsonville. Piles on the left bridge separated from the bent, displaced, and punched through the deck slab as the superstructure fell to the ground (photo courtesy EQE Engineering).

5.9 Interstate 280

Aside from the damage to I-880 and to the San Francisco-Oakland Bay Bridge, structural damage at four other locations was investigated. These locations are shown in figure 5.9.1, and the nature of the damage are described in this section and the sections to follow.

Interstate 280 (I-280) traverses the southern part of San Francisco from west to east and proceeds in a northern direction along the eastern shoreline. The highway was named the Southern Freeway when it was designed. The portion south of Army Street was designed according to the 1961 AASHO Specifications (AASHO, 1961), and the portion near Sixth Street was designed according to the 1965 AASHO Specifications (AASHO, 1965). Damage was observed at two locations: several blocks south of Army Street and at the Sixth Street ramp (see fig. 5.9.1).

Figure 5.9.2 is an aerial view, looking south, of I-280 south of Army Street. At this location a two-level elevated highway (to the south) transforms into to a single level divided highway (to the north). In addition, there is an exit ramp for the lower level northbound section. Damage was observed at Bent numbers 48, 51, and 52.

Figure 5.9.3 is a schematic elevation view (looking north) of Bent 48. The top girder is post-tensioned and supports at the columns are designed as pinned connections, with details similar to those used on I-880. The column reinforcement includes #18 longitudinal bars and #4 ties at 12 in. (0.30 m) spacing. The damage occurred at the top of the west-side column. Figure 5.9.4 shows the nature of the damage, which appears to be a combination of diagonal tension failure and splitting parallel to the longitudinal column steel. Note that the girder is permanently displaced toward the east.

Figure 5.9.5 is a schematic elevation view of Bent 52. The configuration of Bent 51 is similar. The upper, post-tensioned girder is monolithic with the column on the west side and is supported as a pinned connection on the east side. Figure 5.9.6 is view (looking south) as seen from the lower northbound lanes; the upper girder of Bent 52 is in clear view. Damage occurred to the east-side columns of Bents 51 and 52 at approximately the elevation of the roadway. Figure 5.9.7 shows the damage in Bent 52 as it appeared on the northern column face. The damage in Bent 51 was similar as can be seen in figure 5.9.8, which shows that southern column face. Figure 5.9.9 is a close-up view of the damage zone in Bent 51. It is seen that the concrete is extensively fractured and the #4 ties lost their effectiveness because of the inadequate anchorage provided by the 90-degree hooks. The corner #18 bar also appears to have buckled.

Some minor damage occurred due to pounding. It is seen in figure 5.9.2 that where the roadways become side-by-side, the columns supporting the upper roadway are close to the lower roadway. One of these columns which support the upper roadway was damaged due to pounding with the lower roadway, as can be seen in figure 5.9.10.

The complex geometry of this portion of I-280 is likely to be a factor in explaining the causes of the damage. Figure 5.9.11 is a schematic to illustrate the changing structural configuration as the highway changes from a two-level elevated structure to a single-level divided structure. In part (c) of the figure, a tall structure is connected to a short structure. The natural period of vibration of the short structure is shorter than the natural period of the tall structure. Hence it is likely that at some time during the shaking, the roadways were moving in opposite directions. This would lead to high lateral forces at the junction of the two structures, which is consistent with the location of the observed damage. Where the two roadways are completely separated, as in figure 5.9.11(d), motion in opposite directions would lead to pounding as was observed.

The other damage to I-280 was observed at the Sixth Street ramp, where the highway crosses China Basin. Figure 5.9.12 is an aerial view of the site showing the elevated exit ramp crossing over the main highway. Figure 5.9.13 is a ground-level view (looking west) showing the exit ramp above the northbound lane of I-280 exit. The photograph was taken several weeks after the earthquake, and wooden cribbing was being positioned to provide temporary support. The exit ramp is typically supported by a single pier except at this location, where it is supported by a bent (number N-35). The supporting structure for the high-level ramp is attached to the lower highway in a manner similar to that shown in figure 5.9.11(c), i.e., one column is part of the bent for the main roadway, and the other column is free-standing. Damage occurred in the girder supporting the ramp. Figures 5.9.14(a) and 5.9.14(b) show the nature of the damage on the east side and west side of the bent, respectively. On the east-side, diagonal cracks developed in the girder with a major crack running diagonally across the corner. On the west side, many cracks developed toward the corner.

The other place of observed damage at the Sixth Street exit was at Bent 32 of the main highway. Figure 5.9.15(a) shows the appearance of this portion of the structure. The roadway is placed unsymmetrically with respect to the bent. On the east side, a portion of the bent extends beyond the boundary of the roadway. Figure 5.9.15(b) is a close-up view of the girder showing the series of diagonal cracks that developed.

The damage to these portions of I-280 is likely the result of several factors: the structures were designed before modern seismic provisions had been adopted; they were located in areas of deep soil deposits which probably experienced large ground displacements; and the structures had complex geometries in which components with different natural frequencies were joined. To arrive at adequate methods for repair and strengthening, it will be necessary to perform dynamic analyses, using realistic models, of these structures to arrive at realistic estimates of the forces and displacements that might occur in future earthquakes.

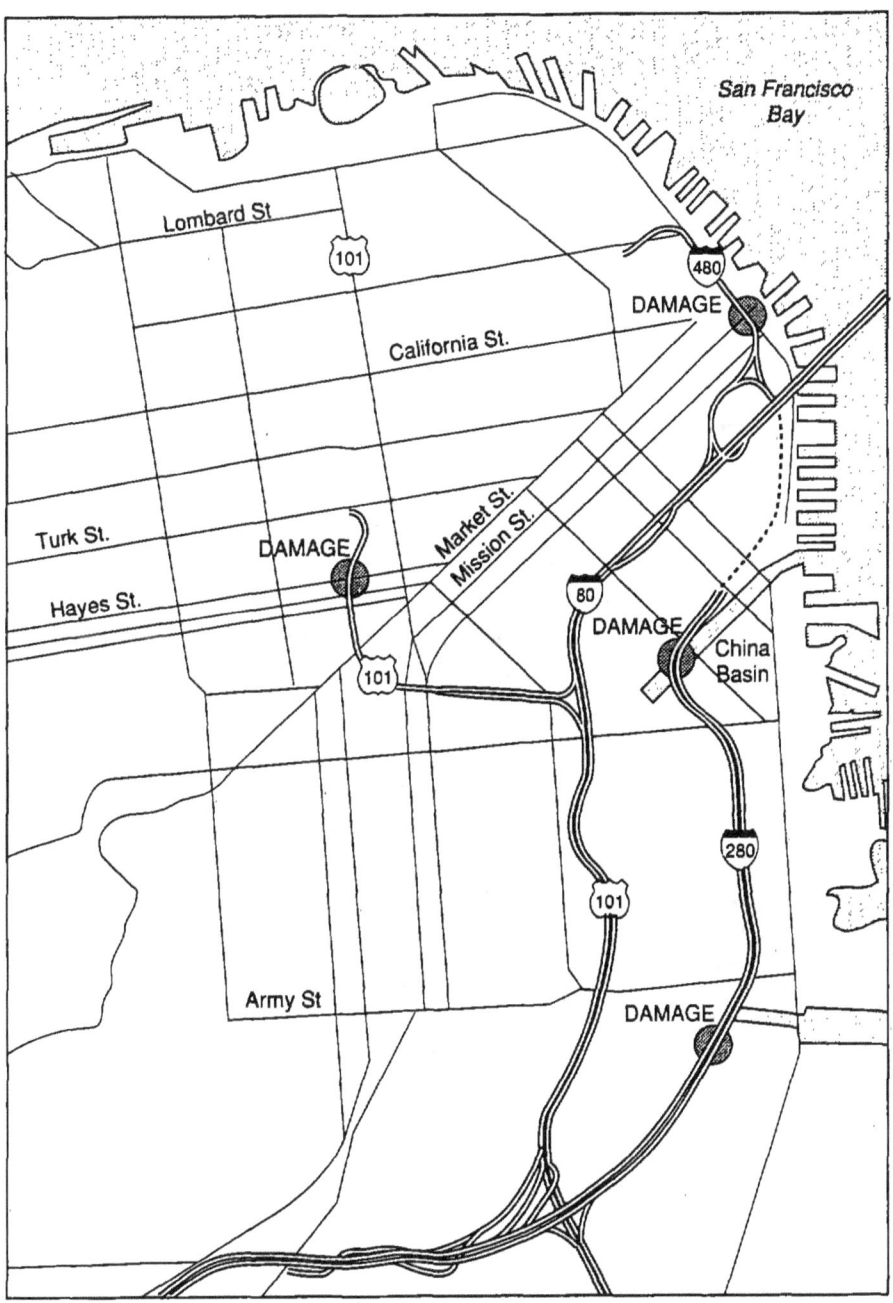

Figure 5.9.1   Location of damage to elevated highway structures in San Francisco.

Figure 5.9.2   Aerial view of I-280 south of Army St., note the transition from a two-level elevated structure to a single-level, divided structure (view is looking south).

BENT 48

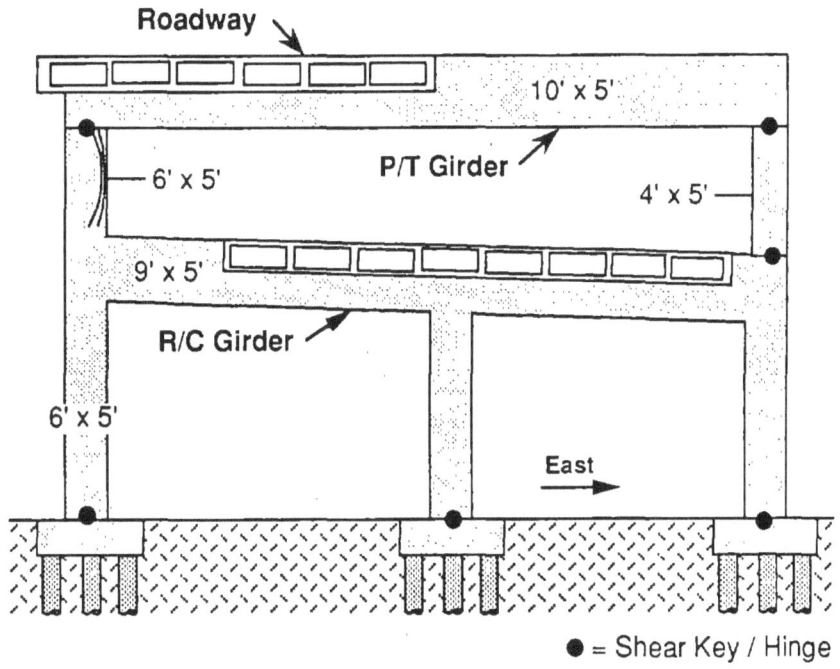

Figure 5.9.3   Schematic elevation view of Bent 48 of I-280 (looking north).

Figure 5.9.4   Damage to west-side column of Bent 48 (looking toward south).

5-75

BENT 52

Roadway

10' x 4.5'

P/T Girder

4' x 4.5'

6' x 4.5'

5' x 4.5'

6' x 4.5'

● = Shear Key / Hinge

Figure 5.9.5   Schematic elevation view of Bent 52 of I-280 (looking north).

Figure 5.9.6   View looking south on I-280 showing the upper girder of Bent 52.

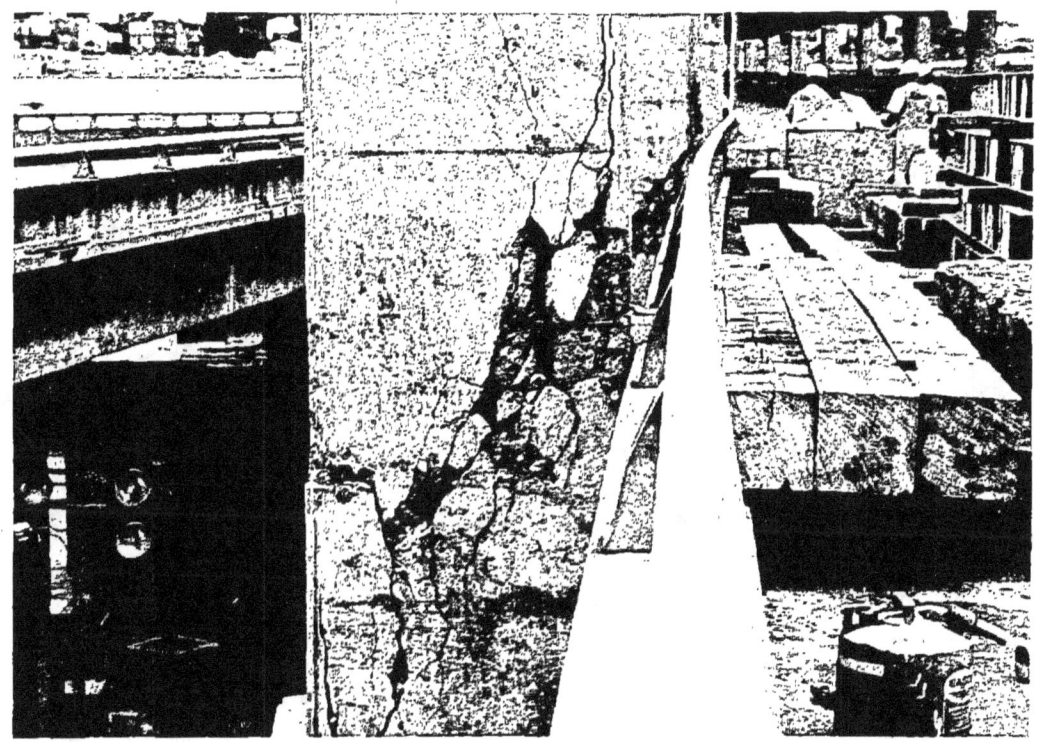

Figure 5.9.7   Diagonal cracking of the east-side column of Bent 52 (north face).

Figure 5.9.8   Diagonal cracking of the east-side column of Bent 51 (south face).

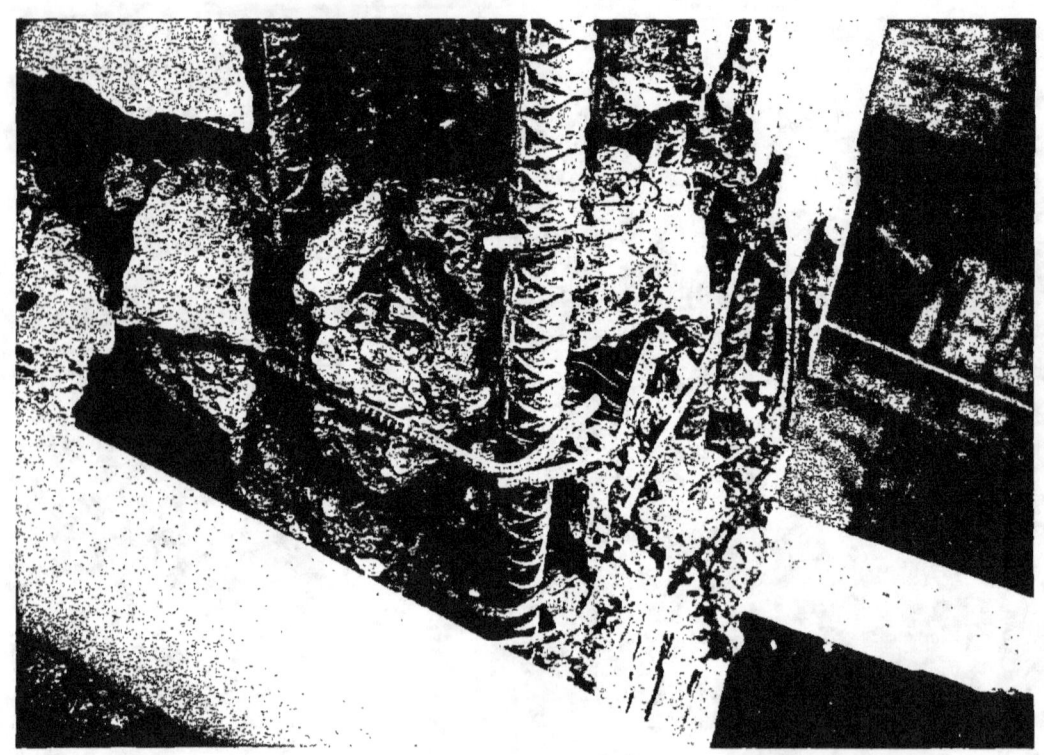

Figure 5.9.9   Close-up view of the failure zone of Bent 51, showing anchorage failure of ties.

Figure 5.9.10   Pounding damage at I-280 south of Army Street.

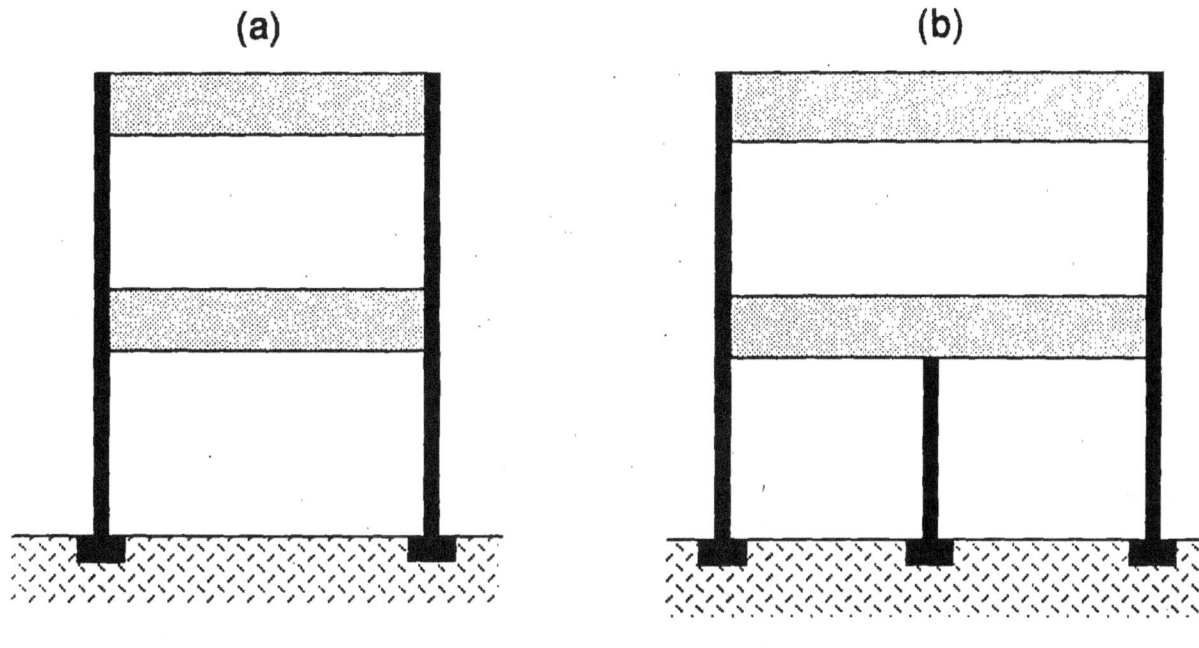

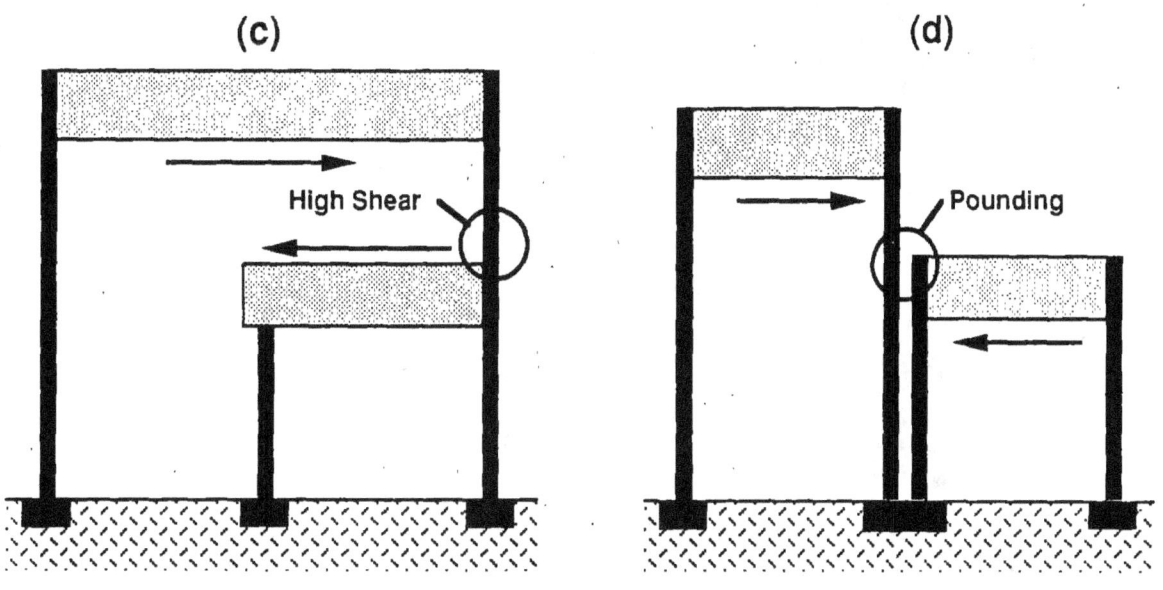

Figure 5.9.11   Schematic illustration of the various structural configurations as I-280 undergoes transition from a two-level to a single-level elevated highway.

Bent N 35

Figure 5.9.12   Aerial view of the Sixth St. exit of I-280.

Figure 5.9.13   The Sixth St. exit ramp where it passes over the northbound lanes of I-280. (View is toward west; cribbing was added to provide temporary support.)

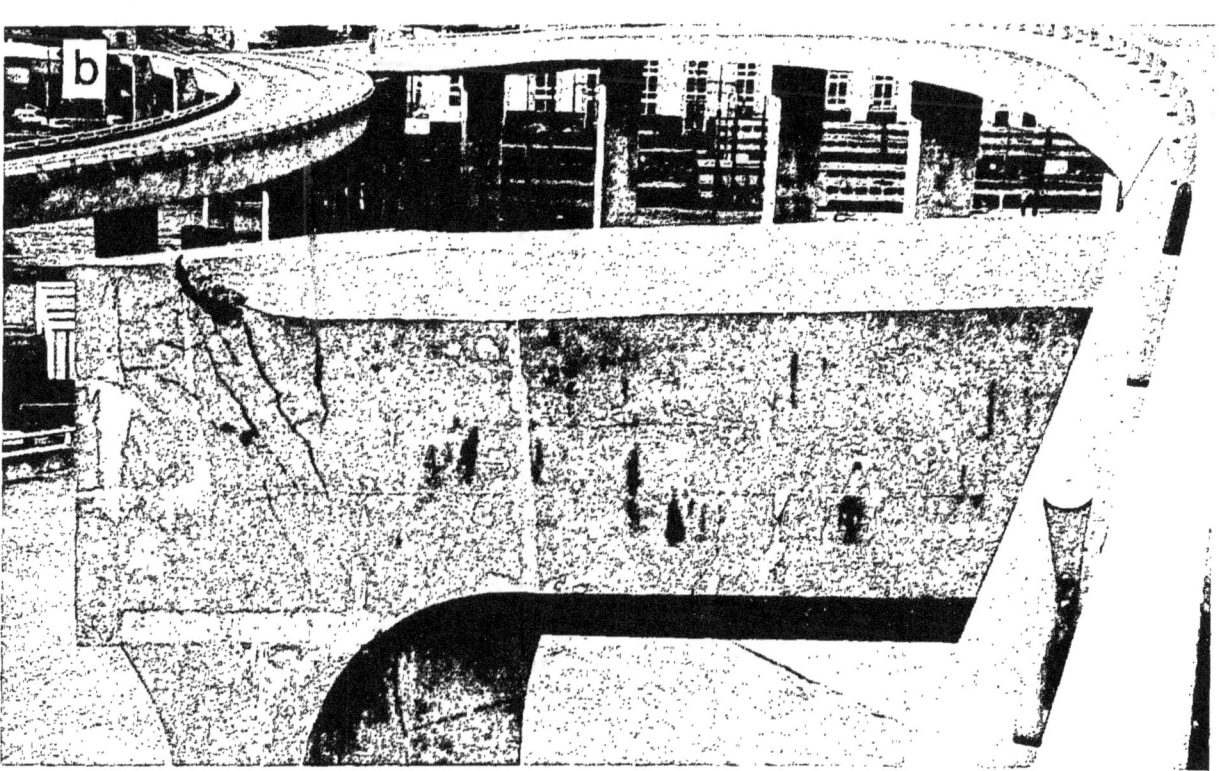

Figure 5.9.14   Damage to girder supporting exit ramp: (a) eastern portion and (b) western portion.

Figure 5.9.15   (a) Bent 32 supporting I-280 at Sixth St. exit ramp and (b) close-up of girder showing diagonal cracking.

5.10 Embarcadero Freeway (I-480)

The Embarcadero Freeway (I-480) is a two-level elevated highway which provides the Financial District with access to the San Francisco-Oakland Bay Bridge. According to the as-built drawings supplied by Caltrans, the freeway was designed according to the 1953 AASHO Specifications (AASHO, 1953). Figure 5.10.1 is an aerial view of the portion of I-480 north of Mission Street. The historic Ferry Building is east of the freeway.

Figure 5.10.2 is a ground-level view looking north along the west side of the freeway; Bent 76 is in the foreground. The vertical metal covers which can be seen at the top girder-column joints protect restraining tendons which were added during the earthquake upgrading in 1972. Figure 5.10.3 is a ground-level view from the east side looking north; Bent 78 is in the foreground. Mission Street is located between Bents 78 and 79 (numbers increase toward the north). The observed damage occurred at the lower girder-column joints in bents located north and south of Mission Street.

Figure 5.10.4 shows the configurations of the bents to the north and south of Mission Street. As can be seen at the bottom of the aerial photograph in figure 5.10.1, the Embarcadero Freeway undergoes a transition in width south of Mission Street, and this is the reason for the different bent configurations. For the wide portion of the freeway, the upper girder is post-tensioned and supported on pinned joints. A detail similar to that used in the design of I-880 was used for the pinned joints. Likewise, for bents with post-tensioned girders, column segments were pinned at both ends on one of side of the bent. The predominant damage was in the form diagonal cracking within the lower girder-column joint, as indicated by the heavy lines in figure 5.10.4. This indicates that the weakness of the Embarcadero Freeway is similar to that of the collapsed portion of I-880. In no cases were the cracks as severe as those observed in the columns of I-280.

Figure 5.10.5(a) is a close-up view of the damaged joint on the west side of Bent 78. Cracking was observed in the joints at both sides of the bent. Diagonal cracks in the joint were in the opposite direction to those at other joints on the west side of the bents. On the south face of the column in figure 5.10.5(a), the cracking was more severe and some of the concrete cover had spalled. Figure 5.10.5(b) is a close-up view of the joint of Bent 79 on the east side. This was the most severe damage observed on the east side of the freeway.

Cracks were observed in the asphalt pavements and concrete sidewalks beneath the freeway, indicating that there were large ground movements during the earthquake. For example, figure 5.10.6 shows a cracked concrete slab at the base of Bent 77 on the east side. The scrape marks on the column are a permanent record of the amount of relative movement that occurred during the earthquake. It also appears that the ground has settled about 1 inch (25 mm).

The reasons for the damage to the Embarcadero Freeway are likely the same as the reasons for the damage to I-280. The structure was built prior to the adoption of modern seismic design criteria, and the structure is located in an area which experienced large ground displacements. While not as obvious as in I-280, the damage occurred in that portion of the Embarcadero Freeway where a transition in the bent configurations occurred. Thus dynamic analyses, using accurate structural models, are needed to determine the response of the structure for earthquake loading.

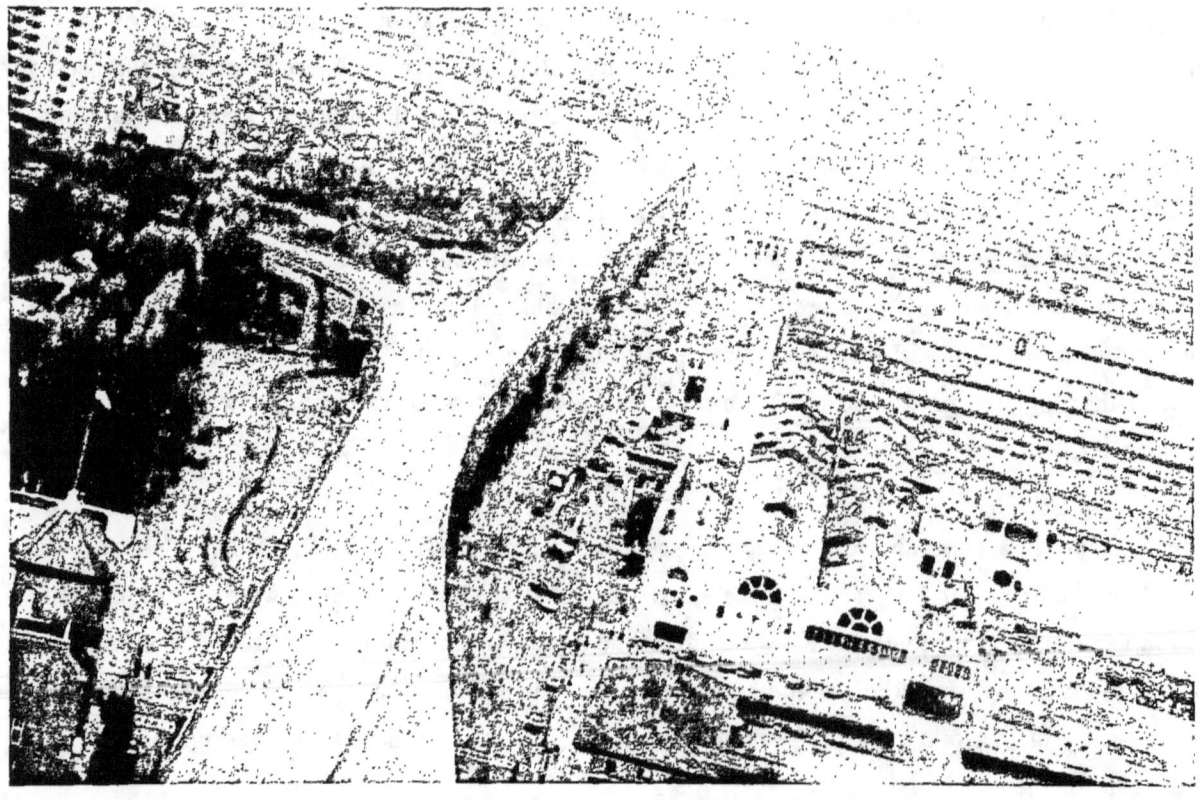

Figure 5.10.1   Aerial view of the Embarcadero Freeway north of Mission St.

Diagonal Cracking

Figure 5.10.2　West side of Embarcadero Freeway south of Mission St., Bent 76 is in foreground.

Figure 5.10.3　East side of Embarcadero Freeway at Mission St., Bent 78 is in foreground.

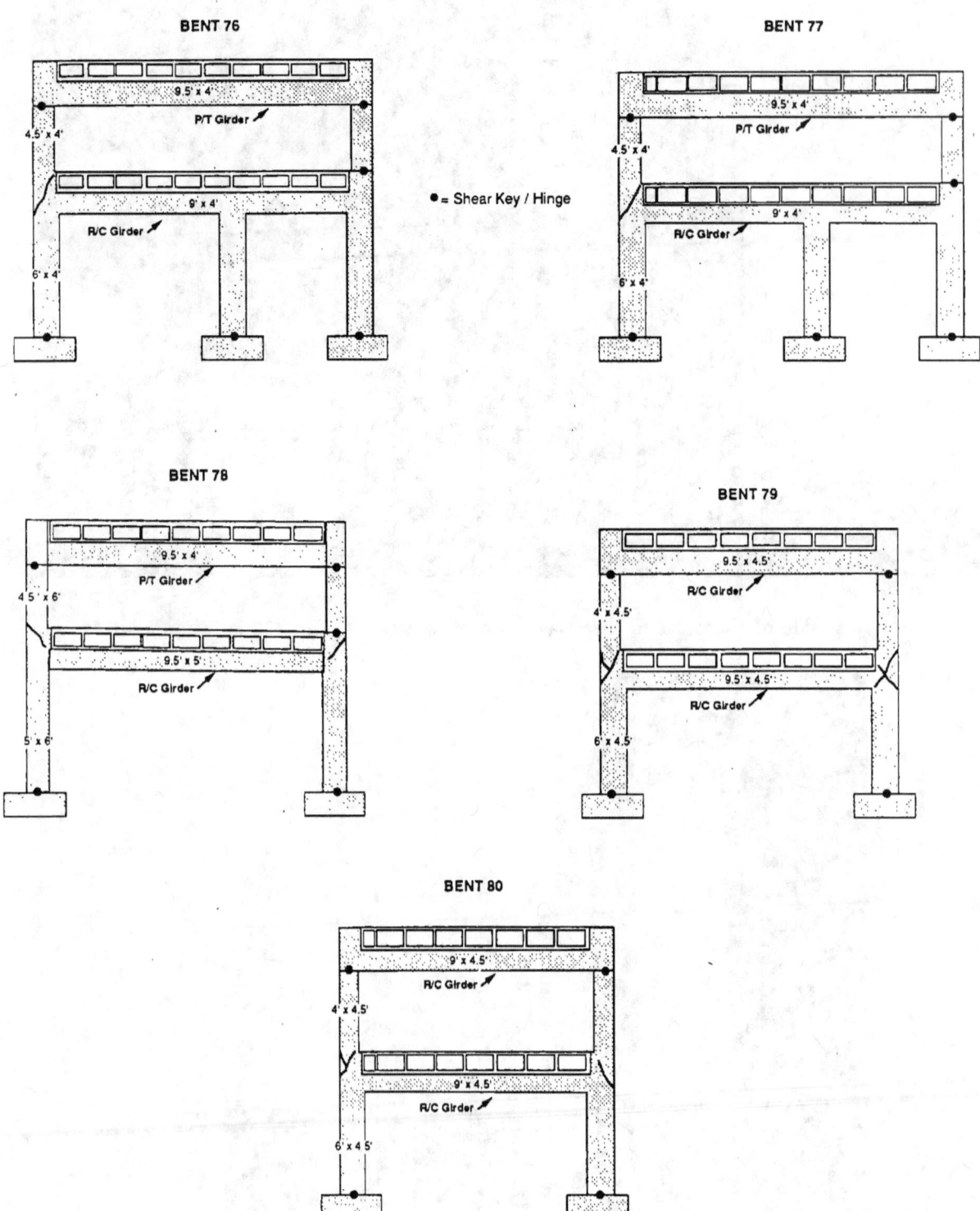

Figure 5.10.4   Schematic of bent configurations and damage at lower girder-column joints.

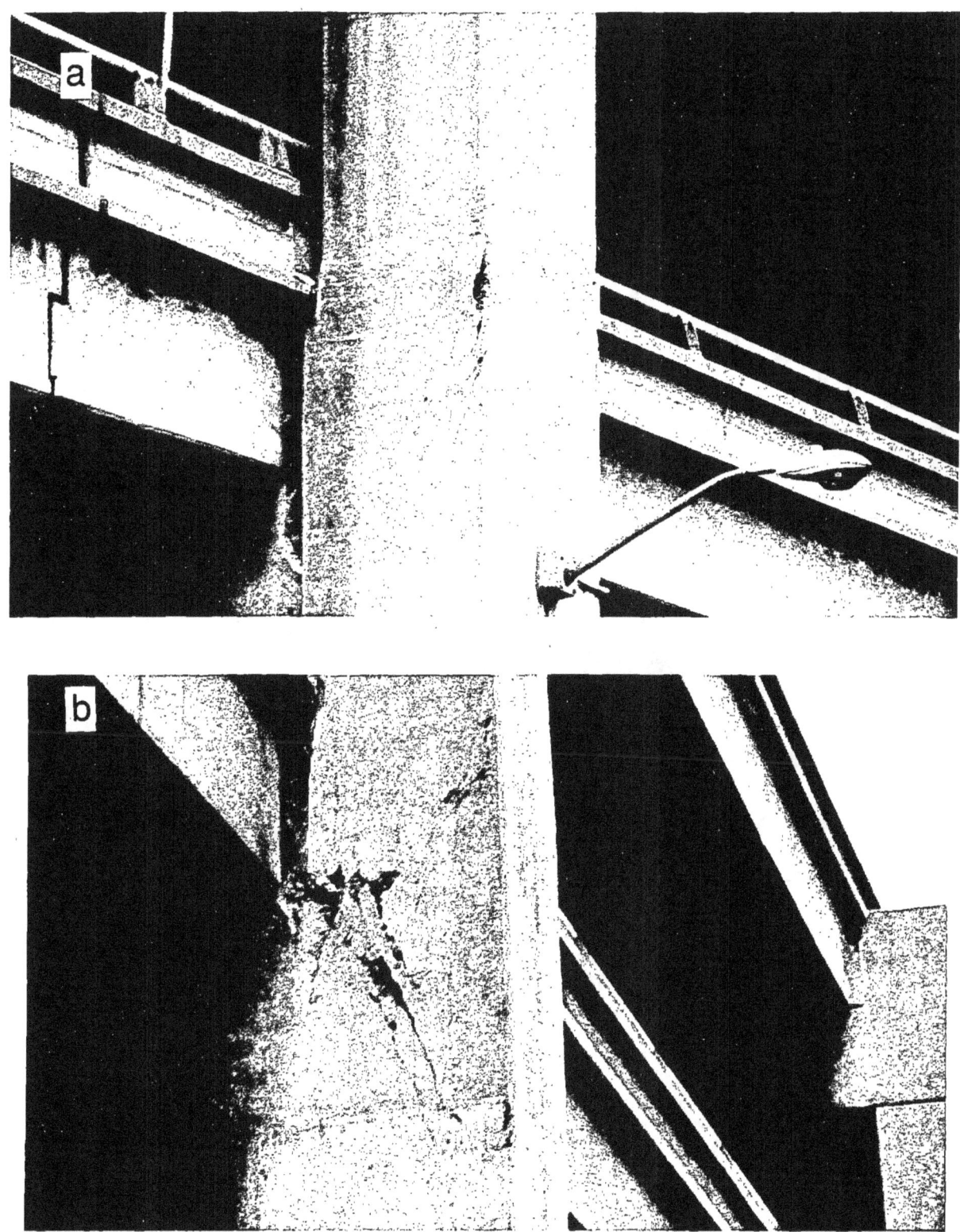

Figure 5.10.5   (a) Close-up view of west side of Bent 78 showing diagonal cracking in joint and vertical cracking at girder-column boundary; (b) close-up view of east side of Bent 79 showing diagonal cracking in joint.

Figure 5.10.6   Evidence of large ground movement at east side base of Bent 77.

5.11 U.S. Highway 101

The northernmost portion of U.S. 101 (originally named as the Central Viaduct) was designed according to the 1953 AASHO Specifications (AASHO, 1953). This was the last section of the highway to be built and extends from South Van Ness Avenue to Turk Street. At the southern end, U.S 101 is a divided, elevated highway. It undergoes a transition to a two-level elevated highway as its direction changes from east-west to north-south. At the southern end near Van Ness Avenue, the concrete roadway is supported by a steel frame. From north of Mission street, the roadway is supported by concrete structures.

One block south of Hayes Street, the highway becomes two lanes in each direction. At Bent 40, the roadway widens to accommodate additional lanes in the future. Damage was observed in the widened, elevated section at Bents 42 and 43, which are located north of Hayes Street. These are shown in figure 5.11.1, a view of the east side of the highway. Figure 5.11.2 is a schematic of the configuration of Bent 43 where serious damage was observed. The configuration of Bent 42 is similar to Bent 43 except that the bent is skewed to the direction of the roadway. The design was similar to the other elevated highways built in the mid 50's. The post-tensioned girders are supported on columns with pinned connections.

Figure 5.11.3(a) is close-up view of the east-side column of Bent 42. A series of diagonal cracks occurred at the middle of the column, and finer cracks developed at the top of the column inclined in the opposite direction. The more serious damage was observed at Bent 43. As shown in figure 5.11.3(b), extensive diagonal cracking developed just above the roadway.

The damaged portion of U.S. 101 is similar in design to the other damaged highway structures that have been discussed. The minimal transverse column reinforcement provided little shear strength for the columns. Further analysis is needed to explain why failure was concentrated within the columns rather than the girder-column joint, as was observed in other damaged elevated highways of similar design.

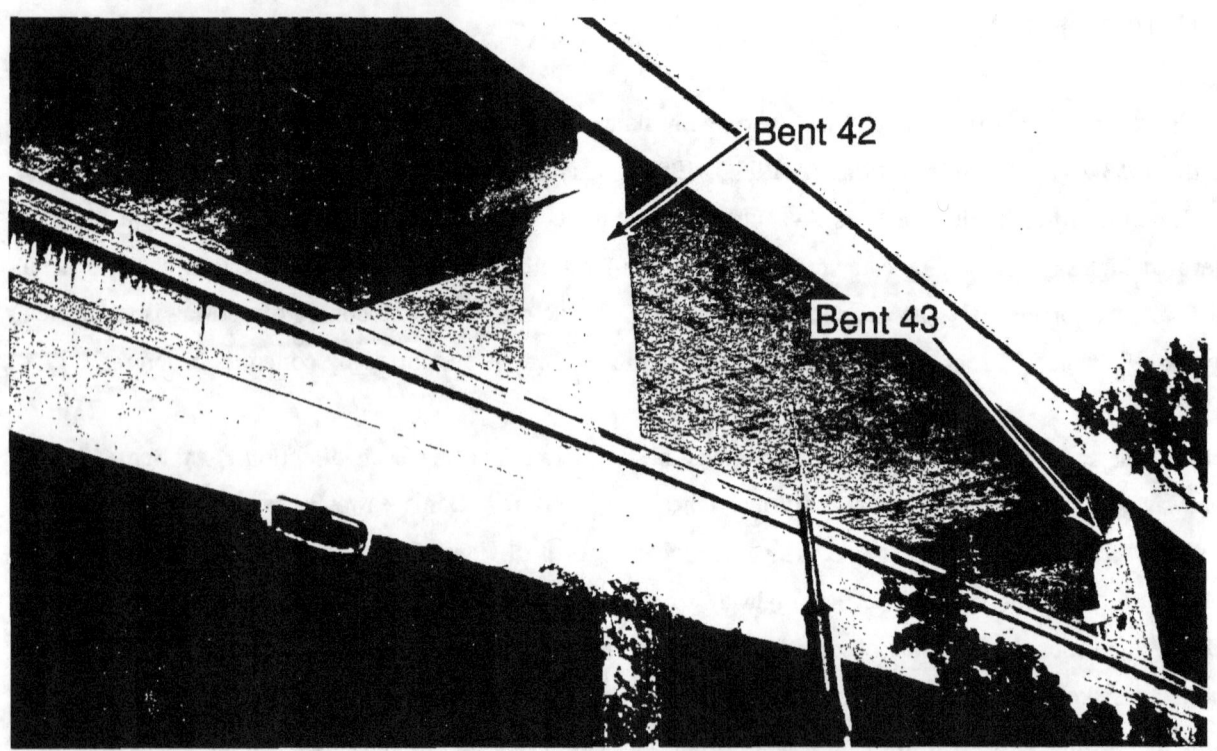

Figure 5.11.1   View of east side U.S. 101 north of Hayes St. showing damaged Bents 42 and 43.

BENT 43

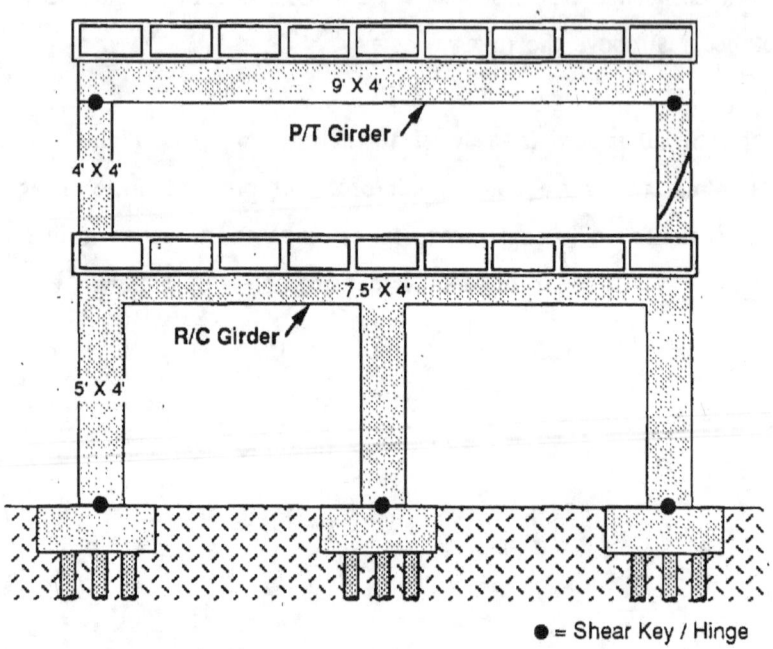

● = Shear Key / Hinge

Figure 5.11.2   Schematic of Bent 43, which had the more severe damage.

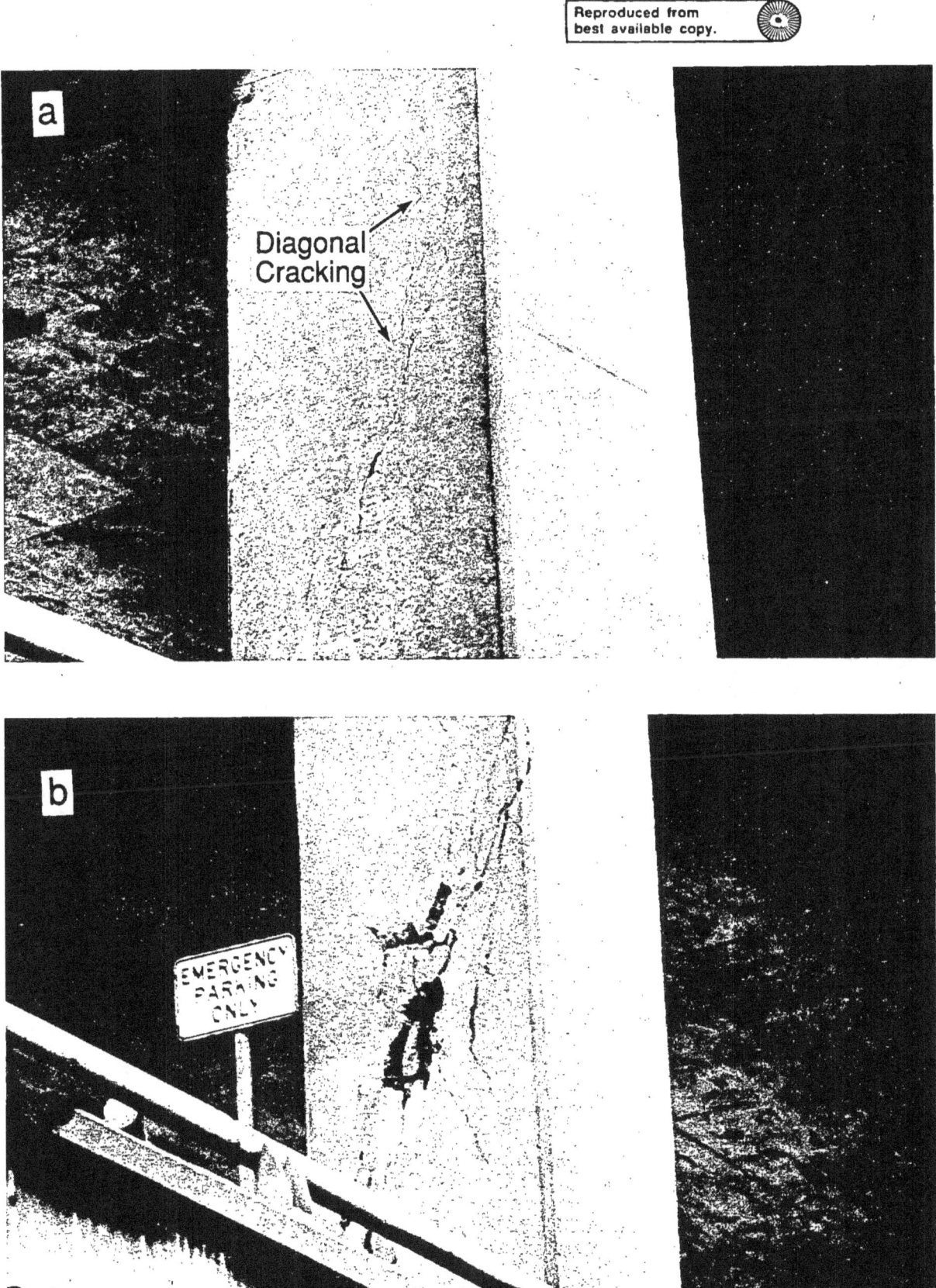

Figure 5.11.3   Close-up views of east side columns of (a) Bent 42 and (b) Bent 43.

5.12 References

AASHO, 1953, "Bridge Design Specifications Manual," Standard Specifications for Highway Bridges, American Association of State Highway Officials, Washington, D.C.

AASHO, 1958-59, "Interim Specifications, Bridges 1950-1959," Subcommittee on Bridges and Structures, American Association of State Highway Officials, Washington, D.C.

AASHO, 1961, "Bridge Design Specifications Manual," Standard Specifications for Highway Bridges, American Association of State Highway Officials, Washington, D.C.

AASHO, 1965, "Bridge Design Specifications Manual," Standard Specifications for Highway Bridges, American Association of State Highway Officials, Washington, D.C.

AASHTO, 1977, "Bridge Design Specification Manual," Standard Specifications for Highway Bridges, American Association of State Highway and Transportation Officials, 12th Edition.

ACI, 1989, "Building Code Requirements for Reinforced Concrete (ACI 318-83)," American Concrete Institute, Detroit, MI.

ATC 1978, "Tentative Provisions for the Development of Seismic Regulations for Buildings," Applied Technology Council, Palo Alto, CA.

Bertero, V., et al., 1989, "The Collapse of I-880 as a Result of the October 17, 1989 Loma Prieta Earthquake," University of California at Berkeley Research Report #89-14.

Caltrans, 1949, "Caltrans Bridge Department Design Supplement for Earthquake Loads, 1949 Edition." California Department of Transportation, Sacramento, CA.

CDMG, 1989a, "A Quick Report on CSMIP Strong-Motion Records from the October 17, 1989 Earthquake in the Santa Cruz Mountains," State of California, Department of Conservation, Division of Mines and Geology, Office of Strong Motion Studies.

CDMG, 1989b, "Strong Ground Shaking from the Loma Prieta Earthquake of October 17, 1989 and its Relation to Near-Surface Geology in the Oakland Area," A Preliminary Report to the Governor's Board of Inquiry on the 1989 Loma Prieta Earthquake. California Department of Conservation, Division of Mines and Geology.

Civil Engineering, 1989, "The Great Quake: On-Site Reports," *Civil Engineering*, December, 1989, American Society of Civil Engineers (ASCE), New York, NY, pp 44-47.

CSSC, 1988, "California at Risk: Reducing Earthquake Hazards 1987-1992," A Report of the California Seismic Safety Commission, Report No. SSC 88-02.

EERC, 1989, "Preliminary Report on the Seismological and Engineering Aspects of the October 17, 1989 Santa Cruz (Loma Prieta) Earthquake," EERC, College of Engineering, University of California at Berkeley, Report No. UCB/EERC-89/14, October, 1989.

Earthquake Engineering Research Institute, EERI 1989, EERI-NRC-NCEER Congressional Briefing, "Loma Prieta (Northern California) Earthquake," Senate Russell Office Building, Room 253, November 30, 1989.

Priestley, M. J. N., Seible, F., and Chal, Y. H., 1989, "Collapse of the Cypress Viaduct," Final Report to Caltrans Office of Structural Design, November 9, 1989.

Uniform Building Code, 1988 Edition, International Conference of Building Officials, 5360 South Workman Mill Road, Whittier, CA 90601, Section 2312.

6. PERFORMANCE OF FIRE PROTECTION SYSTEMS

by Harold E. Nelson

6.1 Introduction

In general, private fire protection facilities survived the earthquake without interruption while public fire protection systems were severely interrupted. Private fire protection systems are limited to a single facility and mostly within buildings while public fire protection systems are external, community wide, and often underground. Several affected communities, including San Francisco, were left in a condition where it is doubtful that they could have halted a serious spreading fire. The absence of a serious spreading fire (other than the one in the Marina District of San Francisco) is believed to be a combination of factors including:

- Prompt shut down of electric power (by the utilities).
- Modern safeguards on burners and pilots on water heaters and other gas fired appliances in service at the time.
- Warm weather (i.e. lack of use of heating equipment).
- Absence of wind (a major fire spread factor if present).
- High moisture content in ground and wild lands (relates to lack of significant wild fire problems).
- The occurrence of moderate earthquake with a short duration of strong ground shaking which caused limited damage on buildings and utility structures in the affected communities.
- Good fortune.

6.2 General Observations

Fire claimed one life, the destruction of a row of about eight apartment buildings in the Marina District, the loss of a auto repair facility in Berkeley, the loss of a single-family dwelling in Los Gatos, and the loss of a single-family dwelling in Watsonville. In general, the losses due to fire were minor as compared to structural damage in this earthquake. This is in contrast to the San Francisco earthquake of 1906 where fire was a major factor. A number of factors including force of the earthquake, wind conditions, moisture content in the wild lands, and differences in the type and arrangement of heating, lighting, and cooking facilities.

It is fortunate that the number of fires were small. Throughout most of the areas struck by the earthquake, the water supplies necessary to combat a significant fire were disrupted and the communications necessary to secure extra resources were either disrupted or so overtaxed as to be of greatly reduced value. In some cases, notably San Francisco and Watsonville, the combination of disrupted facilities and overloaded radio channels virtually halted emergency communications by the fire department.

Throughout the affected region, except Oakland, the power distribution within the communities was immediately ceased. This action eliminated electric power as an ignition source and caused all electrically powered safety valves, (e.g., safety pilots on water heaters, etc.) to close shutting off the pilot and interrupting the flow of gas at that point. It is believed that this action prevented many ignitions in those buildings where there was enough movement to break the internal pipes and sever the electrical wiring. Since the earthquake occurred during daytime, the loss of illumination resulting from the power outage did not appear to have an impact on the safety of individuals.

Except for Oakland, where underground breakage appears to have been very limited, all of the communities visited suffered sufficient underground breakage of utilities to disrupt the water mains including a 12 in. high-pressure line in San Francisco, thereby eliminating the principal source of fire fighting water. Also, the gas mains were disrupted and gas leaks were prevalent, though the removal of power sources and the caution exercised by the citizens was effective in preventing ignition of leaking gas. It is likely that the leakage was distributed widely over the systems, probably concentrated at the points where smaller service pipes are connected to mains. The gas was leaked in a manner that allowed rapid dispersal in the atmosphere. In such case, the odorizing agent tends to remain and encouraged continued precautions.

6.3 Meteorological Effects

At the time of the earthquake and through the next several days there was little wind. This is felt to have been an important factor in the fire which occurred in the Marina District. Had there been a wind, it is quite possible that fire could have developed into a multi-block conflagration. In addition, rains immediately prior to the earthquake had resulted in a high moisture in the ground and wild lands. In areas such as the Santa Cruz mountains, there were ignition sources resulting from downed power lines. Some minor fires did occur. One was significant but still localized. Had the hills been dry and/or a strong wind been present, a different result could well have occurred.

6-2

6.4 Private Fire Protection Systems

The initial data indicates that private fire protection systems such as sprinklers, standpipes, and alarm systems for the most part were not interrupted. This is probably due to both the earthquake bracing requirements included in the fire protection standards governing the installation of these devices in earthquake zones and the fact that most of the buildings where such equipment is involved did not suffer extensive structural damage.

6.5 Summary

This earthquake did not place as much stress on the fire-fighting system as a major earthquake would have. If a major earthquake were to occur, the increased level of destruction of buildings and the resulting increase of available fuel and ignition sources would probably increase the number of fires. If electric power is removed as promptly in such an earthquake, it is likely that many of the potential ignition sources will be interrupted as apparently occurred in this earthquake.

The underground water distribution and gas distribution systems are very vulnerable and generally showed extensive failure even in this moderate earthquake. It appears that the advances in survival of these systems has not matched the advances in the survival of structures. It is critical to conduct further investigation of the impact of the earthquake on the existing systems and the development of better means to insure continued fire fighting water supply and preventing or minimizing the leakage of gas from the distribution system is critical.

7. CONCLUSIONS AND RECOMMENDATIONS
by Richard N. Wright and H. S. Lew

7.1 Conclusions

The Loma Prieta earthquake of October 17, 1989, can provide significant lessons for public policies and construction practices throughout the United States. While it was the largest earthquake to strike Northern California since the great San Francisco earthquake of 1906, earthquakes of similar or larger magnitude are expected to affect 46 of the 50 states, Puerto Rico and the Virgin Islands (Federal Emergency Management Agency, 1988). Thus, lessons of structural performance, seismology, and geology which can be learned from the Loma Prieta earthquake, can be used to reduce earthquake hazards throughout the United States and the rest of the world.

7.1.1 Performance of All Structures

1.   The Loma Prieta earthquake caused human losses of 62 lives and 3,757 injuries. But for fortunate circumstances, human losses would have been much greater. The unusual event of coincidence with a Bay area World Series baseball game reduced traffic far below normal levels on the I-880 viaduct which collapsed to cause most of the life losses. Although water supplies for fire fighting were lost over much of the Bay area, unusually calm winds avoided uncontrolled spreading of fires. The areas affected by the earthquake are among the best prepared in the United States. Clearly, earthquakes remain the United States' greatest single-event natural hazard threatening losses of life and injuries.

2.   Direct property losses are estimated to exceed $ 6 billion, but these are modest compared to losses projected for earthquakes closer to major metropolitan areas, for instance $40 billion for a magnitude 7.5 earthquake on the eastern Bay area's Hayward fault, (California Department of Conservation, 1987) or $37 billion for a magnitude 7.6 earthquake in the New Madrid area of the Central U.S. (FEMA, 1985). Unless actions are taken to reduce earthquake hazards, nationwide, earthquake property losses can be sufficiently large to seriously impact the U.S. economy (The Earthquake Project, 1989).

3.   Consequent economic losses were apparent in the major disruptions of transportation in the month that the San Francisco-Oakland Bay Bridge was out of service. Dislocations continue with major segments of the Bay area highway system still not functioning. The potential for consequent

economic, national security and societal losses arising from earthquake damages add to the status of earthquakes as the Nation's greatest single-event natural hazard.

4. Most building and lifeline structures in the epicentral and Bay areas performed well. Californian efforts to develop, adopt and enforce up to date seismic design and construction practices for buildings and lifelines deserve great credit for this. However, much structural damage and most losses of lives and property occurred in the Bay area 60 to 70 miles from the earthquake source. At such distances, for this sized earthquake, current seismic design and construction practices were expected to be capable of preventing structural damages. Thus, structural performance in the Loma Prieta earthquake provides important opportunities for the assessment and improvement of national seismic design and construction practices.

5. Most structural damages in the Bay area, 60 to 70 miles from the epicentral area, occurred to structures sited on deep deposits of overburden soils above the bedrock. Such sites are common in other areas of the Nation that also are subject to earthquake hazards. Also, the intensity of bedrock ground shaking was much higher in the Bay area than in other directions from the epicentral area possibly due to directional characteristics of the rupture. Because many records of strong ground motions are available from the main shock and aftershock measurements, there important opportunities exist to develop and verify seismological and engineering practices for prediction of the effects of geological and overburden soil conditions on the intensity of earthquake ground motions.

6. Structural damages and failures in both the epicentral and Bay areas indicate some vulnerability for structures having natural periods less than that of their sites. In-depth studies of responses of damaged and undamaged structures can assess the needs, if any, for revisions of current seismic standards which allow reduced design forces for structures having short natural periods sited on deep, soft soil deposits.

7. Ground failures, including landslides and liquefaction, were frequent in both epicentral and Bay areas. These attest to the potential of ground failures to produce earthquake losses of lives and property and provide opportunities to assess the needs to improve existing criteria for the stability of soils in earthquakes.

7.1.2 Buildings Performance

1.   Buildings designed and constructed in accord with modern seismic design and construction practices generally performed well in both epicentral and Bay areas. This shows the value of adopting and enforcing modern seismic design and construction practices in building codes and in Federal construction. However, examples of successful performance in areas of strong shaking and of failures in areas of moderate shaking provide opportunities to assess needs to improve modern seismic design and construction practices.

2.   Widespread failures of older buildings, such as collapses of unreinforced masonry buildings, failures of cripple stud walls, and losses of chimneys and parapets, reemphasize the need to assess the safety of existing buildings and to correct excessive hazards. It is sobering to note that many modern buildings also have these vulnerabilities in seismically hazardous areas of the United States which have not yet, or only recently have, adopted and enforced seismic design and construction provisions in their building codes.

3.   Many older buildings in the epicentral and Bay areas had been retrofitted to improve seismic resistance prior to the earthquake. Some performed well; some failed. In-depth studies of the performance of retrofit measures can reveal opportunities to affirm or to improve standards for assessment and strengthening of existing buildings that currently are being developed.

4.   Many buildings in urban areas were damaged by pounding against adjacent buildings. In-depth studies of occurrences and non-occurrences of pounding can provide improvements, where needed, in standards for design of new buildings, and in standards for assessment and strengthening of existing buildings.

7.1.3 Lifelines Performance

1.   The severe losses of lives in the collapse of the I-880 viaduct, which were fortuitously far less than the losses would have been under more normal traffic patterns, show the importance of successful performance of lifelines for life safety.

2.   The disruptions of economic activities in the Bay area caused by failures of highway structures, and in the epicentral area caused by the landslides that closed state Highway 17, show the importance of successful performance of lifelines for the avoidance of property losses and consequent damages.

3.   Water distribution system failures in the Bay area show the vulnerability of U.S. cities in areas of seismic hazard to fires following earthquakes. Gas distribution system failures in the Bay and epicentral areas show a significant potential for ignition of fires following earthquakes. These failures were predominately in areas of unstable soils.

7.2 Recommendations

These recommendations are based on the information gained in investigations to date of the Loma Prieta earthquake and on the state of the art of earthquake hazards reduction practices.

7.2.1 Performance of All Structures

1.   In all seismically hazardous areas of the United States, Federal agencies responsible for the seismic safety of Federal or Federally assisted or regulated structures, and state and local governments responsible for regulations for buildings and lifelines should:

Plan and initiate systematic programs to assess the safety of existing buildings and lifelines and to correct those that are considered to be unduly dangerous. Particular attention should be given to structures sited on deep soil deposits which can be vulnerable to both nearby and distant earthquakes. Losses of lives and property and consequent damages in the Loma Prieta earthquake were due primarily to failures of structures not designed and constructed in accord with modern practices for seismic safety. To a large extent, these damages occurred to structures located on deep soil deposits. Those in the Bay area were far from the earthquake source.

Adopt and enforce modern seismic design and construction practices for new buildings and lifelines. Generally good performance of modern buildings in the epicentral area of the Loma Prieta earthquake shows the efficacy of modern design and construction practices. Tragic losses of 242,000 lives in Tangshan, China in 1976 (China Academy of Building Research, 1986) and about 30,000 lives in Soviet Armenia in 1988 (Wyllie and Filson,

1989) show that earthquake losses can be catastrophic in the absence of the adoption and enforcement of good seismic design and construction practices.

Adopt and enforce modern practices for assessment of the stability of slopes and areas potentially susceptible to liquefaction to assure that undue existing hazards are identified and corrected and that new construction is not subject to ground failures in earthquakes. Significant property and consequent losses from ground failures in the Loma Prieta earthquake, and severe life losses in earlier earthquakes show the importance of prevention of ground failures affecting buildings and lifelines.

2. **In-depth studies should be made of amplifications of ground shaking by overburden soils and improved practices should be developed for site-specific design criteria for earthquake loadings.** Information from the Loma Prieta earthquake on main and aftershock ground shaking intensities and on structural performance on deep soil deposits provides a strong data base for such studies. These data can be combined with similar data obtained from the 1967 Caracas, 1985 Mexico, and 1988 Spitak earthquakes.

3. **In-depth studies should be made of the effects of geologic structures and earthquake mechanisms on the directionality of the propagation of strong shaking from earthquake fault areas.** The marked irregularity of the intensity contours for the Loma Prieta earthquake show large potential for savings in costs of earthquake resistance and for reductions in earthquake damages when intensity distributions can be predicted more accurately for use in siting and design of structures.

4. **Methods should be developed for measurement of the properties of existing structures that will allow reliable pre-earthquake assessment of vulnerability and post-earthquake assessment of damages.** Experiences in the Loma Prieta earthquake reemphasize both the need for these assessments and the inadequacies of currently available technologies.

7.2.2 Buildings Performance

1. **Successful and unsuccessful performances of modern buildings in the Loma Prieta earthquake should be studied in depth to formulate improvements for seismic design and construction practices. Recommendations from development of the National Earthquake Hazards Reduction Program (NEHRP) Provisions, (FEMA 1988), emphasize the need to improve standards for the**

energy absorbing capacities of various structural systems. The large variety of quantitative information on building performance in the Loma Prieta earthquake provides data for assessing and confirming analytical models for nonlinear structural performance in earthquakes that in turn can be used in development of improved design criteria.

2.   **Successful and unsuccessful performances of buildings that had been retrofitted prior to the Loma Prieta earthquake should be studied in depth to confirm the validity of, or to improve, standards for the assessment and strengthening of existing buildings that presently are being developed in the NEHRP.** The large variety of data on performance of retrofit buildings available from the Loma Prieta earthquake provides a significant opportunity to evaluate and improve practices for the assessment and strengthening of existing buildings.

3.   **Techniques should be developed for reduction of pounding damages for new and existing buildings.** Substantial pounding damages were observed in the Loma Prieta and in the Mexico City earthquake of 1985. Data are newly available for assessment of the adequacy of current criteria for new buildings design. Research can devise and verify techniques for mitigating potential pounding damages between existing buildings.

7.2.3 Lifelines Performance

1.   **Analytical and laboratory studies of highway structures' supports should be conducted to improve design, assessment and retrofit practices.** Severe collapses and damages in the Loma Prieta earthquake and the fact that most of the U.S. highway system has not been designed for earthquake resistance show the need for these studies.

2.   **Analytical, laboratory and field studies of the performance of gas and water pipelines should be conducted to develop improved design, assessment and retrofit practices.** Extensive failures and consequent fire hazards occurred in areas of unstable soils in the Loma Prieta earthquake. Similar potentials exist in most seismically hazardous areas of the United States.

3.   **Nationally applicable design and construction provisions for new lifelines, and assessment and strengthening provisions for existing lifelines should be developed in the NEHRP.** The Loma Prieta earthquake shows the importance of successful lifelines performance for the mitigation of life, property and consequent losses due to earthquakes. In contrast to buildings, and except for

highway structures, no nationally applicable design and construction practices are available for new and existing lifelines.

7.3 References

Federal Emergency Management Agency, FEMA 1985, "An Assessment of Damage and Casualties for Six Cities in the United States Due to Earthquakes in the New Madrid Seismic Zone," FEMA, Central United States Earthquake Preparedness Project.

California Department of Conservation, 1987, "Earthquake Planning Scenario for a Magnitude 7.5 Earthquake on the Hayward Fault in the San Francisco Bay Area," Special Publication 78.

China Academy of Building Research, 1986, "The Mammoth Tangshan Earthquake of 1976," China Academic Publishers.

The Earthquake Project, 1989, "News."

Federal Emergency Management Agency, 1988, "NEHRP Recommended Provisions for the Development of Seismic Regulations for New Buildings," FEMA 95.

Wyllie, L. A., and J. R., Filson, 1989, "Armenia Earthquake Reconnaissance Report," Earthquake Spectra, August 1989.

NIST Technical Publications

Periodical

Journal of Research of the National Institute of Standards and Technology—Reports NIST research and development in those disciplines of the physical and engineering sciences in which the Institute is active. These include physics, chemistry, engineering, mathematics, and computer sciences. Papers cover a broad range of subjects, with major emphasis on measurement methodology and the basic technology underlying standardization. Also included from time to time are survey articles on topics closely related to the Institute's technical and scientific programs. Issued six times a year.

Nonperiodicals

Monographs—Major contributions to the technical literature on various subjects related to the Institute's scientific and technical activities.

Handbooks—Recommended codes of engineering and industrial practice (including safety codes) developed in cooperation with interested industries, professional organizations, and regulatory bodies.

Special Publications—Include proceedings of conferences sponsored by NIST, NIST annual reports, and other special publications appropriate to this grouping such as wall charts, pocket cards, and bibliographies.

Applied Mathematics Series—Mathematical tables, manuals, and studies of special interest to physicists, engineers, chemists, biologists, mathematicians, computer programmers, and others engaged in scientific and technical work.

National Standard Reference Data Series—Provides quantitative data on the physical and chemical properties of materials, compiled from the world's literature and critically evaluated. Developed under a worldwide program coordinated by NIST under the authority of the National Standard Data Act (Public Law 90-396). NOTE: The Journal of Physical and Chemical Reference Data (JPCRD) is published quarterly for NIST by the American Chemical Society (ACS) and the American Institute of Physics (AIP). Subscriptions, reprints, and supplements are available from ACS, 1155 Sixteenth St., NW., Washington, DC 20056.

Building Science Series—Disseminates technical information developed at the Institute on building materials, components, systems, and whole structures. The series presents research results, test methods, and performance criteria related to the structural and environmental functions and the durability and safety characteristics of building elements and systems.

Technical Notes—Studies or reports which are complete in themselves but restrictive in their treatment of a subject. Analogous to monographs but not so comprehensive in scope or definitive in treatment of the subject area. Often serve as a vehicle for final reports of work performed at NIST under the sponsorship of other government agencies.

Voluntary Product Standards—Developed under procedures published by the Department of Commerce in Part 10, Title 15, of the Code of Federal Regulations. The standards establish nationally recognized requirements for products, and provide all concerned interests with a basis for common understanding of the characteristics of the products. NIST administers this program as a supplement to the activities of the private sector standardizing organizations.

Consumer Information Series—Practical information, based on NIST research and experience, covering areas of interest to the consumer. Easily understandable language and illustrations provide useful background knowledge for shopping in today's technological marketplace.
*Order the **above** NIST publications from: Superintendent of Documents, Government Printing Office, Washington, DC 20402.*
*Order the **following** NIST publications—FIPS and NISTIRs—from the National Technical Information Service, Springfield, VA 22161.*

Federal Information Processing Standards Publications (FIPS PUB)—Publications in this series collectively constitute the Federal Information Processing Standards Register. The Register serves as the official source of information in the Federal Government regarding standards issued by NIST pursuant to the Federal Property and Administrative Services Act of 1949 as amended, Public Law 89-306 (79 Stat. 1127), and as implemented by Executive Order 11717 (38 FR 12315, dated May 11, 1973) and Part 6 of Title 15 CFR (Code of Federal Regulations).

NIST Interagency Reports (NISTIR)—A special series of interim or final reports on work performed by NIST for outside sponsors (both government and non-government). In general, initial distribution is handled by the sponsor; public distribution is by the National Technical Information Service, Springfield, VA 22161, in paper copy or microfiche form.